Teaching Pragmatics and Instructed Second Language Learning

Advances in Instructed Second Language Acquisition Research Series
Series Editor: Alessandro Benati

The mission of this series is to publish new theoretical insights in Instructed Second Language Acquisition research that advance our understanding of how languages are learned and should be taught. Research in Instructed SLA has addressed questions related to the degree to which any form of external manipulation (e.g. grammar instruction, input manipulation, etc.) can affect language development. The main purpose of research in instructed second language acquisition is to establish how classroom language learning takes place and how an understanding of second language acquisition contributes to language teaching.

Despite the clear relationship between theory and research in SLA, and language practice, there are still very few cross-references between these areas. This series will publish research in instructed SLA that bridges this gap and provide academics with a set of theoretical principles for language teaching and acquisition. The calibre of research will inspire scholars and practitioners to learn more about acquisition and to reflect on their language teaching practices more generally.

Task Sequencing and Instructed Second Language Learning
Edited by Melissa Baralt

The Developmental Dimension in Instructed Second Language Learning
Paul A. Malovrh

The Grammar Dimension in Instructed Second Language Learning
Edited by Alessandro Benati, Cécile Laval and María J. Arche

The Interactional Feedback Dimension in Instructed Second Language Learning
Hossein Nassaji

The Metalinguistic Dimension in Instructed Second Language Learning
Edited by Karen Roehr

Teaching Pragmatics and Instructed Second Language Learning

Study Abroad and Technology-Enhanced Teaching

Nicola Halenko

BLOOMSBURY ACADEMIC
LONDON • NEW YORK • OXFORD • NEW DELHI • SYDNEY

BLOOMSBURY ACADEMIC
Bloomsbury Publishing Plc
50 Bedford Square, London, WC1B 3DP, UK
1385 Broadway, New York, NY 10018, USA
29 Earlsfort Terrace, Dublin 2, Ireland

BLOOMSBURY, BLOOMSBURY ACADEMIC and the Diana logo are trademarks of Bloomsbury Publishing Plc

First published in Great Britain 2021
This paperback edition published in 2022

Copyright © Nicola Halenko, 2021

Nicola Halenko has asserted her right under the Copyright, Designs and Patents Act, 1988, to be identified as Author of this work.

For legal purposes the Acknowledgements on p. ix constitute an extension of this copyright page.

All rights reserved. No part of this publication may be reproduced or transmitted in any form or by any means, electronic or mechanical, including photocopying, recording, or any information storage or retrieval system, without prior permission in writing from the publishers.

Bloomsbury Publishing Plc does not have any control over, or responsibility for, any third-party websites referred to or in this book. All internet addresses given in this book were correct at the time of going to press. The author and publisher regret any inconvenience caused if addresses have changed or sites have ceased to exist, but can accept no responsibility for any such changes.

A catalogue record for this book is available from the British Library.

A catalog record for this book is available from the Library of Congress.

ISBN: HB: 978-1-3500-9714-8
       PB: 978-1-3502-0353-2
       ePDF: 978-1-3500-9715-5
       eBook: 978-1-3500-9716-2

Series: Advances in Instructed Second Language Acquisition Research

Typeset by Integra Software Private Limited

To find out more about our authors and books visit www.bloomsbury.com and sign up for our newsletters.

Contents

List of Figures		vi
List of Tables		vii
Acknowledgements		ix
1	Introduction	1
2	Researching L2 pragmatics	13
3	Instructed L2 pragmatics	33
4	Requests and apologies	49
5	Background to the study	67
6	Methodology	77
7	Request and apology findings	101
8	Study abroad language contact findings	129
9	Discussion	147
10	Conclusions and future directions	171
Notes		178
References		180
Appendix 1. Living in the UK questionnaire		203
Appendix 2. Scheme of work for the six-week explicit instructional period		205
Appendix 3. Sample of communicative practice materials		209
Index		210

List of Figures

4.1	Strategy choice for request head acts	50
4.2	Formulaic strategies for the apology speech act (Trosborg 1987)	59
5.1	Common data collection instruments on a scale of authenticity and control	73
6.1	Results of the pilot perception questionnaire	79
6.2	An example of a request scenario from the CAPT	84
6.3	Procedure for completion of the CAPT	84
6.4	An example of an apology scenario from the WDCT	85
6.5	Six-week classroom-based instructional procedure	88
6.6	The instructional framework adopted for teaching request and apology speech acts	89
6.7	Testing procedure over the twelve-week period (T1-T4) for the experimental and control groups	92
7.1	CAPT group performance of request production (T1-T4)	111
7.2	PAPER group performance of request production (T1-T4)	112
7.3	Control group performance of request production (T1-T4)	112
7.4	CAPT group performance of apology production (T1-T4)	124
7.5	PAPER group performance of apology production (T1-T4)	124
7.6	Control group performance of apology production (T1-T4)	125
8.1	Evolution of skills assessment by the experimental groups T1, T2 and T4	145

List of Tables

2.1	Examples of noncongruent requests in academic encounters (data taken from Halenko and Jones (2011, 2017))	29
2.2	Examples of noncongruent apologies in academic encounters (data taken from Halenko 2018)	30
4.1	Non-L2-like features of requests reported for L1 Chinese users	51
4.2	Non-L2-like features of apologies reported for L1 Chinese users	60
6.1	Main study participants	79
6.2	Content of the CAPT and WDCT scenarios	82
6.3	Rating scale to evaluate participant responses	94
6.4	Coding scheme for request strategies	95
6.5	Coding scheme for apology strategies	98
7.1	Descriptive statistics: Raters' scores for request responses from the experimental and control groups T1-T2	102
7.2	Descriptive statistics: Gain scores for request responses from the experimental and control groups T1-T2	102
7.3	Frequency of requisite request strategies: Classroom access scenario	104
7.4	Frequency of requisite request strategies: Essay extension scenario	105
7.5	Frequency of requisite request strategies: Book a study room scenario	106
7.6	Frequency of combined production of all key request strategies by scenario (T1-T4)	110
7.7	Non-target-like features of requests T1-T4	114
7.8	Descriptive statistics: Raters' scores for apology responses from the experimental and control groups T1-T2	116
7.9	Frequency of requisite apology strategies: Lost library book scenario	118
7.10	Frequency of requisite apology strategies: Noisy party at flat scenario	119
7.11	Frequency of requisite apology strategies: Missed appointment with tutor	120
7.12	Frequency of combined production of all key apology strategies by scenario	123
7.13	Non-target-like features of apologies T1-T4	126

8.1	Descriptive statistics: CAPT, PAPER and control groups' self-evaluations of combined productive and receptive English use at T1 and T2	131
8.2	Descriptive statistics: CAPT, PAPER and control groups' self-evaluations of separate productive and receptive English use at T1 and T2	131
8.3	Descriptive statistics: Experimental groups' self-evaluations of productive and receptive English use T1, T2 and T4	133
8.4	Descriptive statistics: Experimental groups' self-evaluations of T1-T4 productive and receptive English use by activity	136
8.5	Descriptive statistics: Paired sample t-tests analysing experimental within-group comparisons for productive and receptive English use T1-T4	139
8.6	Descriptive statistics: Experimental and control groups' T1-T2 self-evaluations of listening, speaking, reading, writing and interaction skills	141
8.7	Descriptive statistics: Experimental groups' T1-T4 self-evaluations by skill	143
8.8	Paired sample t-test results for experimental groups by skill	144
8.9	Independent t-test results for experimental groups by skill	144
9.1	Examples of direct strategy use in the request data	150
9.2	Comparisons of self-criticism strategy use in the request data T1-T2	151
9.3	Examples of non-target-like conventional expressions in the request data	153
9.4	Examples of grounders in the request data	155
9.5	Examples of strategy repetition in the request data	155
9.6	Sequencing pattern of strategy use in the apology data	157
9.7	Non-target-like pattern of strategy use in the apology data	158
9.8	Non-target-like linguistic forms in the apology data	159
9.9	Other non-target-like apology features	160
9.10	Excessive offers of repair in the apology data	160

Acknowledgements

This volume was made possible by the support of many incredible people. I have been fortunate to work with a number of inspirational academics on my doctorate journey. I would first like to thank Dr Gila Schauer, Dr Marije Michel and Dr Jenefer Philp. I'm very grateful for all your expertise and direction through the stages of my thesis on which this book is based. A special thanks also goes to Professor Geoffrey Leech with whom I also began this journey. Your kindness and guidance are greatly missed.

I am very grateful to my fantastic TESOL colleagues at the University of Central Lancashire for their encouragement throughout and allowing me time to complete this volume. Thanks also to Bloomsbury for seeing the potential of the volume for the ISLA series and the support provided to reach this point.

This volume is dedicated to Stephen, Jacob and Emily. Thank you for always being there and making me smile at the right times.

1

Introduction

Over more than forty years, pragmatics has developed into a dynamic research field which continues to expand and diversify. Investigating communicative actions in social contexts is at the heart of pragmatics study and several definitions have been proposed over the years, showing pragmatics to be an ever-evolving research discipline. Both Lo Castro (2003) and Crystal (1997) not only provide the most widely cited definitions but capture well the tripartite importance of the speaker, listener and context which underpin pragmatics study. Lo Castro's (2003: 15) definition of pragmatics highlights the shared endeavours of interlocutors to achieve a communicative goal – 'the study of the speaker and hearer meaning created in their joint actions that include both linguistic and non-linguistic signals in the context of socioculturally organised activities'. Crystal's (1997: 301) earlier definition spotlights the complexities of managing talk that is influenced by a number of external factors: 'pragmatics is the study of language from the point of view of the users, especially of the choices they make, the constraints they encounter in using language in social interaction, and the effects their use of language has on other participants in the act of communication'.

Pragmatics has found a well-established home within second language acquisition (SLA) research. Interlanguage pragmatics (ILP), also known as second language (L2) pragmatics, has evolved as a particular sub-field of SLA whose primary interest is to examine L2 users' knowledge and language use in social interaction, most often investigated from cross-sectional or longitudinal (developmental) perspectives. L2 pragmatics is directly linked to models of communicative competence (see Chapter 2). Thomas (1983) and Leech (1983) are known for distinguishing linguistic knowledge (pragmalinguistic) from sociocultural knowledge (sociopragmatic), meaning in addition to having a command of language forms, having the ability to use language in socially appropriate ways is of, at least, equal importance. For instance, when requesting a favour from someone, aside from knowing what forms and lexis are needed to produce the request (grammatical competence), users need to consider their linguistic choices in light of acceptability of the request according to the local cultural norms, the specific situation, the favour itself, and from whom they are soliciting the favour (pragmatic competence). It is recognized that grammatical and pragmatic competencies are inextricably linked (Kasper & Rose 2002; Taguchi & Roever 2017; Trosborg 2010) and need equal attention in the language learning process.

Over the years, it has been shown that inside the classroom, however, grammatical competence tends to be valued more highly and often receives the greatest attention, at the expense of developing pragmatic knowledge (e.g. Bardovi Harlig & Dörnyei 1998; Schauer 2009). Although pragmatic rules often differ cross-culturally, highlighting the need to develop this skill, specific pragmatic-based instruction rarely appears in foreign language curricula and commercial textbook materials rarely address pragmatic features of the target language in any meaningful depth (Barron 2016; Crandall & Basturkmen 2004; Limberg 2016; Nguyen 2011; Schauer 2019). Outside the classroom, interaction in the target language environment may not easily facilitate the development of pragmatic competence either. First, access to expert language users may be limited, which is particularly difficult when studying in at-home learning environments. Even when learners do have greater access such as during a study period abroad, they may prefer not to take advantage of communicative opportunities for self-discovery (Dörnyei et al. 2004; Kasper & Rose 2002). Second, since no pragmatic rule books exist, pragmatic language features may not be salient to learners so opportunities for advancing pragmatic knowledge may be missed. In authentic interactions, pragmatic feedback may not be readily offered to the learner either due to the sensitive nature of highlighting breaches of cultural norms.

It is perhaps not surprising then that research reports disparities between linguistic proficiency and pragmatic competence to be common, even in advanced-level learners of English (e.g. Bardovi-Harlig 2014; Glaser 2018). Some studies have suggested that, without the aid of instruction, pragmatic development is slow (Barron 2003; Cohen 2008; Taguchi 2010), with some language learners failing to achieve any appropriate level of pragmatic competency despite being long-term members of a target language community (Cohen 2008; Kasper & Rose 2002). The importance of language learners developing a reasonable level of pragmatic competence to avoid communication breakdown is clearly underlined by Thomas (1983). She states that whilst grammatical inaccuracies may be excused and accounted for as part of the language learning process, pragmatic infelicities may be judged as a character flaw. This suggests high-risk consequences for interpersonal relationships when failing to consider local pragmatic norms.

1.1. About this book

L2 pragmatics has been actively investigated since the late 1970s. Early defining volumes such as *Interlanguage Pragmatics* (Kasper & Blum Kulka 1993), *Pragmatics in Language Teaching* (Rose & Kasper 2001) and *Pragmatic Development in a Second Language* (Kasper & Rose 2002) helped elevate the appeal and importance of L2 pragmatics in research communities. These volumes also include some of the major intervention studies of the time and so serve as an important backdrop against which new volumes such as *Teaching Pragmatics* can advance the field. Examining the benefits and limitations to becoming a pragmatically competent language user, and how this might be best achieved inside and outside the classroom are some of the key discussion points in this volume. What we can glean from L2 pragmatics research to date is that it can be learned, and this can have a positive effect on learners' confidence, performance and interaction in the target language. Research also shows that many pragmatic features of language are indeed teachable, and explicit instruction, in particular, has been found to yield the best results (see Plonsky & Zhuang 2019; Taguchi 2015 for reviews). Furthermore, practitioners now have access to a growing body of pragmatics-focused materials thanks to editions such as Ishihara and Cohen (2010), Tatsuki and Houck (2010) and Riddiford and Newton (2010). It is also increasingly apparent that pragmatic performance and development are not at all straightforward. Investigations continue to uncover a wide range of complex influential factors such as individual learner differences, motivation, learner agency, and exposure to and engagement in the L2 environment (e.g. Taguchi 2012).

Overall, research to date has offered many key insights to learning and teaching but much remains under-explored in the areas of intervention studies and technology-enhanced teaching and learning, for example. Taguchi and Roever's (2017) comprehensive monograph, *Second Language Pragmatics*, examines the current research landscape and is a timely marker for opening a new chapter in pragmatics research. *Teaching Pragmatics* aims to operationalize some of the most recent calls for advancing the field (see Chapter 5 for more detail on how this volume addresses current gaps in L2 pragmatics research). Firstly, the volume goes beyond basic explicit classroom interventions to examining pretest and posttest performance across multiple experimental groups, working with multiple speech acts and employing multiple delayed test designs. In doing so, the teachability and learnability of multiple speech acts can be directly compared. This exploration of the amenability of different pragmatic features to instruction has important implications for L2 pedagogy (Plonsky & Zhuang 2019). Secondly, environmental influences are explored by measuring the frequency of experimental group contact with the study abroad (SA) environment and the extent to which a non-instructed control group benefitted from exposure alone. Thirdly, adopting rating scales as a means of assessing performance is showcased in this volume to avoid the well-documented challenges of making direct L1-L2 speaker comparisons to judge pragmatic success.

Finally, an emergent sub-field within L2 pragmatics has been the growing attention paid to the beneficial role technology can play in pragmatics investigations. Taguchi and Sykes's (2013) volume helped synthesize current directions in this area but gaps in the research remain, particularly from the teaching and assessment perspectives, as the authors themselves note. At the heart of *Teaching Pragmatics* is the field's first attempt at directly comparing the effects of technology platforms with traditional paper-based tasks for developing pragmatic competency. This includes a comprehensive look at an innovative oral computer-animated production task (CAPT), designed to enhance learner engagement and performance. Within the instructional study presented in this volume, the CAPT is used for both language practice of speech acts and as an assessment tool to measure pragmatic performance.

All the aforementioned features of this volume either break new ground in pragmatics research or offer new insights into under-explored areas (see also Chapter 5). The intention is to address some of the current shortcomings and offer a replicable contribution to experimental studies. To this end, the volume aims to provide a full account of the study, within the limitations of a publication of this kind. To help further pedagogical development in instructed pragmatics, the main data collection instrument (CAPT) can also be found on the open access IRIS website (a digital repository of instruments and materials for research into second languages) (Marsden et al. 2016).

Since this book is one of only a few volumes dedicated to teaching L2 pragmatics, this is an excellent opportunity to survey and synthesize the current literature in terms of what we know about the *why*, *what* and *how* to teach pragmatics. The aspect of *when* (pragmatics should be taught) is only briefly considered since this is not a primary aim of the study. However, discussions concerning age and proficiency are recurrent themes in the chapters, and readers' attention is also directed to wider reading regarding these issues at strategic points in the book.

1.2. Research scope

It is important to also establish the parameters of the empirical study included in this volume. Participants in this study were adult, international students based in a university setting. Whilst these two variables are probably the most widely researched in the field, the justification for continuing the tradition of investigating speech acts in this way is to improve international students' overseas academic experience at the UK institution where the research was based and to improve the impact and longevity of its study abroad programmes. In terms of international student recruitment, China continues to be the biggest source of non-UK students (21.5 per cent) outside of the EU (30.5 per cent) on a national level (Universities UK 2018). At the local level, Chinese ESL students account for over 50 per cent of the international cohort on the British campus where this study is located so this learner group is worthy of investigation for these reasons.

With the academic HE context in mind, the study investigates L2 pragmatic success within a specific genre of discourse known as institutional talk. Discourse of this type is understood as talk between an institutional representative (e.g. faculty staff, advisor at a job agency) and a client (e.g. a student, job applicant), or between members of the same institution in workplace-type interaction (e.g. a nursing supervisor and nurse, hotel or factory employees) (Bardovi-Harlig & Hartford 2005). This study focuses exclusively on institutional talk between members of university staff, as the institutional representative, and university students, as clients.

Institutional talk is recognized as being quite different from general L2 conversation, which often investigates pragmatics from turntaking and negotiation perspectives. Within institutional talk, there is a need to achieve an end goal (within restricted conventional forms) and the need to recognize there will be constraints and frameworks informing how this end goal is achieved (Drew & Heritage 1992). It is not the case that, as in ELF contexts, interactants have room to negotiate meaning using English as the communicative medium. Within staff-student interactions, in a target language university setting, participants need to be aware of the expected norms of the academic encounter, such as observing social roles and power relationships, and then make corresponding language adjustments based on this knowledge.

Where institutional talk is status-appropriate for the participants' roles and adheres to expectations, the talk is described as congruent (Bardovi-Harlig & Hartford 1990, 1993). An example of congruency might be a student requesting an academic meeting with an advisor. In the event of noncongruent interactions, where the status of the representative is challenged (e.g. a student requests an extension to a deadline), status-preserving strategies (SPS) are required as mitigators to ensure the task is accomplished in a favourable way and to maintain a good academic relationship (Bardovi Harlig 1990). Asking for an extension to a deadline, for example, could be mitigated by making the request in a brief and timely manner (non-linguistic SPS) and by using situationally appropriate request strategies and lexical modifiers (linguistic SPS) for damage control. Failing to negotiate noncongruent encounters in an appropriate way is likely to result in non-completion of the task in the short term (the deadline extension is not granted) but could also risk a lasting negative impression of the student in the long term. It is the negotiation of these noncongruent encounters which L2 learners can find particularly challenging and which are a feature of the empirical study presented in this book. Chen's (2006) longitudinal study of a Taiwanese graduate student's academic emails to faculty at an American institution is a good illustration of these struggles. The 2.5-year study charts how status-unequal e-communication is initially challenging for the student since there are no explicit rules to follow or model practices to imitate. This is because emails between staff and students tend to be private exchanges and feedback is rarely offered. These barriers caused the student's progress in producing pragmatically appropriate emails to be slow and limited. Early emails often drew on L1 practices and were characterized as lengthy (with irrelevant detail), were demanding and needy in terms of tone and linguistic expressions used, contained few reasons or explanations as might be expected, and often failed to demonstrate status-appropriate politeness. The study in this volume aims to help students overcome these linguistic and cultural barriers so struggles of this kind do not impede the study abroad experience.

Research shows producing pragmatically appropriate language in a British context may be particularly problematic for international students from positive politeness[1] cultures (Brown & Levinson 1987) such as Spain (Marquez Reiter 2000), Greece (Economidou-Kogetsidis 2008; Pavlidou 1998; Sifianou 1992), Korea (Kim 2008) and China (Gu 1990) as their language can be perceived as rude if they do not adhere to expectations of the UK's negative politeness[2] host culture (García 1989; Marquez-Reiter 2000; Sifianou 1992). As Sabaté i Dalmau and Curell i Gotor (2007: 293) explain, L1 users belonging to a positive face-based culture often perform speech acts at an inappropriate level of intensity when communicating in a negative-based L2 culture due to applying inadequate sociopragmatic concerns and politeness, relative to the target culture. Put simply, when studying overseas in an L2 environment, learners may get the grammar or words right but the pragmatics wrong and this can have a negative impact on how effective their communication is. The study in this volume also investigates the extent to which Chinese speakers from positive politeness cultures manage L2 pragmatic output in a UK-based negative politeness environment.

In terms of measuring the pragmatic success of the participants in this study, the historical practice in L2 pragmatics research is to employ native speaker (NS) norms as a comparative benchmark. Whilst Barron (2003) and Warga (2007), amongst others, argue that some kind of baseline is a useful or unavoidable yardstick (Roever 2011) against which to measure L2 learner performance, the concept of the NS norm must also be viewed with caution. Within intercultural communication studies, the ongoing debates of what it means to be interculturally competent regularly profile the issues surrounding using a NS model, yet these discussions are only recently beginning to resonate in second language pragmatics research. Specifically, critics outline the following difficulties with positing a NS ideal: First, selecting the appropriate L2 norm in a principled manner is a challenging task given the range of language varieties available, within which social class, gender and age-based variation are also likely (House & Kasper 2000). Second, NS themselves also deviate from the standard norm so L2 speakers should be afforded the same concessions, given they are also multicompetent L2 users (Cook 2002). Third is the case of L2 users exercising learner agency and intentionally opting out from convergence to the L2 norm in order to preserve and promote their own L1 identities (Kasper 1997). In such cases, non-L2-like behaviour is a conscious decision rather than being attributed to gaps in pragmatic knowledge. Finally, research has shown acquiring pragmatic knowledge to be a lengthy process, particularly in the absence of instruction. Whether L2 speakers wish to achieve L2-like levels or not may therefore be an unrealistic goal. This may be why some degree of convergence is advocated as a preferable aim (Giles et al. 1991; Kasper 1997; Sabaté i Dalmau & Curell i Gotor 2007).

For the reasons described above, and the caution attached to using L1 comparative data, the study in this volume adopts a stance which avoids the promotion of direct L1 and L2 comparisons. Instead, the aim is to focus on the distinctiveness of the learners' request and apology realizations in this study.

Specifically, what pragmatic features make a successful request or apology? In this study, success is conceptualized as the degree to which L1 English users evaluate L2 learner requests and apologies as being appropriate for a given context. For instance, the rating scale adopted in this study defines a highly appropriate request or apology as one where the interlocutor feels completely satisfied because the levels of directness, politeness and formality are almost entirely appropriate and effective for the situation (see Chapter 6 for details of the rating scale).

In addition, this study will also highlight which aspects of non-L2-like performance are considered inappropriate or hearer-alienating (Sabaté i Dalmau & Curell i Gotor 2007) and may therefore directly affect the outcome of each request or apology. For instance, interlocutors are arguably less likely to react negatively to an unfamiliar address term, such as 'Dear teacher' as an opening to a request, than a direct demand for help, such as 'I need a reference.' Judging the appropriacy of the speech acts is achieved by replacing measurements of comparable NS data with rating the learner data in terms of appropriacy of content for the given scenarios. This approach assumes not all non-L2-like features matter in the sense that some may not directly affect the outcome of the request or apology, or cause communication breakdown, as the previous examples show. In this way, the study aligns itself more to the concept of communicative adequacy, understood as 'the degree to which a learner's performance is more or less successful in achieving the task's goals efficiently' (Pallotti 2009: 596). The study in this volume hopes to shed more light on which pragmatic choices most affect pragmatic success in order to better inform future teaching practices.

Finally, in line with Dewaele (2018), this volume also replaces the terms 'native' and 'non-native speaker' in favour of L1 and L2 user. This shift is to avoid the connotation that the former is more superior than the latter and that being a non-native speaker inherently suggests deficiency rather than celebrating multicompetency, as Cook (2002) also argues. For clarification, the majority of participants in this study are users of English as a second language in its true sense as opposed to the label L2 used as a cover to capture all languages other than the first.

1.3. Research aims

The main objectives of this study are threefold. The first aim is to expand the body of research investigating the effects of explicit instruction on two specific speech acts, namely requests and apologies. Given the motivation for this study is to improve communication between British HE staff and international students on campus, these two speech acts were selected after being identified by academic colleagues, through a short email questionnaire, as being the most common in oral and written communication with their international students. Furthermore, both requests and apologies are associated with negative politeness (Brown & Levinson 1987; Leech 1983). These two speech acts may be seen as particularly challenging for speakers from positive-politeness cultures such as China, as indicated earlier, so are deserved of empirical investigation.

Secondly, a methodological innovation of this research is the design of an oral CAPT. The CAPT was devised to bring the real-world context to the students with the aim of developing and assessing their pragmatic skills. This mode of delivery was chosen for language development purposes: (i) given the propensity for learners to actively use digital technologies outside of the classroom and (ii) for the additional interactive, audio-visual element provided in the material which was thought to be a more stimulating learning mode. For testing purposes, few attempts have been made in the last ten years to widen the range of data collection instruments despite encouragement to do so (e.g. Bardovi-Harlig 2018; Trosborg 2010). The CAPT then also aims to fill this research gap by providing an innovative data collection tool for developing and assessing pragmatic competence, in addition to investigating if technology-enhanced practice improves learning.

Finally, the study seeks to identify if interaction in the study abroad environment, without the aid of instruction, is sufficient for developing pragmatic skills as empirical studies report mixed results, as described in Chapter 2. These three aims can be summarized as follows:

1. To investigate the effectiveness of a six-week explicit instructional period for developing pragmatic competence in the production of requests and apologies amongst Chinese learners of English at a British HE institution during their study abroad stay.
2. To analyse the effects of the differentiated training material; traditional paper-based activities (PAPER group) versus computer-animated versions of the training material (CAPT group), by employing a pretest, posttest and delayed test design.
3. To determine to what extent pragmatic knowledge of requests and apologies can be acquired naturally in the L2 environment by employing a non-instructed control group.

1.4. Organization of the book

The remaining part of this book has nine additional chapters. Chapters 2–4 provide background reading to L2 pragmatics as a research field with a specific focus on instructional pragmatics. Chapters 5–10 detail the empirical study aiming to identify the effectiveness of a differentiated explicit intervention on the oral production of requests and apologies with Chinese ESL users in a study abroad context. Details of these two aspects of the volume are provided below.

L2 Pragmatics as a research field

Chapter 2 begins with addressing some of the theories and principles behind L2 pragmatics and ends with establishing a case for the importance of including pragmatics on teaching curricula. Chapter 3 extends the pedagogical discussion to modes of delivery and instructional content. The chapter covers initial key considerations for teaching pragmatics, before addressing the specifics of study abroad instruction and teaching techniques. Speech acts, pragmatics routines and technology-enhanced language practice are discussed in this chapter for their relevancy to the empirical study. Chapter 4 summarizes current research from Chinese ESL users and what we know about the developmental features of oral and written request and apology production with this learner group.

The empirical study

Chapter 5 provides context to the empirical study by describing the methodological approach adopted and reviewing common data collection techniques to foreground the innovative virtual role-plays (CAPT) designed to elicit oral responses. The chapter concludes by identifying current gaps in L2 pragmatics research and presenting the three research questions guiding the study. Chapter 6 describes the methodology including information on the participants and the three data collection instruments. This chapter also details the instructional and testing phases, in addition to the request and apology coding schemes adopted to analyse the data.

The next two chapters summarize the findings from the data. Chapter 7 presents the request and apology data from two perspectives: the qualitative results from rater evaluations of appropriacy and the quantitative results following a linguistic content analysis. The aim was to identify what are considered the essential components of request and apology language in a range of situations in an academic environment and which components are considered non-target-like which may affect the outcome of the request or apology. Chapter 8 focuses on the data from the study abroad contact questionnaire, elicited to determine to what extent request and apology language could be acquired from the study abroad environment alone.

Chapter 9 discusses the three sets of results in light of the existing literature and the original three research questions posed. Finally, Chapter 10 presents a summary of the study and offers pedagogical implications for language teachers. The chapter concludes with limitations and suggestions for future research.

2

Researching L2 pragmatics

This chapter introduces several key principles behind L2 pragmatics research. The chapter begins by briefly charting early language competency models alongside more detailed accounts of contemporary schools of thought regarding what makes a successful twenty-first-century L2 language user. This is followed by an overview of pragmatics-related SLA theories which help us gain a better understanding of language learning processes to facilitate more effective research and pedagogical practice. The chapter concludes with building a case for why pragmatics instruction is needed in the context of an academic setting within a study abroad (SA) sojourn.

2.1. Pragmatics and language learning

The notion of communicative competence in language learning was first introduced by Hymes (1972) as a shift away from the Chomskyian (1965) view of language as a system isolated from context and use. Hymes introduced the importance of situating both the knowledge of language and the ability to use it in social contexts within the construct of communicative competence, thereby guiding the design of later influential frameworks. Researchers such as Canale and Swain (1980), Canale (1983), Bachman (1990), Bachman and Palmer (1996, 2010) are among those credited with attempting to capture the essential components of communicative competence in second language acquisition (SLA). Whilst Canale and Swain's (1980) and Canale's (1983) work implicitly embeds a pragmatic component, referring to the rules of use and appropriateness within sociolinguistic competence, Bachman and Palmer (1982), subsequently Bachman (1990), were the first to explicitly categorize it as a discrete element.

Collectively, these models of communicative competence demonstrated that it is not only grammatical knowledge that is a key tenet to communicative competence, but the acquisition of a functional and sociolinguistic control of language. The importance of the social aspects of interaction is echoed by a number of researchers who suggest that pragmatic competence must be reasonably well developed for successful communication in the L2 (Bardovi-Harlig 2001; Kasper & Rose 2002; Rose 2005).

In today's globalized world, where multilingual and multicultural interactions are commonplace, research is increasingly drawing upon alternate competency theories which more adequately reflect the modern-day language user. Early frameworks of the 1980s and 1990s, as described above, overlooked the importance of both the situational context and dynamic, interpersonal nature of communicative encounters. Also spurred on by English as a lingua franca (ELF) debates and English user demographics, pragmatics research is aligning itself more to the idea of multiculturalism (e.g. Culpeper et al. 2018; Kecskes & Assimakopoulos 2017; McConachy 2018). More recent pragmatic investigations are rightly concerned with how today's intercultural speakers achieve success through co-constructed understanding, social actions and shared goals. This contrasts with the historical focus on the individual and their interlanguage shortfalls, often measured against a fixed set of competencies or a native speaker ideal. With this revised positioning, communicative competency is now being analysed through a multilingual lens, underpinned by notions of *interactional* and *intercultural competencies*, for instance, and situated within branches of SLA such as *intercultural pragmatics*. These three areas will be addressed briefly in the next sections.

Ishida (2009), Masuda (2011) and Taguchi (2014b) are recent examples of investigations in the study abroad context which incorporate interactional competency models to developmental second language pragmatics investigations (see Hall et al. 2011 for a review of other studies). Interactional competency is characterized as learners bringing a variety of linguistic and semiotic resources to jointly contribute to ongoing discourse and co-accomplish specific language goals (Young 2002). It is differentiated from communicative competency in the following way: 'Interactional competency is not what a person *knows*. It is what a person *does* together with others' (Young 2011: 430, emphasis in the original). This view of L2 pragmatics is rooted in sociocultural theory where participants draw on each other's knowledge and resources to co-construct meaning and understanding. The scaffolding supplied as part of this co-collaboration allows interactants to move beyond their current limitations with the assistance of others (Ohta 2005).

Applying an interactional competency framework to pragmatics study has a considerable role to play from an L2 instructional perspective. Adopting teaching approaches and implementing instructional materials which help develop interactional competence may already be salient techniques to classroom practitioners. For instance, incorporating authentic written and spoken samples to contextualize language and encouraging learners to notice target language features through guided self-discovery are already considered good practice in language learning. Similarly, studying transcriptions of naturally recorded data with language learners or eliciting recent interactions in the target language for reflective purposes (as adopted in the present volume) have been advocated as beneficial teaching tools for enhancing pragmatic development for some time.

In the field of language learning and teaching, studies underpinned by the notion of intercultural competence are also gaining traction. Intercultural competence involves 'a complex of abilities needed to perform effectively and appropriately when interacting with others who are linguistically and culturally different from oneself' (Fantini & Tirmizi 2006: 12). Theorizing intercultural (communicative) competence most often draws on the work of Byram (1997, 2012) who attempts to integrate both communicative competence and intercultural competence within a set of *savoirs* (knowledge) about oneself and others. Most influentially, Byram's model acknowledges the importance of how communicative actions are managed between intercultural speakers whose diverse set of language, culture and belief systems will affect participant interaction. Recent studies adopting an intercultural stance in pragmatics investigations include McConachy (2018), Sánchez-Hernández and Alcón-Soler (2018), Shively and Cohen (2008) and Taguchi et al. (2016).

The complex nature of understanding, theorizing and articulating the specifics of intercultural competency makes the task of promoting it in the language classroom more challenging for teachers and curriculum designers. As Liddicoat (2011) notes, intercultural language teaching and learning does not come with a standardized set of pedagogical techniques which can be adopted wholesale into the language classroom. Instead, practitioners should be led by a mutual understanding of what it means to teach language in an intercultural way in order to inform their own classroom practices. In terms of operationalizing this intercultural understanding, Liddicoat and Scarino (2013) offer a useful starting point by encouraging the design of activities which engage learners to 'notice', 'compare', 'reflect' and 'interact' with language materials to explore and advance their own intercultural experiences. By initiating this sequence of steps, learning becomes meaningful, contextualized, thought-provoking and personal. These four steps are, not dissimilar to existing frameworks designed to support pragmatics instruction (as discussed in Chapter 3) and underline the existing interrelationship between intercultural and pragmatic competencies.

Within the field of SLA, intercultural pragmatics is broadly defined as 'the way in which the language system is put to use in social encounters between human beings who have different first languages, but communicate in a common language, and, usually represent different cultures' (Kecskes & Assimakopoulos 2017: 1). At the heart of this post-2000 discipline is a socio-cognitive approach which encapsulates the modern, multilingual language user. Intercultural pragmatics outlines the process by which participants of different linguistic and cultural backgrounds establish common ground by negotiating their way through the influences of their unique cultural and linguistic groups to bring about a shared understanding and communicative goal. This co-constructed 'third way' (House 2008), or 'third culture' (Kecskes 2014), involves L2 speakers establishing their own 'intercultural positions' (McConachy 2018) within shared communicative spaces. As a sub-field of pragmatics with a multilingual focus, intercultural pragmatics seems fit for purpose to represent today's L2 users, as well as providing a growing discipline within which the next wave of L2 pragmatics research can be taken forward. For the reasons described above, studies aligned to the concepts of interactional and intercultural competencies, as well as intercultural pragmatics as a disciplinary field, are likely to continue gaining momentum in the coming years. Since L2 language behaviour needs to be increasingly explained and understood in multilingual and multicultural terms, these are areas of SLA within which we should all consider grounding our future research and teaching practices.

In addition to SLA theory noted above, research initiatives also typically draw on relevant theory from language learning and teaching disciplines, as discussed in the following section.

2.2. Some theoretical links for pragmatics research

For those less familiar with L2 pragmatics research, it is timely to consider some of the key theoretical frameworks typically associated with the field which are used to ensure research design is approached in a principled way. As is the case with this volume, reviewing related teaching and learning theory helps frame the analysis and understanding of pragmatic behaviour. Some of the key SLA and pragmatic-related theories, which are pertinent to the empirical study, are described below as an introduction for further reading outside of this volume.

Given the classroom setting of the present investigation, research into *instructed second language acquisition* (ISLA) is the obvious first link to be made.

ISLA is most often linked to acquisition in the formal L2 classroom, but it could equally occur as a result of exposure to the target environment or through self-directed study. According to Loewen (2014: 2) ISLA 'aims to understand how the systematic manipulation of the mechanisms of learning and/or the conditions under which they occur enable or facilitate the development and acquisition of a language other than one's first'. Manipulation can occur by altering the instructional input to facilitate learning (e.g. this study's manipulation of authentic written and spoken dialogues to include a range of request and apology expressions) or altering how learners engage with the input (e.g. the differentiated training materials in this study comparing the effectiveness of paper-based vs computer-based learning activities). Research linking ISLA and pragmatics has received only limited attention, despite pragmatic development being a key component for successful communication and the well-documented challenges of acquiring pragmatic knowledge without planned instructional intervention.

Regarding the language learning process, Kasper and Rose (2002) contend interventionist studies are generally underpinned by three interrelated SLA hypotheses; Schmidt's (1993, 2001) *noticing hypothesis*, Swain's (1996) *output hypothesis* and Long's (1996) *interaction hypothesis*. The study in this volume is no exception. The first two hypotheses relate to separate stages in the language learning process. Firstly, given the explicit instructional approach adopted in this study, the proposal in the noticing hypothesis that linguistic forms can only serve as intake for learning if learners 'notice' them drives this present investigation. Secondly, the output hypothesis suggests several acquisitional roles for second language production, namely learners may notice gaps in their interlanguage during utterance production, learners require analysed knowledge for productive language use beyond formulaic speech, and repeated productive language use is requisite for automatization. The third, the interaction hypothesis draws on Schmidt and Swain by positing that negotiation of meaning through interactional adjustments facilitates acquisition by connecting input, output and learner internal capacities. The metapragmatic input and reflective discussions, followed by opportunities for collaborative communicative practice which were incorporated into this study, attend to these acquisitional needs outlined in these hypotheses.

New trends in pragmatics investigations have also begun to draw on *skills acquisition processing* (Anderson 1993) and *input processing* (VanPatten 1996) theories to describe and better understand the cognitive mechanisms underlying the acquisition and processing of pragmatic rules. Pragmatic studies applying skills acquisition theory have focused on tracking learners' growth from conscious learning of pragmatic rules (declarative knowledge) to automatic application of these rules in real time (procedural knowledge) as a result of repeated activation (see studies by Li 2012, 2013). As an alternative cognitive focus, input processing theory which seeks to understand how learners process input, make form-meaning connections and manage syntactic structures can be found in pragmatic studies such as Takimoto (2009).

For studies situated in the study abroad (SA) context like the present volume, language socialization theory (e.g. Duff 2007; Schiefflin & Ochs 1986), which argues the acquisition of linguistic and sociocultural knowledge is simultaneously achieved through social interaction, is a necessary consideration. As is claimed, 'pragmatic skills develop through socialisation in the given speech community' (Kesckes 2014: 65) and the community functions as a place 'where novices participate in concrete activities with experts' (Kasper & Rose 2002: 42). In this sense, language is both a means and a goal of socialization, and activity is fundamental to its success. The SA language contact survey conducted with participants in the present investigation aims to assess the extent of this activity in social interaction with members of the ESL community and its effect on pragmatic development.

2.3. Speech act and politeness theories

Speech act studies principally draw on the work of Austin (1962) and Searle (1969) who are credited with developing speech act theory to provide a clearer understanding of what is required for effective and appropriate communication. It is problematic to assign a clear definition of a speech act given that it is not a sentence or an utterance, but an act in itself. As Austin (1962) describes, language is more than making statements of fact; it has a performative function to carry out social actions such as in stating 'I apologise' has both a linguistic and social function. With this in mind, Austin (1962) posited that when producing utterances, a speaker actually performs three acts; the locutionary act (the utterances themselves), the illocutionary act (the speaker's intention behind the words, such as requesting or apologizing) and the perlocutionary act (the effect of the utterance on the hearer).

Of the three acts described above, the illocutionary act is said to be the underlying focus of speech act theory. Building on Austin's (1962) classifications of illocutionary acts, Searle's (1969) revised taxonomy is based on functional characteristics and incorporates five major groups: representatives (e.g. assertions), directives (e.g. requests), expressives (e.g. apologies), commisives (e.g. promises) and declarations (e.g. vows). The illocutionary act, also known as illocutionary force, provides a signal as to how the speaker wishes the utterance to be interpreted (Barron 2003) and is typically realized by illocutionary force indicating devices (IFIDs) such as performative verbs (e.g. requesting or apologizing), word order or intonation. For instance, 'Would it be possible to have an extension for my assignment?' functions as a request by the speaker. An IFID is considered successful if the listener obliges and complies with the request. The success of utilizing IFIDs appropriately, however, is less commonly achieved by learners of other languages (Barron 2003), the reasons for which have been one of the motivating drives for ILP investigations.

In order to realize the speech act itself, a number of speech act strategies (consisting of a word, phrase or sentence) may be chosen (Cohen 2018). Yet it is problematic to define an absolute set for any speech act since the choice of formulae depends on a number of factors. At best, we can estimate through empirical studies which formulae we would expect to encounter in given situations, as will be presented in Chapter 6. Early research by Searle (1976) and Fraser (1985) proposed that strategies for the realization of speech acts across languages are essentially universal, or non-language specific, but their appropriate use may differ across cultures.

This notion of universality is reinforced to some degree in some of the earliest work on L2 pragmatics such as Olshtain (1989) where strong similarities in the realization of apologies were found between Hebrew, Canadian-French, Australian English and German speakers. Around the same period, this idea was strongly contested, however, in a number of studies which attributed language differences to cultural norms and values (Blum-Kulka & Olshtain 1986; Wierzbicka 1985). This suggests speech act strategies are in fact culture- and language-specific – a claim also investigated in this volume. Speech acts are often performed indirectly (Searle 1976) due to the expectancy that politeness be observed during verbal interaction with others. The principles of politeness and its influence on language use are considered in the proceeding sections.

Speech act studies are closely aligned to the concept of politeness. Many empirical studies evaluate pragmatic performance on the basis of politeness theory and the interactants perceptions of politeness relative to the home and target language communities. A comprehensive review of politeness is beyond the scope of this volume but given its prominence in L2 pragmatics research, key principles of politeness do need to be considered in light of their importance in understanding what successful communication entails.

Leech (2014: 3) suggests being polite means 'to speak or behave in such a way as to (appear to) give benefit or value not to yourself but to the other person(s)'. As introduced in Chapter 1, politeness is characterized as both a linguistic and social/cultural phenomenon, organized by Leech (1983) and Thomas (1983) as *pragmalinguistics* (the range of lexico-grammatical resources) and *sociopragmatics* (the sociocultural context). Acquisition of the former is said to be facilitated more easily as learners can be introduced to different degrees of politeness and their relevant linguistic forms. The latter is based on social and contextual judgements and is, therefore, a more difficult skill to acquire, as empirical research has reported (e.g. Barron 2003; Fukuya & Zhang 2002; Shardakova 2005; Taguchi 2015). Both, however, work in conjunction with one another so competency in both pragmalinguistic and sociopragmatic features of language is requisite for successful pragmatic performance.

Culture, in particular, has a strong influence on politeness and is a factor which occupies much of the debate when analysing language from a cross-cultural perspective. The acknowledgement that there are different ways of performing politeness in different cultures is recognized as one of the main sources of pragmatic miscommunication. For instance, the notion of directness (Searle 1976) underpins both Leech's (1983) and Brown and Levinson's (1987) widely cited politeness theories. Both comment on the close relationship between politeness and indirectness in many Western traditions, yet this is not the case for all cultures. China and Japan, for instance, are said to value directness as a key principle to being polite under the tenets of economy and clarity of language use, most apparent when performing requests (Lee-Wong 1994). What is problematic for L2 communication is when this cross-cultural variation is applied incorrectly to the target culture – a common feature of pragmatics research.

Central to the concept of politeness within Brown and Levinson's work, developed from Goffman (1967), is the notion of 'face'. Parallels between this concept and the phrase 'losing face' can be drawn. When loss of face occurs, we damage our public self-image which can lead to embarrassment so maintaining face is a sensitive issue. In Brown and Levinson's model, face comprises 'negative face' (the right to privacy and freedom, unimpeded by others) and 'positive face' (the desire to be liked and approved of by others). For Brown and Levinson, acts which fail to satisfy face needs are termed 'face threatening acts' (FTAs), which also underpin politeness theory. The speech acts of request and apology, which form the basis to the present study, are both considered inherently face threatening (see Chapter 4). To counter this effect, participants must engage in redressive action to maintain polite behaviour and social harmony.

Further important components of the Brown and Levinson model, which are likely to influence a speaker's linguistic choices, are the social variables of power (P): interpreted as power of control, social rank or authority, distance (D): classified as social similarity or familiarity, and imposition (R): understood as the burden placed on the addressee in terms of time, effort, financial or psychological cost. Furthermore, the model suggests a positive correlation between these variables and the degree of indirectness employed so that the greater the hearer's power, social distance and degree of imposition in a request act, for instance, the greater the face threat will be. A greater threat leads to increased indirectness in the strategies employed. For instance, a request to borrow a book from an academic tutor, with whom you are not very familiar, is likely to be formulated with more indirectness than borrowing a book from a friend. Partial support for this correlation between politeness and indirectness has been identified in a number of pragmatic request studies, with a range of languages: Spanish (Félix-Brasdefer 2006; Marquez Reiter 2000); Hebrew, German, Argentinian (Blum-Kulka et al. 1989); Greek (Economidou-Kogetsidis 2010); and Chinese (Chen, He & Hu 2013). As for social variables, what is problematic for L2 communication is the different perceptions of power, distance and imposition amongst different cultures and speech communities.

Exploring politeness theory as a means of understanding its function within language, Brown and Levinson's landmark work has encouraged discussions around politeness to flourish, whilst, at the same time, been subject to heavy criticism. The main areas of critique include failure to acknowledge the social interdependence of 'face' (e.g. Spencer-Oatey 2000), the emphasis on politeness as means of mitigation for face-threatening acts (e.g. Leech 2014), and the *universal* claim of politeness theory (e.g. Wierzbicka 1985), specifically its Western (Anglo-Saxon) bias (e.g. Matsumoto 1988) which promotes an overemphasis on individual freedom and autonomy (e.g. Gu 1990). Contemporary alternate perspectives on the constituents of politeness have been motivated by this early work such as Spencer-Oatey's (2000) 'rapport management'[1] and Watts's (2003) 'politic behaviour'[2] which underline the interpersonal and social perspectives of interaction. From an East Asian perspective, Gu (1990) and Ide (1993) maintain politeness needs to be considered in relation to cultural traditions which concern the role individuals play within the larger context of the group and the traditional hierarchical society.

As noted, the Brown and Levinson model is said to place an unbalanced emphasis on the rights of the individual without due consideration of how politeness operates in other cultures. Such distinctions have naturally led to cultural labels or stereotypes, such as many Western European societies being considered negative-politeness oriented (focusing on the individual and their rights of privacy) (e.g. Marquez Reiter 2000; Sifianou 1992) and non-Western East Asian societies such as China and Japan, positive-politeness oriented (emphasizing a 'collectivist' group culture) (e.g. Gu 1990; Yu 1999). To some degree, the notion that English-speaking countries operate within the norms of negative politeness has been empirically confirmed in terms of social behaviour (e.g. Hofstede 2005; Ogiermann 2009), and production of request language showing a greater preference for indirect strategies (e.g. Blum-Kulka et al. 1989; Sifianou 1992). Equally, in terms of categorization, empirical research also applies the terms 'positive-politeness' and 'collectivist' to many non-Western societies, particularly in China, Japan and Korea in East Asia (Gu 1990; Mao 1994; Matsumoto 1989; Yu 1999, 2011). These findings need to be viewed, however, under the caveat that there will be group differences within societies which do not necessarily conform and fall neatly into one or the other category. For instance, Culpeper and Haugh (2014) note that in the North of England, where the present study is based, terms of endearment such as 'love' (e.g. Can I help you, love?) and 'pet' (e.g. Are you OK, pet?) are common features of discourse within the public domain (as opposed to academia) which, in fact, relate more to aspects of positive rather than negative politeness. Regarding the East/West debate, Leech (2014: 83) invites us to consider the concepts of Eastern group culture and Western individualist, egalitarian culture as simply positions on a scale, rather than absolutes. Since, he argues, all polite communication involves observation of both individual and group values, it appears that group values appear to dominate in Eastern cultures and individual values appear to dominate in the West. In considering the evidence, this stance seems a good starting point for understanding politeness and its variant forms.

In line with the aforementioned studies, the study in this volume will continue to adopt the terms 'positive' and 'negative politeness' in the ways described for convenience and general understanding, whilst acknowledging that these categorizations can be oversimplistic. Despite the criticism levied towards Brown and Levinson's politeness theory, this too will be the main theory applied to the current data and utilized in the discussions for three main reasons. Firstly, as Locher and Watts (2005: 10) maintain, Brown and Levinson's theory is 'in a class of its own in terms of its comprehensiveness, operationalizability, thoroughness and level of argumentation'. Secondly, to maintain cross-research comparisons, this model most favoured in ILP research is also adopted here to contextualize the current findings amongst existing investigations on requests and apologies. Finally, Chen and Hu's (2013) recent study suggests that a number of features of request behaviour such as high frequency of indirectness and observation of power and distance show little variation between American and Chinese speakers, in spite of previous claims. Chen and Hu contend cultural differences may not be as extreme as to lead to the conclusion that there is an East-West divide in terms of politeness, at least as defined by Brown and Levinson. Determining the extent to which the notions described so far have a bearing on the linguistic output of the Chinese learners employed in this study is also a valuable area of investigation – determining the extent to which the notions described so far have a bearing on the linguistic output of the Chinese learners employed in this study.

2.4. Politeness and culture

A number of researchers investigating cross-cultural and interlanguage behaviour in Chinese cultures have contributed to the debate of universality versus cultural specificity, arguing that deep-rooted cultural values and conventions directly affect pragmalinguistic and sociopragmatic behaviour in the L2. Whilst Yu (2003), amongst others, suggests the ultimate goals of polite facework proposed by Brown and Levinson are not so different from those of Chinese speakers, researchers suggest that the concepts of face are fundamentally based on Western cultural norms which prioritize the self (Gu 1990; Lin 2009; Wang 2011; Yu 1999; Zhang 1995). In contrast, social harmony and seeking the respect of the group are central to Chinese culture (positive politeness), rather than accommodating individual desires and freedoms (negative politeness) which are said to be more of a concern in Western societies (Gu 1990; Lin 2009; Wang 2011; Zhang 1995). The Chinese appear to be motivated by being part of the whole and are communally driven in direct contrast to the self-oriented image of a Western society. In this case, it is unreasonable to assume Chinese speakers will automatically enter into and participate in interactions in this same way as L1 speakers of English in Western cultures.

Research on other non-English-speaking cultures has also contested the applicability of Brown and Levinson's theories, supported by empirical evidence which suggests they have negligible relevance in collectivist societies such as Japan (Hill et al. 1986; Matsumoto 1988, 1989), Poland and Hungary (Suszcyznska 1999; Wierzbicka 1991), Greece and Germany (Pavlidou 1994), and China (Gu 1990; Mao 1994). Secondly, Lee-Wong (1994) and Yu (1999) are among studies reporting directness as a common strategy for Chinese speakers in conversation – a marker of both politeness and sincerity in Chinese culture. Yu (2011) claims that whilst the typical conventionally indirect structure using the modal *could* may be regarded as an acceptable request by English speakers, this tentativeness potentially questions the sincerity of the interlocutor in Chinese culture and may therefore cause offence. As a result, Chinese beliefs heavily influence the semantics of their utterances adopting brevity and directness to display politeness: a feature of positive politeness societies. Kasper and Zhang (1995) note study abroad students in China concluded the interpretation of politeness in China was very different to their Western expectations. The students reported comments concerning age, salary and obesity were approached in too direct a manner in China compared to Western conventions, e.g. 'you are really fat', 'you have a big nose' (1995: 18), in addition to suggestions being perceived as directives because of the linguistic forms chosen. Such statements are not impolite in China and directives, in certain contexts, are considered appropriate in Chinese culture but can be unfamiliar and uncomfortable for Westerners.

As noted above, politeness is generally considered to be marked by indirectness in Western societies. Whilst a shared belief exists that indirectness does play a role in polite behaviour in China, the most important point here is that politeness is realized in a different way. In request language, for instance, it is suggested indirectness is measured by the framework of the utterance (Yu 2011; Zhang 1995). External modification devices such as small talk and supportive moves, preceding the proposition, are fundamental to conveying indirectness, rather than internal modification such as modals and pronouns as evidenced in Western utterances. Examining a range of Western cultures, Faerch and Kasper (1989) found that for British English, German and Danish groups, internal modification is obligatory but external modification is optional. Such an emphasis on internal modification for L1 English speakers is also confirmed in more recent studies (Octu & Zeyrek 2008; Woodfield & Economidou-Kogetsidis 2010). According to Yu (2011) and Zhang (1995), amongst others, the opposite is true in Chinese culture, with external modification being the preferred mitigating technique. This difference in linguistic sequencing may have a significant impact on the success of the utterance if these are facilitated by negative L1 transfer.

From a cultural perspective, social structures may also play a key role in how interactions are managed in the East and West. Japan and China are described as 'vertical societies' (e.g. Matsumoto 1988; O'Driscoll 1996) where a clear hierarchy exists between social groupings. In contrast, 'horizontal' societies of the West have relatively weak vertical ties and members of groups feel closest to those of the same rank and role. In this case, obligations are few between high-status and low-status members in comparison to vertical societies (O'Driscoll 1996).

A small number of studies also report the significance of non-verbal apologetic behaviour in Eastern cultures has been found to be widely misinterpreted by English speakers (Hall 1977; Kim 2008). Hall (1977) describes Japan, South Korea and China as 'high-context' cultures where implicit understanding of the context may negate the requirement of an overt verbal apology, particular amongst in-group members. In the case of minor offences, this is commonly replaced by bowing, smiling and even silence – the latter considered to be one of the most important apologizing strategies amongst intimates in South Korea (Kim 2008). By contrast, 'low-context' Western cultures value clarity through explicit verbal communication and it is the speaker's responsibility to ensure meaning is conveyed through these means ((Kim 2008). Kim suggests misinterpretation by English speakers is common when a smile is used whilst making an apology. For South Koreans this relates to the 'desire for rapid conflict resolution' (2008: 268) but is likely to offend English speakers who may doubt the sincerity of the apology and question the speaker's motives.

As in all of the above cultural variations, there is potential for mismatch between the approaches taken by learners of English from Japan, Korea and China and those from Western societies. In each case there are defined cultural expectations for what constitutes a successful exchange from both pragmalinguistic and sociopragmatic perspectives. There is a need, therefore, for learners to understand how politeness is realized in the target culture, particularly when undertaking a period abroad where L2 interaction occurs on a daily basis. When interacting in the L2, Chinese learners of English are perhaps in a disadvantaged position unless politeness strategies from Western cultures are known, and learners are equipped with the linguistic devices and understanding to manage their utterances. At this point, the next section reviews some of the broader issues associated with study abroad and L2 interaction to further build the case for instructional intervention.

2.5. The case for instructed L2 pragmatics

As summarized in Chapter 1, challenges to improving pragmatic performance exist for both learners (e.g. issues with meaningful pragmatic input and feedback) and teachers (e.g. a paucity of readily available pragmatics-focused teaching materials). For the reasons highlighted in Chapter 1, there is already a valid argument for a focus on pragmatics as part of the learning curriculum. However, since the present study is situated in an academic setting, within a study abroad (SA) environment, an insight into the need for intervention within these two learning contexts will each be addressed in the following sections.

Beginning with the wider study abroad context, Kinginger's (2009: 11) definition of SA suits the purposes of this volume by emphasizing the educational context of the period abroad; 'a temporary sojourn of pre-defined duration, undertaken for educational purposes'. Many language learners are keen to exploit L2 opportunities for language development and raising cross-cultural awareness. This is evidenced in the continued popularity of SA and high international student mobility for these purposes,[3] though shorter-term sojourns of up to six months appear to be increasingly common, for UK students at least. The diversity of opportunities to gain frequent exposure to authentic, contextualized communicative norms means, in principle, the SA environment is an excellent resource. For pragmatic development, the potential for observation of pragmatic norms, situated practice, direct feedback and experiencing real-life consequences of pragmatic behaviour is invaluable (Taguchi 2017).

Xiao's (2015) synthesis of studies tracking acquisitional pragmatic development across multiple languages highlights those with largely positive SA effects (e.g. Matsumura 2001, 2003; Schauer 2006), minimal SA effects (e.g. Barron 2006; Iwasaki 2011) and studies generating a mixed picture (e.g. Barron 2003, 2007; Bataller 2010; Code & Anderson 2001; Schauer 2006, 2007; Warga & Schölmberger 2007). These linear and non-linear developments as a result of the SA stay are also evident when examining L2 requests and apologies. Moves towards more L2-like norms include a greater use of indirect request strategies over time within English-speaking SA stays (Bataller 2010; Code & Anderson 2001; Schauer 2007; Woodfield 2012) and more frequent use of direct requests in Chinese and Spanish contexts (Félix Brasdefer 2007; Li 2014; Shively 2011). An increase in the use of formulaic language in requests has also been observed over time (Bardovi-Harlig & Bastos 2011; Barron 2003, 2019; Schauer 2007; Shively 2011). Use of internal and external modification devices to mitigate or soften requests is reported to be less successful, however. Underuse of modification (Li 2014; Schauer 2007, 2009; Woodfield 2008, 2012; Woodfield & Economidou-Kogetsidis 2010) outnumbers results showing improvement across time (Li 2014; Schauer 2007; Woodfield 2012). Developing pragmatic competency in apology use has also seen mixed results in a range of languages, with negative transfer from L1 norms being one of the most consistently reported explanations for non-L2-like performance (Barron 2019; Sabaté i Dalmau & Currell i Gotor 2007; Shardakova 2005; Shively & Cohen 2008; Warga & Schölmberger 2007).

To summarize, SA gains are characterized by considerable variation, though such mixed results are not exclusive to developing pragmatic competency alone. It is well documented that SA investigations are highly complex (Bardovi-Harlig 2012; Kinginger 2013). Where pragmatic gains are reported, these are said to still fall short of the levels produced by expert users of the target language in almost all of the studies reviewed in this section. A call for targeted instruction to complement the SA experience is therefore a widely recommended conclusion and a line of discussion pursued further in the next chapter.

Turning to the academic context, the empirical study presented in this volume is operationalized within the boundaries of institutional talk (Bardovi-Harlig & Hartford 2005), as described in Chapter 1. This means academic interactions are typically goal-oriented and governed by conventionalized rules and expectations. Here, the pragmatic emphasis is less about negotiating an intercultural middle ground as in L2 exchanges amongst ELF users. In the case of a university setting, it is about knowing the conventionalized rules of academic encounters and applying this knowledge appropriately to achieve the desired outcome whilst maintaining a long-term (and favourable) academic relationship. Although it would be inaccurate to suggest that all international students struggle with adjusting to the host environment in this way, there is sufficient evidence across different languages to suggest that many students lack some pragmalinguistic and sociopragmatic means to better achieving their end goals in academic encounters (e.g. Brown 2013 (L2 Korean); Félix-Brasdefer 2012 (L2 Spanish); Winke & Teng 2010 (L2 Chinese); Barron 2019 (L2 German); Halenko 2018 and Halenko and Jones 2011, 2017 (L2 English)). Examining email requests to faculty in L2 English, for instance, Economidou-Kogetsidis (2011) found her Greek learners of English lacked pragmatic control of acceptable greetings and closings, forms of address, directness and lexical downgraders which impacted on their emails to faculty being perceived as impolite or abrupt. Alcón Soler's (2015) study of Spanish students' L2 English e-requests showed a tendency to rely on directness and only limited internal mitigation. Following a combination of instruction and SA exposure, the Spanish L1 learners recognized the negative impact of these strategies and subsequently changed their email practices in favour of increased mitigation.

For the Chinese ESL study abroad sojourner, studies examining undergraduate students regularly cite challenges with adjusting to cultural differences in academic practices such as learner independence and class participation, understanding unfamiliar academic norms, and socializing with home students when studying overseas (Campbell & Li 2008; Major 2005; Ranta & Meckelborg 2013; Spencer-Oatey et al. 2017; Trice 2003). It is language barriers, however, which are one of the most widely reported factors which can directly affect the day-to-day international student experience. Speech act studies with Asian learners of English almost consistently report that international students, as novice L2 users, are under-prepared to interact in situationally appropriate ways with expert L1 users in many basic academic encounters in study abroad settings, such as producing written or spoken requests or apologies. Evidence suggests that written email requests to faculty by Chinese learners of English are frequently characterized by directness (Chen 2006, 2015a; Lee 2004), verbosity (Chen 2006), incorrect address forms (Chen 2015a; Rau & Rau 2016), limited variance in request strategies, mitigation and politeness devices (Chen 2006, 2015a; Zhu 2012) and frequently display inadequate sociopragmatic competence to recognize imposition and politeness variables (Chen 2006; Zhu 2012). Oral requests in L2 English between staff and students have also been reported to lack an appropriate range of mitigating strategies and satisfactory levels of internal and external modification in comparison to expert users (Lee-Wong 1994; Wang 2011; Yu 1999; Zhang 1995). A series of studies by Halenko (2018) and Halenko and Jones (2011, 2017) revealed that, without the help of instruction, L1 Chinese ESL learners tended to formulate situationally inappropriate oral requests which overlooked both the status of the interlocutor and the imposition of the request in academic interactions. The hearer-alienating request components, indicated by low rating scores, included an overreliance on modals (typically *can, could)*, instances of direct strategies (*I want, I need)*, and an insufficient range of appropriate mitigating strategies such as grounders (explanations). As highlighted by these, and other authors, the pragmatic gaps in knowledge for Chinese learners of English can be traced back to L1 transfer in many cases. Examples of noncongruent oral requests in academic encounters can be found in Table 2.1.

Producing L2 English apologies which meet academics' expectations has proven to be equally problematic for L1 Chinese learners. Investigations of this speech act are fewer in number but report similar findings between them. Chang et al. (2016) reported verbosity to be a key feature of email apologies, whilst Cheng's learners (2017a) lacked the sociopragmatic knowledge needed to make effective apologies in terms of taking responsibility and making adequate repairs. Added to this, Halenko's (2018) Chinese ESL participants tended to undersupply explanations or promises not to repeat the offence and oversupply repeated, direct apologies (Table 2.2).

Table 2.1 Examples of noncongruent requests in academic encounters (data taken from Halenko and Jones (2011, 2017))

Description of academic request encounter	Sample learner request	Appropriacy rating score* by an ESL tutor
Ask a tutor to write a same-day reference for you	Hi teacher. I need a reference today for my new boss. Thank you for doing this for me.	1 (completely unsatisfactory)
Ask a librarian to extend a library loan beyond the date	Because I need to write my essay in one days so I want to borrow this book for some more time to finish my essay. Is this ok?	2 (unsatisfactory)
Ask a tutor to change the time of your presentation	Hi teacher. I am very busy now and I think a new time would be better for me for my presentation. I cannot do this presentation in this time. Can I change the time?	1 (completely unsatisfactory)
Ask the accommodation office to delay your rent payment	Hello. I do not want to pay my accommodation now and I want to pay it next time so is this ok for me?	2 (unsatisfactory)

* Appropriacy rating scores based on a 5-point Likert scale (5 = completely satisfactory, 1 = completely unsatisfactory)

As indicated earlier, pragmatic underperformance in a SA academic context may mean international students are left without their desired intended outcome. More costly might be a negative effect on a student's academic trajectory or damage to the longer-term academic relationship, if functions such as requests or apologies are not handled well and are perceived to be abrupt, demanding or discourteous. There is empirical evidence to suggest that faculty members can indeed feel aggrieved or frustrated when academic interactions do not unfold according to expectations (e.g. Akikawa & Ishihara 2010; Alcón Soler 2015; Economidou-Kogetsidis 2011). As examples, qualitative case studies such as Trice (2003) more broadly indicate that faculty perceive 'functioning in English' and 'cultural adjustment' to be the biggest challenges for international students, causing both personal and academic issues inside and outside the classroom. Directly related to pragmatic success in academic interaction, Cheng's (2017b) survey of instructors found effective email and spoken apologies from international students necessitated, but commonly lacked, the following components: responsibility-taking, acknowledgement of possible consequences

Table 2.2 Examples of noncongruent apologies in academic encounters (data taken from Halenko 2018)

Description of academic apology encounter	Sample learner apology	Appropriacy rating score* by an ESL tutor
Apologize for lost library book	Hello madam. I have to make an apologize to you. You know I have borrowed a book from the library but I lost it. I'm so sorry and wish your forgive.	2 (unsatisfactory)
Apologize for late submission of assignment	I'm really sorry for I did not complete my essay. Sorry and I try to want to ask for extra time for you.	1 (completely unsatisfactory)
Apologize for missing a meeting with tutor	I am so sorry about that. I was too tired at that day and after that there are so many thing I need to do so I forgot to email you to explain.	1 (completely unsatisfactory)
Apologize for forgetting payment for accommodation	I'm really sorry for I did not complete have the payment. I want to ask for extra time from you.	2 (unsatisfactory)

* Appropriacy rating scores based on a 5-point Likert scale (5 = completely satisfactory, 1 = completely unsatisfactory)

and initiating repair (sociopragmatic), in addition to being grammatically sound, and employing appropriate linguistic devices to avoid threatening negative face (pragmalinguistic). Conversely, poorly rated e-apologies, which were common amongst the international group sampled, did not contain these features. Consequently, instructors' negative reactions included questioning students' overall academic potential and recommending remedial help. It is not generally the case that learners intend to convey pragmatically infelicitous messages, but, as discussed in Chapter 2, indirectness and politeness may be realized in different ways in the L1 and L2, suggesting a need to formally address this knowledge gap.

All the above studies generally agree that learners need pedagogical intervention to advance their pragmatic development since exposure to the L2 environment alone does not facilitate this knowledge to the same high levels as structured input provides. This is critical for enhancing the academic study abroad experience for learners and allowing them to interact confidently and competently in status-unequal encounters. The question of opportune timing for instruction is often dictated by external forces and the logistics of organizing an intervention is not a simple task. However, it is suggested that pragmatic instruction should ideally be initiated at the pre-departure stage so early cross-cultural connections can be made in the at-home environment and then revisited post-arrival in the host country (see Chapter 3 for further discussion). This timing of pre-arrival instruction is likely to maximize its effectiveness, is likely to provide a considerable confidence boost for learners at a difficult early stage of adjustment to a new environment, and is likely to help prime learners to notice, and implement, pragmatics in action from day one. The next chapter addresses these points in more detail.

3

Instructed L2 pragmatics

The history of instructed L2 pragmatics is brief in comparison to the focus on comparative studies (see Bardovi Harlig 2015; Takahashi 2010b for more on intervention studies). Research on the effectiveness of instruction has targeted the development of a variety of language functions, across multiple languages, but speech acts remain the most popular area of investigation: compliments (Billmyer 1990; Rose & Ng 2001), refusals (Alcón Soler & Guzman Pitarch 2013; Kondo 2010; Usó Juan 2013), requests (Alcón-Soler 2015; Codina-Espurz 2008; Cohen & Shively 2007; Fukuya & Clark 2001; Li 2012; Martínez-Flor 2012; Takahashi 2001) and apologies (Cohen & Shively 2007; Kondo 1997; Olshtain & Cohen 1990; Tateyama 2001). Notably, despite the variability in lengths of instructional treatments of 45-minute sessions over three weeks (Li 2012) to 120-minute sessions over a 15-week semester (Alcón Soler 2005), positive treatment effects, using a variety of teaching approaches, are still evident in most studies.

Having established the importance of developing pragmatic knowledge as a language learner and SA sojourner, this chapter moves on to highlight the what and how of teaching pragmatics. Since there is much overlap, the chapter is not divided in this way, but the sections cover the essential aspects of these two areas. The chapter begins with a set of basic principles for teaching pragmatics before moving on to reviewing aspects relevant to the empirical study: study abroad instruction, teaching techniques, speech acts and pragmatics routines as a focus for instruction. The chapter concludes with a review of technology-enhanced input and practice.

3.1. Initial considerations for teaching pragmatics

One of the difficulties surrounding classroom instruction in pragmatics is where to start. This may be one reason for the relative few interventional studies in comparison to the many contrastive studies undertaken. The large number of language functions, speech acts, contexts and purposes do not facilitate this task easily. Until recently, this was further complicated by the lack of resources and methodological approach, though research in these areas is still not developing as quickly as we might hope. A fundamental first step in pragmatics instruction is to raise students' awareness that pragmatic functions exist, rather than to prescriptively teach L2 norms and insist learners approximate them in L2 interaction (Kasper & Rose 2002). Early calls such as those by Kasper (1996) to equip learners with the tools to analyse their own pragmatic development, allowing space to make informed choices on the basis of L1 identity and values, are now prominent and growing features of L2 pragmatics research. Taking issues of promoting L1 identity further, studies such as Davis (2007), Ishihara and Tarone (2009), Kim (2014) and LoCastro (2001) foreground investigating resistance to L2 pragmatic norms whilst other studies suggest resistance (partially) explicates differing levels of L2 pragmatic performance (e.g. Eslami 2010; Hassall 2013; Masuda 2011; Shively 2011). Increasingly, the issues of learner identity, subjectivity and agency are discussed in the wider movement towards understanding today's intercultural language user. What is ever more apparent is that learners sometimes choose to project their sense of self and L1 cultural identity through their pragmatic choices. Divergence from L2 practices cannot then always be dismissed as lacking relevant pragmatic knowledge and linguistic know-how, but rather a conscious attempt to preserve and emphasize L1-ness (see Gomez-Laich 2016; Taguchi & Roever 2017).

With this awareness-raising approach in mind, Taguchi (2011) advocates that the key elements of learner-centred teaching materials should include (i) social context, (ii) functional language use and (iii) interaction within frameworks which promote pragmatic and intercultural competencies. Such frameworks include those developed by Martínez-Flor and Usó-Juan (2006), Ishihara and Cohen (2010) and Kondo (2008). As an example, Martínez-Flor and Usó-Juan (2006) framework comprises six main stages which in fact appear common to many teaching frameworks: researching and reflecting on pragmatic concepts, receiving instruction, analysing pragmatic data, participating in communicative practice and receiving feedback. Teaching frameworks can also be student-led, rather than teacher-led. In this way, learners are trained to take the initiative and responsibility for their own pragmatic development. Cohen (2005) applied the principles of strategy instruction to pragmatics by outlining a set of speech act learning strategies to encourage learners to form self-directed learning habits where they monitor, control and evaluate their own pragmatic development. Shively's (2010) investigation, which encouraged learners to collect naturalistic data and participate in the local target community using the speech acts studied, is an example of applying strategy instruction to good effect. The main benefits of strategy instruction are the development of autonomous learning, task-based activities which encourage participation in the host environment and the development of independent learning which accommodates individual learner differences.

The takeaway points here are that through awareness-raising activities and adopting frameworks which promote the (self-) development of pragmatic knowledge alongside intercultural skills, practitioners can facilitate pragmatic discussions and prompt self-reflection, so learners are equipped with the necessary tools to make informed pragmatic choices. Opportunities for practice are also considered vital for pragmatic development (Plonsky & Zhuang 2019). These basic principles must act as the starting point for pragmatic interventions with the end goal being that the L2 user becomes the enabler of their own pragmatic actions. A review of the small collection of L2 instruction studies which have adopted such techniques continues in the next section.

3.2. L2 Instructional studies during study abroad

As described in Kasper and Rose (2002), instructional studies can be broadly categorized into three types: (i) 'teachability studies' (e.g. Martínez-Flor 2008b), examining the extent to which pragmatic items are teachable in a classroom setting and typically adopting a one-group, pre-posttest design; (ii) 'instruction versus exposure studies' (e.g. Fukuya & Zhang 2002), comparing an experimental group, receiving instruction with a no-instruction control group; and (iii) 'studies incorporating a variety of instructional techniques to determine method-effect' (e.g. Takimoto 2009). The study presented in this volume examines both instruction versus exposure and measures the effectiveness of differentiated teaching materials, thereby combining study types two and three described above. As the SA setting is the context for the instructional intervention conducted in this volume, this section will review the small body of SA instructional studies for comparability purposes.

Study abroad instructional studies are still limited in number in comparison to research on acquisitional pragmatic development during SA. Existing SA instructional studies can be either categorized into those focusing on a 'pre-departure' instructional stage, with the presence or absence of further instruction during SA, or 'in-country' instruction once learners have arrived in the target language community. The former, pre-arrival category of studies is clearly under-represented in existing L2 pragmatics literature and limited to a handful of investigations such as Cohen and Shively (2007), Halenko and Jones (2017), Halenko et al. (2019), Hernández and Boero (2018) and Wang and Halenko (2019). This small collection has the distinct benefits of directly comparing before-and-after instructional effects. Some studies also correlate findings with the effects of exposure and engagement in the host environment. This longitudinal approach provides a much richer data set of the learners' experiences and pragmatic growth. Operationally, these studies have administered different lengths and modes of pre-departure treatment (perhaps indicative of the challenging nature of design and delivery of this type of research), but all still report considerable learner benefits. For instance, Hernández and Boero (2018) reported that their pre-departure L2 Spanish instruction as short as ninety minutes was helpful with request planning and production during SA. Halenko and Jones (2017) also established significant short-term post-instructional gains with reference to L2 English request modification, range of request formulae and sensitivity to the imposition of requests, following a five-hour intervention.

Post-arrival 'in country' instructional studies combine participant instruction with direct and immediate exposure to the target language – an advantageous addition to the at-home language learning experience. Guiding learners to become ethnographers[1] themselves to record or discuss their observations and experiences adds a further valuable dimension to exploit the advantageous position the SA experience offers. Measuring effects across different L2 contexts (China, France, Spain, UK) and over a range of time periods (eight weeks to one academic year), these examples of intervention studies have reported successful learning effects over a number of areas: pragmalinguistic production (Alcón Soler 2015; Cohen & Shively 2007; Halenko 2018; Halenko & Jones 2011; Li & Gao 2017; Morris 2017; Winke & Teng 2010), metapragmatic awareness (Henery 2015; Li & Gao 2017; Morris 2017), cross-cultural understanding (Halenko 2018; Winke & Teng 2010) and confidence-building to deal with unfamiliar local conventions (Shively 2011). To illustrate these successes with Chinese learners of English, instructional effects were reported for oral request production in Halenko and Jones (2011) and oral apology production in Halenko (2018). Both studies sampled young adult participants from mainland China, undertaking one academic year at a British university. The learners shared a similar upper intermediate level of English (approximately IELTS 5) and had no previous study abroad experience. Pragmatic performance was measured on the frequency and quality of linguistic strategies employed in both cases. Following weekly classes totalling six hours and eight hours respectively, the explicitly instructed groups significantly outperformed their non-instructed counterparts in each request and apology study. In practical terms, this means the participants in both studies demonstrated a heightened awareness of which pragmatics forms to use for the best pragmatic effect – gains not observed in either of the control groups' data sets. Specifically, in Halenko and Jones' (2011) request study, an increase in pre-request supportive moves (e.g. *I can't access my university email account ...*), alerters (e.g. *Sorry to bother you*) and use of bi-clausals (e.g. *Would you mind ...*) were evident in the requests receiving the highest rating scores, though these gains were not sustained in the long term. The participants in Halenko's (2018) study on apology language also showed marked increases in the use of explanations, mitigators and more varied intensifiers such as 'terribly' across all post and delayed tests as a result of instruction. A declining effect of L1-influencing strategies was also reported in the reduction of multiple apologies, inappropriate requests for forgiveness, choice of alerters and information sequencing.

Whilst classroom-based input remains the main forum for pragmatic instruction and has proved highly beneficial, results are inconclusive regarding the most effective instructional technique. What follows is an exploration of the main teaching approaches adopted in intervention studies.

3.3. Explicit and implicit teaching approaches

Discussions over the benefits of explicit versus implicit teaching approaches occupy much of the debate concerning the effectiveness of instructed L2 pragmatics and ISLA in general. These two techniques are differentiated by the presence (explicit) or absence (implicit) of metapragmatic information as part of the instructional input (Alcón-Soler & Martínez-Flor 2008). Most studies to date incorporating EFL/ESL learners have adopted an explicit teaching approach (Jeon & Kaya 2006; Taguchi 2015; Takahashi 2010a), which is often characterized by teacher-led introduction of the pragmalinguistic and sociopragmatic goals of the target language. Activities to promote learning in explicit treatments include awareness-raising tasks and activities providing communicative practice such as role-plays.

Overall, findings do show students having profited from explicit instruction (e.g. Bouton 1994; Cohen & Tarone 1994; Fukuya 1998; Iwai 2013; Kondo 2010; Liddicoat & Crozet 2001; Lyster 1994; Usó-Juan 2013; Wishnoff 2000). Studies specifically targeting request and apology language also follow this positive trend:

Eslami and Eslami-Rasekh (2008, requests and apologies), Eslami et al. (2015, requests), Halenko and Jones (2011, requests), Johnson and deHaan (2013, requests and apologies), Martínez-Flor (2008b, requests), Safont Jordá (2004, requests). As examples, both Safont Jordá (2004) and Martínez-Flor (2008b) employed low proficiency level EFL groups of Spanish students. Receiving one semester of explicit request instruction versus six hours of treatment respectively, findings revealed a higher frequency of conventionally indirect strategies and fewer direct strategies (Safont Jordá 2004) and a greater number and variety of modifiers, and frequent instances of fixed expressions. Halenko and Jones (2011) adopted a similar methodological approach with six hours of instruction on requests but included a control group and delayed test to determine short- and long-term instructional effects, and focus group data on the benefits of pragmatic classroom input. As in the previous studies, similar post-instructional gains were evident, but these declined following a six-week period. The authors proposed that even a short-term focus on pragmatics embedded within existing language programmes can be beneficial, as also reflected in the learner interview comments. However, the authors suggested that sustained practice is required for long-term retention of pragmatic request knowledge.

According to the most recent review of intervention studies employing designs suitable for measuring true explicit instructional effects (Taguchi 2015), only two studies include a focus on apology language. First, Eslami and Eslami-Rasekh (2008) examined the teaching of both requests and apologies to an under-explored group of Iranian postgraduate non-native English-speaking teacher candidates (NNESTCs) (experimental group = 25, control group = 27). Following seven hours of instruction, the responses from an error recognition task (judging pragmatic awareness) and a written production task (judging pragmatic production) were assessed for appropriacy on a five-point Likert scale. The treatment was declared to be highly effective for both production and awareness of request and apology language due to the instrumental motivation as pre-service English teachers to engage in the intervention.

Secondly, Johnson and deHaan (2013) illustrate the potential of technology-enhanced instruction for advancing requests and apologies (see Section 3.6 for further discussion of technology-based pragmatic input). Utilizing model conversations with twenty-two undergraduate computer science students, a classroom online Wikispaces and digital video software, learners were able to perform, record, self-correct and reflect on their pragmatic outputs within business contexts, under the instructor's guidance. Pretest-posttest NS assessments revealed improved levels of accuracy and appropriacy for request and apology language, post-instruction. Statistical differences were only noted in appropriacy, however, realized through fewer direct, simplistic formulations (as found in the pretest), replaced by increased modality, conventionally indirect language and fixed expressions such as 'I was wondering if'. For both apology studies, delayed-posttests were not administered, nor was the value or effectiveness of teaching multiple speech acts investigated.

Explicit instruction has not consistently been found to be superior, as several studies comparing the explicit and implicit approaches have found. Kubota (1995), for instance, found initial gains from explicit instruction had disappeared by the time a delayed posttest was employed, Rose and Ng's (2001) pre- and posttests did not produce positive results on all of the assessment measures employed, and Martínez-Flor (2006) reported similar levels of effectiveness for both explicit and implicit treatments. Variability in operationalizing these two methods is a suggested cause of the discrepancy in results (Taguchi 2015). Implicit interventions have yielded positive results in their own right so this instructional approach cannot be entirely dismissed (e.g. Fukuya & Zhang 2002; Takimoto 2009).

What links the success of the implicit treatments in the above studies is that simple exposure is not sufficient. There is a need to first ensure learners' attention and then direct this to noticing and to subsequent processing of the information to induce rules, given no overt explanation of the target features is available in this approach. This indicates, regardless of teaching method, Schmidt's (1993) hypothesis of noticing and processing information still needs to be observed. Put simply, when implicit instruction versus no-instruction designs are investigated, treatment gains are generally exhibited, but performances by explicitly instructed groups generally surpass those receiving implicit treatment (Plonsky & Zhuang 2019; Taguchi 2010 provide comprehensive reviews). Given the available evidence showing the superiority of explicit over implicit treatments, the explicit teaching approach was adopted for the instructional phase of this study.

The reported variability of instructional success may also be attributable to an interplay between instructional method and other external factors. Firstly, research evidences pragmatic instruction should be at least five hours to be effective (Jeon & Kaya 2006; Salazar 2003; Usó-Juan 2013). Secondly, individual learner differences such as proficiency (e.g. Codina-Espurz 2008) motivation (e.g. Takahashi 2012) and learner agency and identity (e.g. Kim 2014) are also reported to have an impact on pragmatic development. Finally, in addition to teachability, 'learnability' of the target feature is said to affect instructional success (Taguchi 2010). Few studies have adopted this kind of analysis, however, as most pragmatics investigations are isolated to one speech act or area of pragmatic concern. Exceptions are Johnson and De Haan (2013) who reported greater semantic gains at the macro-level when testing for appropriateness of request and apology production than at the micro-level when measuring accuracy of response. In other words, politeness strategies and discourse moves were more easily retained and recalled from the instruction than knowledge of the linguistic form. A similar trend was evidenced in Sykes's (2009, 2013) online studies into developing request and apology behaviour. Findings revealed minimal change in choice of request strategies, in contrast to clear improvements in some aspects of apology language such as head acts. Sykes claims the structural and functional simplicity of apology formula at the lexical-level facilitated learning.

Findings such as these widen the debate concerning the benefits of teaching and learning speech acts, using a formulaic approach as a means of achieving this, the need for teacher training and how an array of technologically enhanced solutions are now available to facilitate pragmatics development. The chapter closes with an overview of these four areas since they are key features of this volume's study.

3.4. Teaching speech acts

Adopting a speech act focus for studying pragmatics is advantageous for several reasons. First, since speech acts such as requesting and apologizing function as social actions, and social actions are carried out daily, using speech acts as a starting point for instruction seems a sound pedagogical decision. Second, extensive research exists to support the claim that speech acts are troublesome for language learners since they are culturally and contextually dependent (e.g. Bardovi-Harlig 2015; Hinkel 2018; LoCastro 2001; Rose & Kasper 2001). Navigating one's way through initiating and responding to speech acts in another language is tricky and can be a slow process without specific attention (Cohen 2008; Taguchi 2010). Third, textbooks frequently refer to speech acts such as requests and apologies, but mostly fail to deal with them in any meaningful depth (Barron 2016; Crandall & Basturkmen 2004; Limberg 2016; Nguyen 2011; Schauer 2019). Teacher-led tasks and discussion could usefully enhance textbook material to facilitate pragmatic development. In this way, practitioners with already heavy teaching loads and limited class time could pause at opportune moments to highlight the value of, and promote extended reflections on, a specific pragmatic feature, using additional exercises which could be sourced online (see the American CARLA website as an example of this kind of resource).

Finally, speech acts are a very accessible area of language. Thanks to extensive cross-cultural research over the past four decades, speech acts have been helpfully coded and packaged in an accessible way, making teaching and learning a much easier task. Instructors cannot be expected to know or teach all the ins and outs of every speech act so the considerable research data now available are a valuable information source.

The number of journal articles providing samples or suggestions for teaching activities also continues to grow (e.g. Alcón Soler 2005; Bardovi-Harlig & Mahan-Taylor 2003; Eslami-Rasekh et al. 2004; Limberg 2015; Martínez-Flor & Usó-Juan 2010; Siegel et al. 2019), in addition to commercially published volumes with ready-to-go activities (Houck & Tatsuki 2011; Ishihara & Cohen 2010; Riddiford & Newton 2010; Tatsuki & Houck 2010). Contextualized speech act samples for use in pragmatics activities have been successfully sourced from feature films (Abrams 2013; Martínez-Flor 2008a; Rose & Ng 2001), sitcoms (Alcón Soler 2012; Alcón Soler & Guzman Pitarch 2010) and TV shows (Alcón Soler 2005; Codina-Espurz 2008). Other studies have relied on excerpts of naturally occurring data presented in oral form (Cohen & Ishihara 2005; Teng & Fei 2013) or written form (Félix-Brasdefer 2008; Li 2012; Nguyen et al. 2013). More recently, Bardovi-Harlig et al. (2015) also illustrated how corpus tools can be used effectively in guided discussion tasks. Thankfully, there is now a much greater range of meaningful, contextualized resources to draw on for teaching speech acts, and pragmatics more generally, although there is still work to be done. Using this information, instructors can assess which pragmatic targets are important for their learner groups and help them develop useful strategies to deal with these in real-life encounters. In this way, learners can be empowered to assess, and appropriately respond to, a variety of communicative situations.

3.5. Teaching pragmatic routines

Pragmatic routines or formulaic language is seldom a focus of mainstream L2 pragmatics studies, despite its acknowledgement as a central component for effective and efficient communication as many leading authorities maintain (e.g. Pawley & Syder 1983; Schmitt 2004; Sinclair & Sinclair 1991; Wray 2008). The teaching and learning of formulaic language is closely connected to Lewis's (1993) lexical approach which advocates that much communication is expediated through lexical phrases or chunks, characterized as multi-word units, but remembered and deployed as single lexical items. Defining formulaic language is problematic due to its diversity (Schmitt & Carter 2004) and the fact that numerous terms exist to describe it (Wray 2002). In the area of pragmatics, labels such as conversational routines, conventional expressions (Bardovi-Harlig 2009), formulaic expressions (Taguchi et al. 2013) situation-bound utterances (Kesckes 2000a, b, 2010) and pragmatic routines (Sánchez-Hernández & Alcón Soler 2018) are used to describe these recurrent expressions used for pragmatic purposes. This book adopts the terms 'formulaic language' and 'pragmatic routines' since the latter also makes an explicit link between the everyday occurrence of these expressions and the research area itself.

For language users, retrieving and producing highly routinized language chunks saves both time (Pawley & Syder 1983) and effort (Wray 2000). For foreign language learners in particular, formulaic language can save mental capacity (Wang 2011), reduces the amount of time planning and processing (Hinkel 2018), and improves fluency (Nattinger & DeCarrico 1992). For these reasons, language learning from a formulae-based approach can be an effective learning strategy by forming the basic building blocks from which learners can develop more creative ways of using language as they extend and diversify their linguistic repertoire (Nattinger & DeCarrico 1992). Interlocutors also easily recognize formulaic language and, in fact, have an expectation that formulaic language is used in order to expedite effective communication in many formal and informal situations.

The issue of conventional versus literal meaning is one of the key challenges for many language learners. Novice language users may focus on literal interpretation (Kecskes 2000a, 2000b), whilst expert users typically recognize such a sequence as a conventionalized routine from its social context. This indicates that pragmatic routines are culture-specific (Kecskes 2015), so an understanding of the social norms of a speech community is dependent on the successful use and interpretation of pragmatic routines. A second challenge is that pragmatic routines require a certain degree of accuracy to be effective (Hinkel 2018), but this is not always achieved from a grammatical perspective (Bardovi-Harlig 2009; Halenko 2018; Qi & Ding 2011; Sabaté i Dalmau & Curell i Gotor), e.g. *I am wonder if…* , or a meaning perspective (Bardovi-Harlig 2009; Hinkel 2018), e.g. *Happy morning.*

Research reports that L1 users employ a greater differentiated range of pragmatic routines whilst L2 users tend to rely on a limited repertoire (e.g. Bardovi-Harlig 2009; Hinkel 2018; Wang 2011; Yu 1999). Mastering pragmatic routines is challenging even for advanced-level language learners (Boers & Lindstromberg 2012; Glaser 2018). Kecskes (2000b) further notes that natural acquisition of pragmatic routines is a slow process due to the need for frequent exposure. He suggests only after two years living in the United States did his eighty-eight multinational English learners begin to develop L2-like control. As many pragmatic routines are found in speech acts such as requests and apologies (Bardovi-Harlig 2012; Schmitt & Carter 2004), but 'instructed L2 learners have an impoverished stock of formulaic expressions' (Wray 2012: 236), point to a need for intervention. Research suggests a lack of familiarity with expressions and sociopragmatic knowledge (Kecskes 2000a), overuse of familiar expressions, level of proficiency (Bardovi-Harlig 2009) and inadequate L2 exposure (Sánchez-Hernández & Alcón-Soler 2018) as factors for this lack of resource.

For language teachers, pragmatic routines offer a promising starting point though a principled approach to teaching in this way is yet to appear. Some of what we know appears to tally with the reported difficulties learners have with comprehension and production of formulaic language. For example, plentiful exposure and regular practice of formulaic language is crucial for long-term retention (Hinkel 2018) though it is advised this should complement, rather than replace, a focus on grammar and vocabulary instruction (Swan 2017). Explicit teaching fares better than textbook exposure for comprehension of form and meaning of sequences (Le-Thi et al. 2017) and shorter routines can be learned more easily (Chang 2010) which is welcome news for younger or lower proficiency level learners. Bardovi-Harlig and Vellenga (2012), Le-Thi and colleagues (2017), and Wang and Halenko (2019) are amongst those demonstrating the positive effects of teaching pragmatic-focused language using a formulae-based approach.

Ascertaining what specific learner groups find challenging with pragmatic routines is a useful starting point for where instruction should be targeted. In the case of EFL learners, Sánchez-Hernández and Alcón Soler (2018) reported the limited exposure to certain pragmatic routines may have resulted in lower recognition in the long term for their Brazilian students, Qi and Ding (2011) found sequences containing prepositions and articles to be problematic for their Chinese EFL learners, and Schauer (2006) noted her German EFL students struggled with producing pragmatically appropriate language due to reliance on L1 strategies. Given the variability of learning trajectories and goals, motivation, individual learner differences, intensity of L2 interaction and length of L2 exposure, it seems appropriate to first conduct a needs analysis of learners' start and preferred end points. This initial assessment ensures pragmatic instruction is meaningful and valuable to the participants, and class time is used effectively.

3.6. Pragmatics in teacher education

The accessibility of speech act material and pragmatic routines can also be usefully applied to teacher development since it has been found that teacher training programmes sadly lack much reference to the why and how of pragmatics instruction (Halenko & Aslan – forthcoming UK-based survey; Vásquez & Sharpless 2009 – US-based survey). This inadequate level of training may partially account for why many educators remain unconvinced and unprepared for pragmatics instruction. This state of affairs needs urgent review if pragmatics is to gain the legitimacy it needs in teaching curricula and commercial language learning material. It is unfortunate that this volume cannot extend the debate very much beyond joining the calls for action and highlighting some of the major concerns, as summarized in the next section.

In her review of primary teacher training programmes in Germany, Glaser (2018) reports pragmatics to be a neglected area. Glaser suggests this situation is due to the marginal role assigned to pragmatics as a core skill in language development, teachers' previous language learning experiences (which, presumably, also lacked a pragmatics focus), (perceived) issues with their own linguistic competence to provide adequate models and a lack of available teaching resources. Teacher training investigations with Greek (Savvidou & Economidou-Kogetsidis 2019), Japanese (Ishihara 2010) and other international teacher groups (Cohen 2016) report almost identical challenges.

It is further reported that to be an effective L2 pragmatics teacher requires an awareness of pragmatics norms and variation, practical skills to provide focused pragmatics instruction and assessment, and a sensitivity to learners' culture and subjectivity (Ishihara 2011; Limberg 2015). Gaining expertise in these areas is certainly best achieved through targeted teacher training programmes since pragmatics is an area of language which is nuanced, variable and influenced by a range of contextual factors. Pragmatic decisions require simultaneously managing three equally important elements of form, function and context, making it a particularly complex area of language development for teachers to pursue without adequate knowledge and practical teaching solutions. Yet whilst the evidence appears to warrant a focus on pragmatics in teacher education, the support and training offered to teachers are not currently commensurate with the continued growth of the research field (Cohen 2016). The outcome is that the default position for L1 teachers is to rely on intuition about pragmatics (which may or may not be reliable) or L2 speaker teachers may simply avoid teaching pragmatics altogether. Since teachers are the primary agents for instructional pragmatics and the evidence, as outlined above, points to a need for specific teacher preparation, this situation is in need of reform.

The limited role of pragmatics in teacher training programmes has been repeatedly highlighted (Cohen 2005; Eslami 2011; Glaser 2018; Ishihara 2010, 2011; Savić 2016; Vásquez & Sharpless 2009). The same concerns that pragmatics is typically dealt with in an incidental rather than a systematic fashion in language learning materials (Vásquez & Sharpless 2009) are also mirrored at the teacher development stage. Some attempts have been made to effectuate change, but these are typically isolated efforts, although their success is encouraging (Eslami 2011; Eslami & Eslami Rasekh 2008; Vellenga 2011; Yates & Wrigglesworth 2005). Pragmatics training is yet to appear as a basic component of teacher training programmes despite the demand and responsibility to professionally prepare teachers to teach and assess pragmatics in their own specific contexts. Further research into pragmatics and teacher education is needed to help build a more convincing case.

3.7. Teaching with technology

How the digital world shapes and influences our lives continues to be of great interest and importance to researchers, educators and learners. Within education, digitally mediated platforms have advanced the possibilities for greater interaction and access to authentic, context-rich input facilitated through tele-collaboration, social networking, digital games and blogs (see Chapelle & Sauro 2017). This expansion in technology-enhanced pedagogy is matched by a continued growth in technology-related literature tracking the highs and lows of its evolution. Teaching and researching L2 pragmatics have also been influenced by the technological wave. This section limits itself to a discussion of computer-assisted language learning (CALL) tools, given their use in the present study.

Extensive research demonstrates clear benefits to facilitating instruction via CALL technologies (e.g. Belz 2007; Cohen 2008; De Freitas 2006; Gee 2005; Sykes et al. 2008; Taguchi 2015). Firstly, authentic, meaningful interaction can be created through the use of online materials (Belz 2007), enhanced by, arguably, a more dynamic and motivating learning environment (Taguchi 2015). As in this study, interaction may be further stimulated by animated interlocutors who are also able to display a range of non-verbal signals such as facial expressions and gestures, thought to be as powerful as verbal cues, to enhance authenticity

(Wik & Hjalmarsson 2009; Yang & Zapata-Rivera 2010). Pressures from the face-threatening nature of apologies and requests, for instance, are alleviated in simulated contexts, allowing for a stress-free, 'low-risk' learning experience (Sykes et al. 2008), with a high emotional connection (De Freitas 2006), which can be individualized and paced (De Freitas 2006; Gee 2005). Many of these advantages are illustrated in recent works employing a range of online technologies for developing pragmatic competence, as the following studies illustrate.

Developing speech act performance through the medium of technology has received some attention in L2 pragmatics literature (e.g. Halenko & Flores Salgado 2019 – disagreements and refusals; Tsai & Kinginger 2015 – advice) but requests and apologies are still relatively under-explored pragmatic targets. The small collection of studies reviewed here covers a variety of both web-based written communication and real-time oral communication, but all seek to investigate the value of technology-enhanced tools for the development of request and apology behaviour (see also Johnson and De Haan (2013) reviewed earlier).

Mirroring the instructional delivery to multiple groups with differentiated training materials as adopted in the study in this volume, Eslami and Liu (2013) and Sydorenko (2015) investigated the request performance of two experimental groups from Taiwan and China respectively. The learners in the former study ($n = 78$) participated in either teacher-led classroom instruction or online group emails/discussions delivered by American graduate students. Measured against a control group ($n = 36$), the ten-week programme increased both experimental groups' request performance, which was not found for the control group. Though the teacher-led instruction appeared more beneficial than the CMC delivery, no statistically significant between-group differences were reported at the posttest stage, suggesting online modes of delivery may prove as effective as face-to-face interventions (see also Cunningham 2016 for a study with similar outcomes). In the latter study, Sydorenko's groups received the same explicit pragmatic input on requests and then engaged in language practice facilitated by either computer-delivered structured tasks (CASTs) using native-speaker models or learner-learner open-ended role-plays. Both sets of practice materials were found to have particular strengths. Specifically, CASTs proved more beneficial for improving pragmalinguistic aspects of requests as learners emulated the native speaker models, whilst the role-plays allowed for more language creativity and authentic turn-taking practices.

The possibilities of applying digital game and play activity to teaching and learning have also seen growing interest in L2 pragmatics literature. According to Reinhardt and Sykes (2014), this move includes *game-enhanced* research (exploring the use of commercial entertainment games being used for pedagogical purposes), *game-based* research (designing online educational games such as immersive environments) and *game-informed* research (applying game and play principles to a pedagogical activity). Several L2 pragmatics studies (including this volume) have explored request and apology development in one of these three areas. Yang and Zapata-Rivera (2010) devised an innovative educational game to raise learner awareness of request language. Similar to the study in this volume, the request game incorporated problem-solving tasks within a simulated academic context and included an animated agent as interlocutor. In contrast to this volume's study, which focused on oral exchanges, learners engaged in asynchronous conversation via cyber chat and were provided with corrective formative and summative feedback on their written output. Questionnaire results from fifteen students (mainly from East Asia), studying on a US-based ESL programme, reported a high percentage of learner motivation and increased knowledge of formulating requests, following a forty-five-minute experience of using the game.

A digital game was also the basis for Sykes (2009, 2013) who explored the use of multi-user virtual environments for pragmatic development. In this study, a three-dimensional immersive environment named 'Croquelandia' was devised for learners of Spanish to improve their use of requests and apologies. Participants navigated a series of goal-directed activities or 'quests' with behaviour-based feedback provided by other group members or computer-generated players. Pretest and posttest DCT measures revealed little change in the strategies chosen to perform requests and apologies, though learners' pragmatic awareness revealed distinct improvements.

Assessing L2 pragmatic performance has generally been dominated by written-based tests but the affordances of technology offer promising alternatives as a way of increasing learner engagement and addressing historical issues with test validity, for instance (see Chapter 5 for an overview of L2 pragmatics testing instruments). Computer-based testing can be effective in terms of maximizing content and format, optimizing set-up, delivery and analysis of tests, and capturing a greater range of performance measures. These benefits are summarized by Roever (2013) as follows: Referring to the advantages of online activities identified at the start of this section, Roever highlights the increase in opportunities for enhanced contextualization, authenticity of content and potential for adding audio and visual material, as seen in many of the studies reviewed earlier. Administratively, greater control of time limits, start and end points, and sequencing of computer-based tests are also noted as methodologically sound features to reduce external variables. These benefits can also be extended to the potential for immediate scoring, analysis and feedback. Finally, Roever emphasizes the ability to capture a broader range of performance indices such as response planning time and fluency. These aspects widen our understanding of other areas of language performance, as initiated in some L2 pragmatics studies already (e.g. Li & Taguchi 2014). So far, the indications are that technology can play a crucial role in moving research forward so it is good news that the short-term challenges associated with designing computer-based tests may be offset against longer-term rewards.

4

Requests and apologies

As a reminder, request and apology speech acts were selected for this study because they are highly frequent in academic staff-student interactions but have been found to be problematic to execute for international students. This chapter provides an overview of each speech act, followed by a review of empirical work in these areas. The empirical studies reviewed in this chapter will be limited to request and apology investigations located in East Asian cultures, namely Japan, South Korea and China who are said to share similar cultural and positive politeness values influencing behaviour and language within these two speech acts (e.g. Gu 1990; Lin 2009; Wang 2011).

4.1. The speech act of requests

Derived from Searle's (1976) classification of 'directives', requests are seen as illocutionary acts in which a speaker (or writer) conveys to a hearer (or reader) his/her wish for the hearer to perform an act which is of cost to them but has benefit to the speaker. This can be a request for verbal goods, such as information, or non-verbal goods, such as an object or service (Trosborg 1995). It is characterized as a pre-event act given the expectation that the act will take place in the immediate or near future time. As the request imposes on the hearer, it is also, by nature, a face-threatening act (FTA). Within Brown and Levinson (1987) theory of politeness, a request specifically threatens the hearer's negative face (the freedom to be unimpeded by others) by creating this imposition.

To mitigate this FTA, a number of strategies can be undertaken to minimize the request, whilst maximizing politeness at the same time. Drawing on Austin (1962) and Searle's (1976) theories, as reformulated by Brown and Levinson (1987), Blum-Kulka and Olshtain (1986) and Trosborg (1995), the following summarizes a basic taxonomy of requests on which the current study is based. A comprehensive table of classifications used to code the data in the present study can be found in Chapter 6. One of the most common ways a request may be minimized is through indirectness within the core component of the request, the head act, which conveys the speaker's wish(es). The head act comprises three main strategies; direct, conventionally indirect, and non-conventionally indirect (hints) which increase in indirectness, as outlined in Figure 4.1.

First, direct strategies may be employed when the speaker wishes to explicitly state the illocutionary point of the utterance via performative verbs (e.g. 'I request a lift from you'), imperatives (e.g. 'Give me a lift') or modals expressing obligation (e.g. 'You must give me a lift'). They fail to offer any options to the hearer so are considered the least polite. Next, conventionally indirect strategies (CID) question the hearer's ability and willingness to comply with the request (e.g. 'Could you give me a lift?'). In this case, compliance is not taken for granted and a means to opt out is supplied, thereby lowering the risk of the speaker losing face by increasing indirectness. CID strategies typically comprise routinized formulae and those which are hearer oriented (i.e. 'Could you …') are generally considered less coercive as a compliance option is provided. Finally, the third strategy, non-conventionally indirect or 'hints' are employed when the speaker does not wish to overtly state the desired action but instead prefers to make a statement or ask a question. It requires the hearer's interpretation of the speaker's intent (e.g. 'I'm late for the train') ought to signal to the hearer that he/she might offer the speaker a lift to the train station. In addition to these levels of directness/indirectness, the request can also be analysed from different perspectives: hearer oriented (e.g. 'Can you give

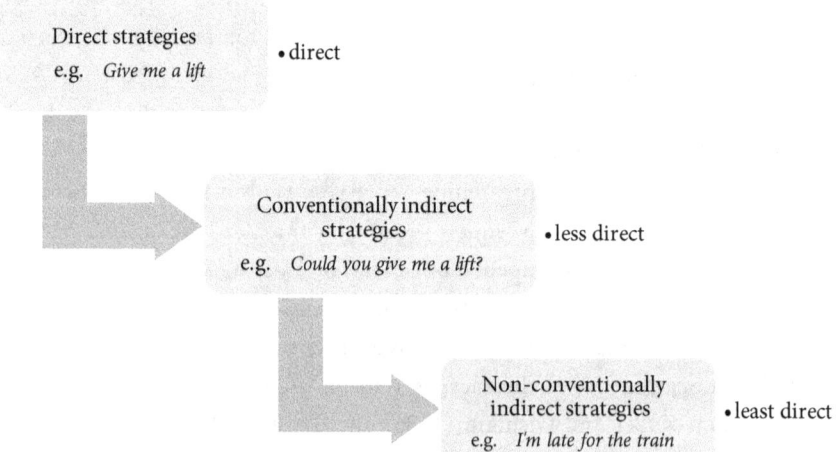

Figure 4.1 Strategy choice for request head acts

Table 4.1 Non-L2-like features of requests reported for L1 Chinese users

Language feature	Explanation	Studies reporting language feature
Overuse of 'can'/'could' as preferred conventionally indirect request strategy	Limited range of conventionally indirect expressions employed with NS-C in comparison to NS-E.	Lin (2009) Rose (2000) Yu (1999) Halenko & Jones (2017) Jones & Halenko (2014) Halenko et al. (2019)
Overreliance on direct strategies	Evidence of more direct strategies employed in comparison to NS-E. In particular, 'want' statements	Chen (2006) Lee-Wong (1994) Wang (2011) Yu (1999) Zhang (1995) Halenko & Jones (2017) Halenko et al. (2019)
Overreliance on speaker-oriented perspective	Requests structured more frequently with 'I' than 'you'	Lin (2009) Zhang (1995)
Verbosity in request structure	Reliance on external modification devices such as grounders leads to lengthier, more verbose constructions	Chen (2006) Yu (1999) Wang (2011) Zhang (1995) Kasper & Zhang (1995)
Use of (multiple) explicit apology to signal politeness	Inclusion of apologies for the ensuing trouble the request may cause. Used as a marker of politeness. No evidence of this in NS-E data	Yu (1999) Zhang (1995)
Little evidence of internal modification	Some NS-E patterns do not exist in Chinese (e.g. verbal conditionals). Not a preferred device for expressing politeness	Yu (1999) Fukushima (2002) Halenko & Jones (2017)
Overreliance on external modification	NS-E rely more on internal modification devices. NS-C rely on external modification devices to show politeness	Wang (2011) Yu (1999) Zhang (1995)
Because-therefore pattern in information sequencing	Reason preceding the problem is common in L1 utterances (apologies and requests). In contrast, the opposite structure (therefore-because) is preferred by L1 English speakers.	Chen (2006) Kirkpatrick (1991, 1992) Wang (2011) Yu (1999) Jones & Halenko (2014) Halenko et al. (2019)

Note: NS-E = English L1 speakers
NS-C = Chinese L1 speakers.

me an extension?'), speaker oriented (e.g. 'Can I have an extension?'), those taking a joint perspective (e.g. 'Could we make the hand in date next week?' or impersonal stance (e.g. 'Is there any chance of an extension?').

The head act can function independently but is typically embedded within a range of mitigating supportive moves which serve to soften the request. These comprise internal and external modifiers. Internal modifiers are those which form part of the head act itself and include softeners which reduce the impositive force (e.g. 'Could you possibly ... '), fillers, items used to fill in the gaps of the utterance (e.g. 'Could you, erm, possibly ... ') or alerters which serve to gain the interlocutor's attention (e.g. 'Excuse me ... '). In contrast, external modifiers surround the head act, serving to further absorb the impact of the impending imposition. These include preparators, employed to set up the request (e.g. 'Mr Waters, I've got a question about my assignment ... ') and grounders, devices used to provide a reason or explanation for the request (e.g. 'Could I have an extension? I've had computer problems'). Observations about the context and social environment need to be made before deciding on the appropriate construction of the request itself.

Within existing request literature, a number of non-L2-like language features have been reported as being culture- and language-specific for many Chinese L1 users when formulating L2 requests. Features which have been reported more than once in existing literature have been selected as foci for this thesis and are summarized in Table 4.1. These language features were included within the intervention to satisfy the pedagogical aim of this study: enhancing the quality (and quantity) of interaction between staff and students on a SA sojourn. With this in mind, non-L2-like features which are most likely to trigger negative reactions and affect the outcome of the request are of most interest in this study.

4.1.1. Empirical request studies

Over the last three decades a substantial body of research on requests across a number of languages has accumulated. Schauer (2009) claims the overwhelming interest shown in this speech act over any other is probably due to its high frequency of occurrence in daily interaction and the many ways requests can be formulated within a wide variety of contexts. This is particularly true of staff-student exchanges in academia, so it is worthy of further investigation. Findings from request studies repeatedly reveal that regardless of learners' language background and proficiency level, there are clear disparities between L1 and L2 users (e.g. Economidou-Kogetsidis 2012; Octu & Zeyrek 2008; Woodfield & Economidou-Kogetsidis 2010). Differences have been noted in lower frequencies of conventionally indirect strategies and internal modification devices, in addition to higher levels of direct strategies and external modification devices by L2 users when compared with English L1 users.

The development towards L2 norms relative to greater proficiency levels is a trend reported in a number of early studies employing Japanese EFL learners. Hill (1997), for instance, examined Japanese learners' production of requests at low, intermediate and advanced proficiency levels. A move towards NS levels as the learners' interlanguage developed was reported in terms of a decrease in direct strategies and an increase in overall indirectness. Regarding the presence of internal modification, Sasaki's (1998) examination of twelve Japanese EFL learners of English requests reveals a limited repertoire of internal modifiers, including conditionals, 'could'/'would' and the politeness marker 'please'. The author proposed a lack of linguistic development due to low proficiency levels as an explanation for this restricted range.

A second line of request investigations within the Asian context considers the influence of negative language transfer, defined as 'the projection of first language-based sociopragmatic and pragmalinguistic onto second language contexts where such projections results in perceptions and behaviours different from those of second language users' (Maeshiba et al. 1996: 155). Lee-Wong (1994) and Zhang (1995) usefully catalogue L1 Chinese request strategies which provide an important backdrop to then examining the role of L1 interference and transfer. Overall results of these early studies suggest Chinese speakers consistently display a preference for direct forms through imperatives, direct questions and 'want' statements when formulating requests in the L1. This trend is claimed to be attributable to the Chinese preference for linguistic conventions which are economical, clear and explicit, in line with maintaining a positive public self-image, as opposed to the importance of individual self-image proposed through Brown and Levinson's theories (Lee-Wong 1994; Zhang 1995). This strategy is extended to situations involving close social relationships, even between status-unequal members. The closer the relationship, the greater the tendency to be direct and explicit (e.g. 'Give me a lift'), avoiding the need to solicit whether the request can be carried out, which is more common in English (e.g. 'Could you give me a lift?'). Direct strategies can be mitigated in L1 Chinese, though this is typically achieved through external supportive moves and small talk preceding the request, rather than internal modification, preferred by English users. Conventionally indirect structures (e.g. 'could you'/'would you'), which maximize indirectness in English, are deemed more appropriate in situations involving maximum social distance in Chinese. For Chinese users, indirectness, and therefore politeness, is realized through the aforementioned external moves so the necessary face adjustments to others and oneself can be made (Lee-Wong 1994; Zhang 1995).

The findings from subsequent investigations into L2 patterns of request production reveal interesting similarities, said to be traceable to L1 negative transfer (Fukuya & Zhang 2002; Lin 2009; Wang 2011; Yu 1999). From a pragmalinguistic perspective (linguistic forms) pragmatic transfer is understood as 'the illocutionary force or politeness value assigned to a particular linguistic material in L1 which influences learners' perception and production of form-function mappings in L2' (Kasper 1992: 209). From a sociopragmatic perspective (cultural norms), pragmatic transfer occurs when 'the social perceptions underlying language users' interpretations and performance of linguistic action in L2 are influenced by their assessment of subjectively equivalent L1 contexts' (Kasper 1992: 209).

Beginning with Yu (1999), comparisons of linguistic request behaviour were made between forty Chinese ESL learners, forty American L1 speakers and forty L1 Chinese participants using their L1 for analysis of transfer. Similar to the study in this volume, the situations eliciting request forms centred on the role of a university student. Firstly, the findings from the Chinese L1 group were similar to those identified in Lee-Wong (1994) and Zhang (1995). Secondly, the majority of the L2 behaviour was revealed to be appropriated from the L1, including underuse of internal modifiers, more frequent use of direct strategies and external supportive moves such as small talk, 'grounders' and 'please' than the L1 English group. The 'because-therefore' pattern in information sequencing was a further point noted which resembled the learners' L1 style. Lin's (2009) findings also lend further support to the L1-L2 differences in request realization found in Yu's study. In addition, Lin notes that L1 English users employ a much wider range of conventionally indirect strategies in general. Both Yu and Lin, however, may have limited the scope of analysis by solely relying on the Cross-Cultural Speech Act Realisation Project (CCSARP) for data coding which does not include the use of 'want' statements, for instance, often identified in Chinese request language. Furthermore, both studies elicited data via a written production task which has been subject to critique for representing oral output in a written mode (see Chapter 5 for further discussion on test modality).

Fukuya and Zhang (2002) employed a pretest-posttest experimental design to analyse the performance of twenty Chinese learners of English in producing pragmatically appropriate high-risk and low-risk request head acts. In contrast to Yu's (1999) and Lin's (2009) comparative studies, a treatment group receiving implicit corrective feedback via recasts was measured against a non-treatment control group. Following 350 minutes of role-play practice, participants completed a written production task to elicit the requests, in addition to a Likert scale rating of their confidence levels. Pretest results suggested no significant between-group difference in the use of the eight request target forms. Posttest results, however, indicated that the control group lacked the same command of request use as the treatment group in some areas, including fewer instances of the target forms introduced and increased use of query preparatory questions 'can/could/will/would'. The authors claim the success of the implicit treatment was attributable to the recasts encouraging learners to 'notice' the language features and the gap between their interlanguage and target language systems. This strategy was also said to be facilitated by the formulaic nature of request conventions which could be acquired and processed as whole expressions more easily and efficiently than sociopragmatic conventions, for instance (see Chapter 3 on teaching formulaic language). Disappointingly, a delayed test was not conducted to measure long-term effects.

Trends reported in the aforementioned studies are corroborated in a more recent, comprehensive comparative analysis of L1 English and Chinese request production, though this evidence is again extracted from written production tasks. Wang (2011) utilized visual aids (a photographed image depicting the context) alongside ten situational prompts in his enhanced written production task for reinforcement. The results showed his two general English (n = 32) and business English (n = 41) learner groups exhibited a range of request features which diverged from the native Australian English speakers, employed for comparison purposes (n = 32). Specifically, an underdeveloped repertoire of formulae was found, with further evidence of the struggle to master more complex (bi-clausal) expressions, common to the NS group: 'I was wondering if', 'Would it/you be'. According to Lin (2009), Wang (2011) and Yu (1999), this is because bi-clausal structures (main clause + subordinate clause) do not exist in Chinese (e.g. 'I was wondering if (main clause) I could have an extension for my essay?' (subordinate clause)). Internal modification was also employed less frequently by the learner groups. This included suggestions of underdeveloped sociopragmatic knowledge, evidenced in the non-L2-like use of address terms such as 'sir' and 'madam' during service encounters. Corroborating previous studies, external modification was found to be more frequent and elaborate than their NS counterparts in terms of supportive moves, information sequencing and overall utterance length. For Wang, the primary cause of divergence amongst the learner groups at the strategic, lexical and sociopragmatic levels was negative L1 transfer.

A smaller collection of studies, specifically investigating pragmatic performance through email requests to faculty, shows evidence of similar non-L2-like forms occurring in written request production too. Despite a focus on the written medium, this body of studies provides important insights into the causes of pragmatic divergence. Chen (2006) is one of the only longitudinal studies to incorporate a detailed individual case study investigation combined with a series of retrospective verbal reports, conducted at three defined points over a thirty-six-month study period. This approach allowed an in-depth understanding of the changes in an L1 Chinese speaker's cognitive processes and developing discourse practices when formulating email requests over a longitudinal year SA experience in the United States. The 266 emails collected revealed that, without guidance, the participant's implicit learning of appropriate email request practice was slow and limited in scope since there were no models to imitate, no explicit rules to follow as might be introduced in instruction, and rarely were opportunities presented to obtain feedback. Pragmatic problems outlined in the early stages of the participant's email practice included 'want' statements embellished with unnecessary detail, lengthy and inductive structures, reliance on the student-oriented perspective ('I'), and no status-appropriate politeness conventions. Based on the interview data, most of these inappropriate practices could be traced back to the participant's first language pragmalinguistic and sociopragmatic conventions. Slow but gradual improvements in the participant's email practices became evident in the production of shorter messages, greater use of the more indirect query preparatory strategy and more appropriate mitigating supportive moves.

Chen's (2015b) intervention study attempted to address some of the issues concerning infelicitous language use when composing email requests to faculty. Results from 224 email scripts by EFL learners revealed improvements in the framing moves of email requests (subject, greeting and closing), following six hours of explicit instruction. Participants were less successful at adopting the content moves in the form of request strategies and relevant external supportive moves. The former gains were said to be attributable to the ease of acquiring formulaic expressions, whilst the content moves were considered more idiosyncratic and less controllable in a classroom setting. No delayed posttest meant the retention of the input over the long term could not be measured.

Although employing Japanese participants in her study, Taguchi's (2006) methodological approach has direct relevance to this volume due to the inclusion of L1 speaker rating scales to measure pragmatic appropriateness of requests responses, in addition to a linguistic analysis of the oral data. The findings support studies reporting an increase in proficiency levels to be concomitant with the ability to produce more target-like utterances (Hill 1997; Roever 2005; Rose 2000; Trosborg 1995). This trend, however, did not extend to the use of mitigated-preparatory strategies (e.g. 'I'm wondering if ... ', 'Do you mind ... ') suggesting that, despite their high frequency (100 per cent use by the NS group), these complex forms were much more difficult to acquire even for high proficiency learners of English. The use of rating scales in this study uncovered two notable aspects in the measurement of pragmatic performance, absent from most speech act analyses which mainly focus on linguistic performance alone. First, despite noticeable grammatical errors in some responses, these were still evaluated as being pragmatically acceptable. This echoes Bardovi-Harlig and Dornyei's (1998) celebrated study which reported ESL instructors rating pragmatic performance more highly than grammatical accuracy, placing emphasis on the communicative aspect of language production. This is further underlined in the second finding that, despite the core request being realized with appropriate levels of directness and politeness, a number of responses still received low ratings due to poor discourse management, for instance. Overall, this study reveals successful pragmatic performance is dependent on a combination of discourse features and cannot be attributed to linguistic production alone. The study may have benefitted from an oral production task such as the CAPT which would have allowed more efficient capture of data, under controlled conditions, with the fifty-nine participants. Instead, individual role-plays of up to twenty-five minutes were conducted, and participants were permitted unlimited time to prepare.

In summary, research to date reveals several trends outlining non-L2-like performance across a number of languages when investigating the formulation of requests in English. Specifically, learners employ conventionally indirect strategies less frequently than expert users, and internal modification is found to be more challenging to incorporate than external modification devices, particularly for lower proficiency learners. Specific to learners from Chinese backgrounds, negative cultural and linguistic transfer are common explanations for non-standard features of request production such as an overuse of direct strategies, a limited range of conventionally indirect forms and verbosity. The review of requests conducted here is extended to the speech act of apologies in the next section.

4.2. The speech act of apologies

As with requests, apologies are considered face-threatening acts (FTAs). To repair the damage of FTAs, interlocutors may engage in numerous facework strategies, such as apologizing, as corrective measures to re-establish social harmony (Olshtain & Cohen 1983). Apologizing is therefore a post-act event. The conditions to an apology being fulfilled are dependent on the culpable person acknowledging or recognizing the offence has occurred, which may be determined by sociocultural norms just as linguistic norms will determine whether the utterance actually qualifies as an apology (Olshtain & Cohen 1983). In Brown and Levinson's (1987) terms, the act of apologizing is face-saving for the hearer and face-threatening for the speaker. Leech (1983) qualifies this by maintaining there is some kind of benefit for the hearer at a cost for the speaker through the act of apology, unlike requests which are costly in the reverse.

Researchers have posited a number of general and more detailed classifications for the semantic formulae contained in acts of apology. Most build on the influential work of Goffman (1971) who describes apologizing as 'remedial work' accomplished by accounts (excuses/explanations), requests (begging sufferance) and apologies. Goffman classifies apologies as either 'ritual', motivated by social habits, or 'substantive' – the wish to repair any damage or harm caused by the initial act.

The limited categorizations proposed by Goffman have since been modified and expanded by a number of scholars based on cumulative research conducted in the 1980s (Blum-Kulka & Olshtain 1984; Fraser 1981; Olshtain & Cohen 1983; Owen 1983; Trosborg 1987). As a result, these studies have developed and described a range of strategies to be undertaken for appropriate apology behaviour.

As introduced earlier, Blum-Kulka et al.'s (1989) cross-cultural speech act realisation project (CCSARP) is cited as a basic conceptual framework of the semantic formulae involved in apologizing, though this is largely a reformulation of those proposed in the earlier studies (Blum-Kulka & Olshtain 1984; Fraser 1981; Olshtain & Cohen 1983; Owen 1983; Trosborg 1987). It consists of a set of five formulae which individually may be considered sufficient to placate the hearer, although a combination, signifying a more heartfelt apology, is also commonplace (see Figure 4.2). Intensification of apologies ('I'm *very* sorry') are also common to emphasize regret. It is useful to view them on a continuum as Trosborg (1987) suggests. In this case, the cumulative total of formulae (a) to (e) in Figure 4.2 increases in indirectness and potential for placating the recipient.

Explicit expressions of apology (a) are generally realized through performative verbs such as 'apologize' or 'forgive'. An explanation (b) provides a reason for the violation or damage which has occurred and often provides supportive evidence to (a). An admission of responsibility for the offence is realized through strategy (c) which is suggested to be the most explicit and direct and powerful apology strategy (Nureddeen 2008). An offer to repair or pay for the damage caused is

(a). Expression of apology (with intensification)
e.g. *I'm really sorry*

(b). Explanation or account
e.g. *The traffic was awful*

(c). Acknowledgement of responsibility
e.g. *It's my fault*

(d). Offer of repair
e.g. *Let me buy you a coffee. My treat*

(e). Promise of forbearance
e.g. *I'll set off earlier next time*

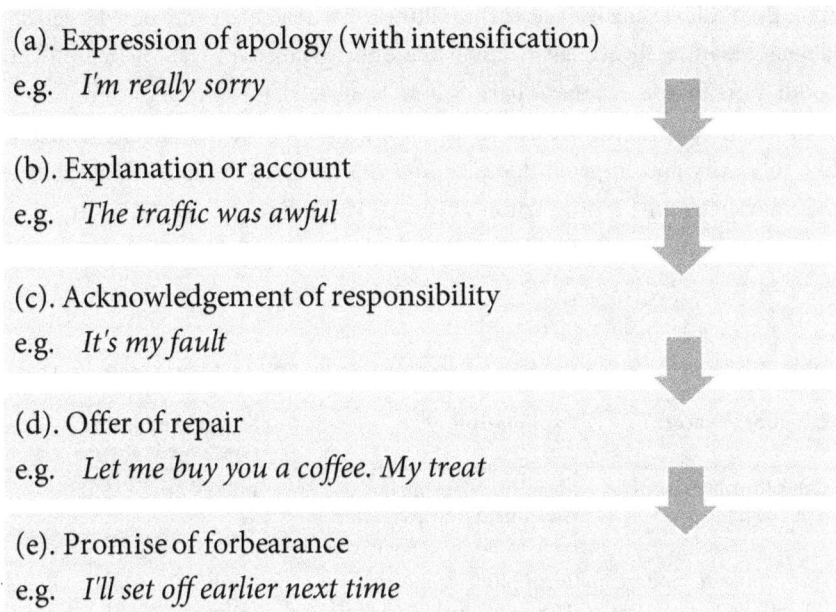

Figure 4.2 Formulaic strategies for the apology speech act (Trosborg 1987)

provided through (d), whilst promising not to repeat the offence in the future is acknowledged in strategy (e).

Strategies (a) and (b) are said to be the basis of any remedial work, whilst (c) to (e) are situation-dependent (Blum-Kulka et al. 1989) in the event further mitigation is required. In contrast, Bergman and Kasper's (1993) review of a range of empirical apology studies has since concluded the essential components of an apology contained strategies (a) and (c) – explicit expressions of apology and statements of responsibility (Holmes 1990; House 1988; Kasper 1989; Trosborg 1987), and it is the severity of the infraction which dictates the redressive strategy preferences (e.g. Brown & Levinson 1987; Holmes 1990; Maeshiba et al. 1996). A single apology in the form of an IFID may be adequate for being slightly late to meet a friend (ritual apology), but a more elaborate formulation incorporating multiple strategies may be required if the offence is much more serious such as misplacing someone's treasured possession (substantive apology). Contextual factors such as power and social distance between interlocutors also influence apology performance (Maeshiba et al. 1996).

Similar to the research on Chinese requests, Table 4.2 summarizes non-L2-like language features reported as being culture- and language-specific for Chinese L1 speakers when formulating L2 apologies. Due to the low number of empirical apology studies exclusively featuring Chinese participants, some non-target-like language features illustrated in Table 4.2 are also gleaned from studies employing South Korean and Japanese participants (italicized in the table). Similarities between these Asian cultures such as sharing common sociolinguistic variables like solidarity and in-group identity, and the reported comparable influences this may have on L2 production (Byon 2004; Fukushima 2002), justify their inclusion as they may provide further clarity on L2 production and a greater

Table 4.2 Non-L2-like features of apologies reported for L1 Chinese users

Language feature	Explanation	Studies reporting language feature
Inappropriate use of 'I apologize'	Socially inappropriate use or use considered 'excessive' for L2 context	Linnell et al. (1992)
Inappropriate request for forgiveness	'Please forgive me' may be socially awkward and/or excessive in certain L2 contexts. Generally reserved for major offences only in the L2	Chang (2010) Halenko (2018)
Inappropriate use of phrase for context	Use of phrase, e.g. 'take it easy' (when speaking to a higher-status interlocutor)	Linnell et al. (1992)
Undersupply of admission of responsibility	*Embedded in the L1 IFID so unlikely to be explicitly repeated as a supportive move (Kim 2008). Negative L1 transfer may explain why L2 use of this strategy is uncommon.* No reason supplied for the Chinese learners in the Linnell et al. (1992) study	Linnell et al. (1992), Kim (2008) Halenko (2018)
Redress an offence with excessive offer of repair	Although the utterance may be functionally adequate, it sounds socially awkward and is likely to have a negative effect on the L2 interlocutor. In contrast, such a move is not uncommon in the L1.	Linnell et al. (1992) Halenko (2018)
Use of an imperative which acts as a directive	Common to learners with a lower-level proficiency. Suggests negative L1 transfer where imperatives are a common linguistic feature.	Linnell et al. (1992)

Because-therefore pattern evident in information sequencing	This syntactic structure where the reason precedes the problem is common in L1 utterances (apologies and requests). In contrast, the opposite structure (therefore-because) is preferred by L1 English speakers.	Yu (1999), Lin (2009) Halenko (2018)
Use of inappropriate address terms	Evidence of negative L1 transfer from the wide range of address terms which exist in Chinese and have a function beyond alerting attention. The selection reflects social relationships (Zhang 1995: 36).	Zhang (1995) Halenko (2018)
Intensification signalled by multiple apologies rather than adverbial internal modifiers	Often replaced by the production of multiple apologies to signal intensification as a result of L1 transfer in comparison to NS who use more adverbial internal modifiers such as 'really' and 'so'.	Chang (2010) Halenko (2018)
'Explanation' strategy uncommon	*Preference for 'compensatory' strategies as producing an 'explanation' shifts the blame from the speaker causing potential to damage the speaker's image or for him/her to appear less sincere.*	Barnlund and Yoshioka (1990), Kim (2008) Halenko (2018)
'Promise of forbearance' strategy uncommon	Promise of forbearance reported to be rarely used as it causes too much humiliation for the speaker	Kim (2008) Halenko (2018)

evidence base from which the present study's results can be analysed. As with the previous chapter on requests, the non-L2-like features which are most likely to trigger negative reactions and affect the outcome of the apology are of most interest in this study.

Performing an apology is complex. Indeed, the combination and sequence of the multiple strategies available to realize these supportive moves differ cross-culturally. Examples of these cross-cultural differences in Western and non-Western contexts can be found even in early empirical research on apologies, as discussed in the next sections. As with requests, the majority of apology studies adopt a L1/L2 comparative stance to assess pragmatic performance.

4.2.1. Empirical apology studies

Since the emergence of the CCSARP (Blum-Kulka et al. 1989) similar smaller-scale studies have established growing evidence that language users signal politeness in apologies in a variety of ways which may differ across languages (e.g. Barron 2019; Nureddeen 2008; Sabaté i Dalmau & Curell i Gotor 2007; Shardakova 2005; Suszcyznska 1999). Investigating apology behaviour in East Asian cultures is under-explored compared to research situated in Western contexts. It is only since a small growth in studies focusing on Japanese, Chinese, and Korean cultures evidencing disparities between East and West cultural values and norms, that increasing attention is being paid to the effect this might have on L2 production. At the same time, as mentioned previously, the evidence provided in these studies leads to questioning the applicability of Brown and Levinson's theory of politeness, at least in these geographical locations.

One of the earliest non-Western apology studies aimed to assess differences in L1 and L2 production of apologies and to what extent this was affected by language proficiency (Linnell et al. 1992). Similar to the present study, the participant data were captured orally in a single-turn interaction but, in Linnell et al.'s case, the twenty English learners (from a range of L1s including Chinese) completed a verbal production task. Although the results need to be considered tentatively given the multilingual background of the participants, and the considerable variation in L2 exposure (two weeks to six years), the authors found some evidence of non-L2-like apology forms in comparison to L1 users. These included the use of imperatives as directives and redressing offences with excessive offers of repair. Significant differences were also noted in the undersupply of explicit apologies, acknowledgements of responsibility and intensifiers.

Park and Guan (2009) aimed to test the hypotheses that Americans were more likely to display apologetic behaviour when their negative face was threatened and, comparably, that L1 Chinese speakers would display similar behaviour when their positive face was threatened. Though some similarities between the two cultures were evident with regard to levels of intentions to apologize, results showed that the 'individualistic' American participants reacted more strongly when their negative face was threatened in a 'stepping on someone's foot' scenario, for instance. In contrast, when presented with a 'laughing when someone belches' scenario, the Chinese had stronger intentions to apologize in positive face-threatening situations such as this. Measuring actual apology behaviour, as in the present study, would have allowed more concrete conclusions to be drawn.

From a pragmalinguistic perspective, Tanaka et al. (2000) provided counter-evidence to the stereotypical perception that the Japanese apologize more frequently than English speakers. They suggest this myth is based on the Japanese 'sumimasen' being regarded as equivalent to the English 'I'm sorry' when, in fact, it serves a number of functions in addition to an apology: expressing thanks, as a preface to a request, as an attention-getter or as a leave-taking device. Their study reported the use of explicit expressions of apology in the form of IFIDs was not significantly more frequent overall when compared to responses from British or Canadian L1 English users. In fact, in specific scenarios where the complainant was at fault, the Japanese were much more reluctant to overtly apologize than the English-speaking respondents.

Kim (2008) offered a similar account of the South Korean phrase 'mianhada' and how the meaning is under-represented by the simplistic English translation of 'I'm sorry'. It, too, is multi-functional in its semantic meaning which includes thanking and requesting, in addition to apologizing. When comparing the semantic formulae used to produce an apology in Korean, repair and use of intensifiers were more evident in the Korean data in comparison to Olshtain's (1989) data from Australian English, Canadian French and Hebrew. The forbearance strategy, however, rarely appeared as the author cited this was likely to cause excessive humiliation for the speaker. An interesting feature of the data is that the participants in this study relied more heavily on the use of IFIDs which, in Korean, inherently includes a 'responsibility' component. As a result, a separate admission of responsibility was much less frequent than in the other languages so direct comparisons between them were inconclusive. According to Kim, further limitations to cross-cultural comparability lie in the inadequacies of coding schemes which fail to acknowledge the frequent use of non-linguistic devices such as bowing, smiling and silence as a means of apologizing in cultures like South Korea. For both Tanaka et al. (2000) and Kim (2008), achieving L2-like performance may therefore be more complex, rooted in the problematic notion of exactly what constitutes an apology, as noted in some Western languages (e.g. Wierzbicka 1985, 1991).

Following a series of semi-structured interviews with Japanese and American university students to investigate cultural variables affecting forms of apology in both countries, Barnlund and Yoshioka (1990) reported instances of both cultural convergence and divergence. Examples of the former include the overwhelming preference for both groups to initiate apologies with an IFID and to respond to the status and social differences of their interlocutors, for instance. The latter was evidenced in several ways. Firstly, the Japanese participants generally believed the act of apologizing repaired the relationship, rather than improved it, which was the American perspective. Next, the use of more direct and extreme forms of apology expressions was evident in the Japanese data (a feature common to both Japanese and Chinese cultures). Finally, the Japanese opted for a more limited range of apologetic acts such as directly saying 'sorry' and offering to repair the situation. Mirroring Kim's (2008) findings, the Japanese students considered the interlocutor's status to be influential in how apologies were formulated and preferred compensatory strategies (offer of repair) twice as frequently as the Americans who favoured explanations to complement the initial IFID. Kondo (1997) suggests Japanese tend to undersupply explanations and excuses as it conflicts with the cultural expectation of being deferent. Repeated, direct expressions of apology are the preferred option as they humble oneself and appeal to the hearer. The concept of restoring and maintaining group harmony is offered as an explanation for many of the strategies adopted by the Japanese group – a recurring theme in East Asian pragmatic studies.

Of direct relevance to this volume's study, Chang (2010) investigated the acquisitional order of apology sequences and linguistic forms by Chinese learners of English between the ages of nine and nineteen years old, as proficiency levels increased. Perhaps unsurprisingly, results revealed that the IFID 'I'm sorry' was the first emergent interlanguage strategy and the one which proved to be the most frequent in all age groups. 'Explanation' strategies, however, were not evident until the later stages of development. A developmental sequence emerged from the data allowing for the apology strategies to be ranked in order of acquisition from lowest to highest proficiency levels: (1) IFIDs or equivalent expressions of regret, (2) alerters and admissions of fact, (3) intensifiers, expressing concern, minimizing and repairing damage, (4) explanation, lack of intent, promise of forbearance, acknowledgement, blame. This corroborates Sabaté i Dalmau and Curell i Gotor (2007) who suggest that face-threatening acts such as apologies are likely to be acquired very late in the L1 or L2. Chang's study is useful for understanding the benefits of formulaic language at early stages of language development and how linguistic proficiency and cognitive maturity are requisite to achieving more elaborate, and arguably more appropriate, utterances.

To sum up, several features of apologies have been noted in the research to date. For instance, L1 English speakers seem to rely on a limited range of performative verbs to realize apologies and favour internal modification devices as a mitigating strategy. Apologies produced by learners of English from Asian cultures, on the other hand, have been found to exhibit a number of non-L2-like forms: an undersupply of promises of forbearance, admissions of responsibility, and explanations; an oversupply of repeated, direct apologies. What is indicative of many of these studies is a need to consider both form and function of the apology in the first language and target contexts. It would appear the latter is often overlooked as a possible cause of miscommunication, even though in a small number of studies, it has been shown to be a contributory factor.

From discussions so far in this chapter, there is sufficient evidence to suggest that conveying a message, such as a request or apology, may differ across cultures and languages so the presupposition that learners can always rely on their L1 knowledge to inform pragmatic choices should be avoided. Such conclusions arguably support the case for pragmatic instruction with second language learners, as discussed in Chapter 3.

5

Background to the study

Before introducing the empirical study, this chapter foregrounds a number of key areas to set up the investigation. The first section briefly describes the research design employed. This is followed by an exploration of data collection instruments, and their associated benefits and challenges, to rationalize the selection of tools used for the study. The chapter concludes with detailing current shortcomings of L2 pragmatics research and outlining the main research questions adopted for the study.

5.1. Methodological approach

To provide a comprehensive account of the findings and improve validity through triangulation of results, this study adopted a mixed methods design. Combining methods aims to dilute potential biases in any one analytical approach and achieves greater insight into the data by observing them from different angles (House 2018). Within Creswell and Plano Clark's (2010) major mixed method designs, the present study adopts a convergent parallel (QUAL + QUAN) design given both the qualitative and quantitative data were elicited at the same time and relationships between them investigated. Within this overarching design, the present study adopts a quasi-experimental approach of the type described by Creswell (2009), in which the outcome of a treatment on non-randomized subjects is measured – in this case, intact classes of learners on an existing English language programme. Experimental studies such as this volume are characterized by Cohen and Macaro (2010) as the manipulation of a situation to determine if an independent variable (e.g. instruction) has some kind of effect on a dependent variable (e.g. language learning).

5.2. Data collection in L2 pragmatics research

It is the dichotomy of controlling variables whilst seeking authenticity of data which overshadows data collection in L2 pragmatics studies. An overview of archetypal written and oral data collection instruments will be briefly presented in the following sections as a means of highlighting the gap in the data collection pool to be filled by the computer-animated production task (CAPT) implemented in this investigation.

5.2.1. Written discourse completion task

The written discourse completion task (WDCT), also known as a production task or production test, is one of the earliest instruments devised to elicit L2 responses and is still by far the most frequently used data collection instrument in L2 pragmatics research (Jeon & Kaya 2006; Labben 2016). In WDCTs, participants are presented with a situation in paper-based format in which a request (or other speech act), for instance, is believed to be the next relevant action; e.g. 'You have not completed your essay. You go to your tutor's office to ask for extra time.' Participants are then invited to note in written form what they might say or how they might react. Since the participant responses to the situations need to be assessed, WDCTs typically contain no more than twelve situations (see Jeon & Kaya's 2006 meta-analysis). The situations also typically include a range of interlocutors to examine if learners are able to adjust their interlanguage based on the social context and with whom they are speaking.

Administratively, WDCTs offer ways to assess pragmatic performance within short periods of time, with large numbers of L2 learner cohorts, and are able to control the sociolinguistic variables of the respondents (age, background, gender, linguistic profile) and interlocutor (including social distance and status). Nevertheless, the written-for-oral mode (Bardovi-Harlig 2015) calls its construct validity into question, and the non-interactive format, failing to replicate real-life interaction, means the data captured may not truly represent what would be produced in an authentic exchange (Golato 2003). Further concerns lie in the variability of the DCT design in terms of the quality and quantity of the contextual information presented (e.g. Billmyer & Varghese 2000), the presence of single or multiple turns (e.g. Bardovi-Harlig & Hartford 1993) and even the amount of space available for the written response (e.g. Rintell & Mitchell 1989). Given the affordances technology now offers for capturing data has led to suggestions that written DCTs should now be retired (Bardovi-Harlig

2018; House 2018) where possible, though Labben (2016) argues that the WDCT may remain the most utilized data collection instrument since not all teaching and research contexts can access the tools or facilities needed for alternative methods. Ways to capture more naturally occurring discourse in the form of oral production tasks have long been encouraged but equally present their own challenges, as discussed in the following section.

5.2.2. Oral discourse completion task

That oral discourse completion tasks (ODCT) are also known as 'closed role plays' suggests, by definition, enhanced interaction between interlocutors in comparison to the WDCT due to the turn-taking format. Added to this, the oral-for-oral mode (Bardovi-Harlig 2015), by which the data are elicited, means that construct validity of this instrument is also optimized in comparison to the WDCT. Unlike the WDCT, however, no standardized format seems to exist for the closed ODCT, and methodological details in empirical studies are often vague.

Whilst the format of providing a response in an interaction with a predetermined course and outcome remains the same as the WDCT, studies to date largely support the use of the ODCTs as a means of collecting more natural speech (e.g. Yuan 2001). Versions of the ODCT were used as early as the 1980s (Olshtain & Cohen 1981) but have failed to generate the same interest as the WDCT. This could be because the administration is logistically more complex with a need for multiple sets of audio recorders or language laboratory facilities. Data analyses are potentially more time-consuming too if transcription is required. Studies incorporating the ODCT have also focused on its value in comparison to other instruments. The findings suggest oral responses tend to be longer than their written counterparts (e.g. Rintell & Mitchell 1989; Yuan 2001), provide data which have more features of spoken discourse (Eisenstein & Bodman 1993; Yuan 2001) and are less direct in content (Rintell & Mitchell 1989).

The advantages of capturing oral data within face-to-face interactions have also been explored. Simulations of communicative interactions via open role-plays, where a negotiated outcome is required, are perhaps the closest approximation to achieving authentic spoken data in an environment with some degree of control (Golato 2003). Indeed, the stimulus for oral production, the opportunity for multiple turn-taking, the online planning and decision-making, in addition to the face-to-face interaction, are all typical features of authentic encounters and are likely reasons for the popularity of open role-plays. Plonsky and Zhuang's (2019) meta-analysis also found free outcome measures such as role-plays yielded larger effects in empirical studies than more controlled outcome measures such as multiple-choice questions and WDCTs. From a procedural perspective, however, role-plays are more time-consuming to operationalize, as is data transcription and coding. The cognitive strain on the participants as they perform a specific role, whilst simultaneously online planning and processing information to produce a response, may also lead learners to underperform and fail to demonstrate their true capabilities (Kasper & Rose 2002; Yuan 2001).

5.2.3. Collecting naturally occurring data

Whilst naturally occurring data potentially present the best sample of what actually takes place in authentic conversation, the methodological issues attached pose a number of obstacles for the researcher: (i) accessing the authentic settings and isolating sufficient interlocutors and 'events' in order to obtain the data, (ii) ensuring that the data yield sufficient samples of the particular speech act under investigation, and (iii) controlling sociolinguistic variables to ensure data comparability (Golato 2003; Kasper & Rose 2002). These features are much easier to control using simulated elicitations which add to their appeal over ethnographical studies. Utilizing field notes and audio recordings are typical approaches employed for capturing authentic discourse but are few in number in comparison to other methods discussed here. Field notes and recordings are largely employed as benchmarks against which other methods can be measured to determine data authenticity since naturally occurring data are considered to be truly representative of actual language use. Multi-method investigations include Beebe and Cummings (1996), Félix-Brasdefer (2007), Golato (2003) and Yuan (2001). One major drawback noted, however, is that studies eliciting natural data are typically context-sensitive such as Beebe and Cummings' (1996) telephone conversations and Hartford and Bardovi-Harlig's (1992) academic advising sessions whose interlocutors and linguistic context are very specific. Results are therefore more difficult to generalize as the speech act is limited to one main context or setting which may produce different results when investigated elsewhere.

5.2.4. Innovative data collection instruments

The landscape of new and innovative data collection instruments is changing but development is slow in this area. Rose's (2000) cartoon oral production task (COPT), modified by Flores-Salgado (2011), paved the way for the introduction of more innovative measures of data elicitation and enhancing learner interactivity by providing a visual stimulus to elicit oral data. Cartoon illustrations representing different social situations were depicted as the stimuli to capture the data, supported by brief L1 captions of the context. Participants were then recorded producing a range of requests, apologies and compliment responses. Although the primary school participants employed in Rose's study may have been the chief motivation behind the COPT's design, it illustrates an effective means of eliciting large amounts of spoken data under controlled conditions and was generally considered a success by the researchers, though the instrument itself was not under the spotlight. A further appeal is its potential with beginner-level learners, since there is no specific requirement for reading, writing or listening with this task.

Schauer's (2004) multimedia elicitation task (MET) refines the COPT further by adding an audiovisual element to a computer-based task, motivated by the need to address standardization of instruments to ensure equal conditions amongst participant groups: a limitation previously highlighted in other instruments as well as in the early COPT study. In the MET, oral data are elicited via a set of timed slides. Each scenario is presented through a content slide which provides a brief description of the event. Several seconds later, this is followed by a photographic image of the situation which is supported by an audio description. Schauer claims that both standardization and learner engagement are enhanced through this instrument.

Both the COPT and MET have made worthwhile modifications to data collection design by promoting learner interactivity and considering data comparability. CALL tools, in particular, continue to be refined and improved in an effort to find a rigorous means of data elicitation which can stand up to scrutiny. The CAPT instrument employed in this volume also operates via a computerized presentation format to address issues around standardization yet improves the work to date by its unique features of combining an audiovisual element with synchronous exchange of dialogue. The CAPT can be broadly categorized as a *game- (and play-) informed* pedagogical tool, of the kind described by Reinhardt and Sykes (2014) and discussed briefly in Chapter 4. Game-informed tools integrate the elements of game and play within an activity designed to meet a specific pedagogical goal. By integrating what is known about game and play research, pragmatics materials can be designed and manipulated to maximize teaching and learning. The CAPT is a product of this approach and its success as a teaching and assessment tool has been demonstrated across several studies investigating speech act performance (Halenko 2013, 2018; Halenko & Flores Salgado 2019; Halenko & Jones 2017; Halenko et al. 2019).

In the CAPT, though the interaction is limited to a single turn in this and previous studies, the exchange increases the opportunities for eliciting authentic, naturally occurring discourse, but in more controlled, comparable conditions than those presented through role-plays or ethnographic recordings (see Figure 5.1). The added dimension of incorporating virtual reality seeks to increase student engagement and refines previous attempts of enhancing the stimuli by uniquely incorporating both audio and 3D interactive visual elements not seen in the oral DCT, COPT or MET. This allows the interlocutor to enhance the utterances with non-verbal communication cues, for instance, to authenticate the exchange rather than relying on a visual 'still' (MET) or paper-based cartoon (COPT). What the CAPT provides is a range of opportunities for the animated interlocutor to incorporate prosodic features (e.g. stress and intonation of voice) and paralinguistic features of language (e.g. gestures, body movements and facial expressions) which cannot be captured using the aforementioned tools. Including an interlocutor turn at the initial stage also makes the simulation more like conversation (Bardovi-Harlig 2015). In terms of participant output, speech rates, hesitations and prosodic cues that are relevant to pragmatic comprehension can also be captured (Bardovi-Harlig 2018). These features make the CAPT entirely innovative to the current data collection pool which exists in L2 pragmatics research (Chapter 6 details the CAPT design).

To recap, if researchers were to chart the aforementioned L2 pragmatics data collection instruments on a scale of control and authenticity, it might be illustrated as in Figure 5.1. Though this scale considers neither convenience nor practicality for the researcher in terms of operationalizing these approaches, it suggests that WDCTs provide the least suitable means for capturing authentic data to assess pragmatic competence, whilst unscripted and unrehearsed L1-L2 exchanges in real time present the best opportunities. On the other hand, the WDCT gains merit for being better able to control sociolinguistic variables such as age, gender, background and linguistic competence as well as efficiently collecting multiple data sets – variables difficult to manage when collecting naturally occurring discourse.

An important point to note is that the diagonal lines do not represent a particular measure, nor is there a claim that the instruments follow such a uniform pattern or are differentiated in such a linear way as Figure 5.1 suggests. It simply generalizes an increase or decrease in the two variables of control and authenticity but, more importantly, depicts the struggle researchers have in selecting an appropriate data collection method and the compromises which often have to be made when doing so. Careful consideration of purpose is

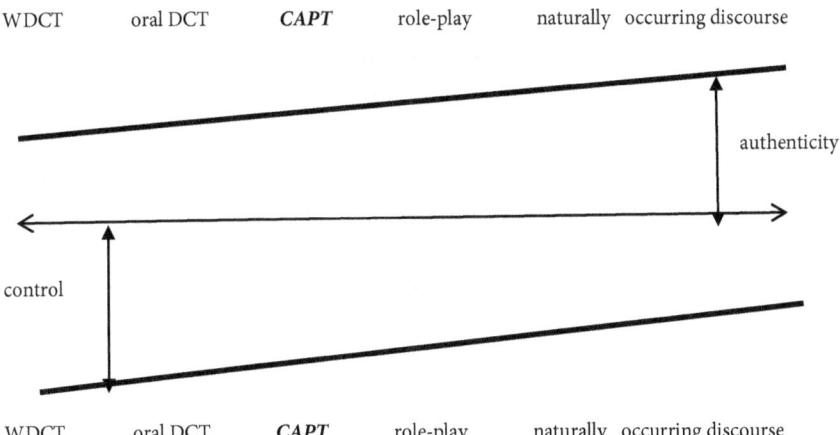
Figure 5.1 Common data collection instruments on a scale of authenticity and control

therefore key, in addition to a multi-method, triangulated approach. Having established a methodological base, the next section describes how the present study addresses existing limitations within L2 pragmatics research and concludes with the research questions applied.

5.3. Research gaps

Methodological shortcomings in L2 pragmatics research are directly addressed in this volume in multiple ways. First, meta-analyses by Llanes (2011) (L2 gains in SA settings) and Plonsky and Zhuang (2019) (L2 pragmatic instruction) report that few pragmatic investigations are situated within a sojourn overseas and most offer an American perspective. The instructional setting within an ongoing UK-based SA sojourn featured here addresses both of these issues.

Second, Taguchi's (2015) meta-analysis of fifty-eight instructional studies found only five which taught more than one pragmatic target. A simultaneous focus on both requests and apologies in this study also fills a much-needed gap in explicit intervention research and can attest to the teachability and learnability of multiple pragmatic targets.

Third, the discussions so far have indicated that technology plays a positive and effective role in language learning. Cohen (2008) and Taguchi (2015) acknowledge, however, that to date no effort has been made to either explore direct comparisons between technology-based learning and other more traditional forms in pragmatics instruction or implement pre-post experimental designs with a control group. The present study is extensive and unique in its comparison of the CAPT with traditional paper-based activities and also expands the range of pragmatic assessment tasks which are said to be slow in their development (Bardovi-Harlig 2015). Using the CAPT as a language practice instrument and assessment task is therefore a unique and innovative contribution to the field of L2 pragmatics research.

Fourth, recruiting two experimental groups and a control group adds to the robustness of the study design for measuring genuine instructional effects. The implementation of two delayed tests to assess the durability of learning is also an under-explored feature of experimental studies. Examining the extent of sustained learning at multiple (post-instructional) points leads to more convincing and insightful findings regarding the nature of pragmatic learnability in classroom settings (Takahashi 2010b).

Fifth, the use of rating scales to assess overall effectiveness of responses, which goes beyond the trend to focus on linguistic forms alone, is also under-represented in speech act analyses. The focus on using rating scales as a means of assessing pragmatic competency further avoids the well-documented challenges raised in Chapter 1 regarding making direct comparisons to NS data to judge pragmatic success.

Finally, it is suggested that production task data alone are too crude a measure of pragmatic development in a SA setting. Research proposes methodological triangulation with data which capture participants' intensity of interaction in the target environment in order to shed more light on the complex interplay between pragmatic development and study abroad (Bardovi-Harlig 2013; Bardovi-Harlig & Bastos 2011; Taguchi 2015). The language contact questionnaire administered during the intervention captures the extent of the participants' self-reported engagement with English in the L2 setting.

5.4. Research questions

The empirical study in this volume is guided by the following research questions. The first research question can be viewed as the primary focus of the study, from which research questions two and three are secondary avenues of exploration.

1. How effective is explicit instruction in developing the pragmatic competence of requests and apologies in Chinese learners of English at a British Higher Education institution during a study abroad stay?

2. To what extent can computer-animated practice materials, eliciting an oral performance, contribute to the short- and long-term production of requests and apologies, in comparison to traditional paper-based activities, eliciting a written performance?
3. What role does the study abroad environment play in the pragmatic development of requests and apologies in Chinese learners of English at a British Higher Education institution during a study abroad stay?

6

Methodology

This chapter first describes the initial pilot phases conducted to validate the instruments and procedural aspects of the study. This is followed by detailing all aspects of the subsequent main study designed to answer the three research questions.

6.1. Pilot study

Two rounds of extensive piloting of the instruments were conducted in the initial phases. The aim of the first round was to experiment with the format of the CAPT and WDCT data collection instruments, to identify the optimum interval times between scenarios on the automated slide sequence and the optimum time needed for participants responses. In the next round, the pilot trialled the CAPT and WDCT in controlled conditions to validate the adjustments made. The participants rehearsed working with two separate CAPT scenarios, depicting situations not used in the main study (apology to tutor for late submission of assignment, request to security guard to unlock flat). In addition, a perception questionnaire was administered at the end of the pilot to gauge participants' motivation and interest in the CAPT as a tool for language practice. None of the seventeen pilot students participated in the main study, but all students were comparable to the final sample employed in terms of age, gender, background and linguistic profile.

A number of revisions were made to the instruments as a result of the pilot rounds. First, three scenarios involving a 'landlady' character were removed as this character and setting did not fit with the other scenarios. Second, with the remaining nine scenarios, the researcher undertook a trial assessment of the responses, using the Likert scale to rate the appropriacy of the request and apology data. To limit the time participants spent completing the tasks as no reward was offered for participation, and the intention was to use a much larger participant sample in the main study, the decision was taken to reduce the final number of scenarios to six. This provided an equal number of scenarios for the three remaining interlocutors and also aimed to reduce the raters' cognitive and physical workload. As six-scenario DCTs had been employed in earlier pragmatic investigations (e.g. Halenko & Jones 2011; Johnson & deHaan, 2013; Shardakova 2005), this was considered an acceptable adjustment. Finally, several lexical items needed clarification on both production tasks which were subsequently revised for the main study (e.g. *assignment* revised to *essay*; *instructor* revised to *tutor*).

6.1.1. Results of the pilot perception questionnaire

Before implementing the CAPT in the main study, a perception questionnaire was also administered to gauge interest and motivation. Learners were asked to compare the computer-animated scenarios with traditional paper-and-pencil activities and base their preferences on the following criteria (the key words in parentheses represent the coding for analysis):

(a) Which is more enjoyable? (enjoyment)
(b) Which is more realistic to a real-life situation? (realism)
(c) Which is easier to complete in terms of task modality – written vs spoken? (ease)
(d) Which has the more interesting format (reading the scenarios or watching the animations)? (content)
(e) Which is more interesting to complete as a language learning activity? (task type)
(f) Which is more helpful for developing skills to interact with L1 speakers? (usefulness)

The results of the questionnaire can be found in Figure 6.1. The experimental group overwhelmingly preferred using computer animation for the language practice of requests and apologies on all but one of the criteria. Results were less decisive regarding 'ease' but as neither instrument seemed to pose any challenges, this was not unexpected. The hypothesis that the CAPT would be a motivating learning tool seems to have been supported in these results.

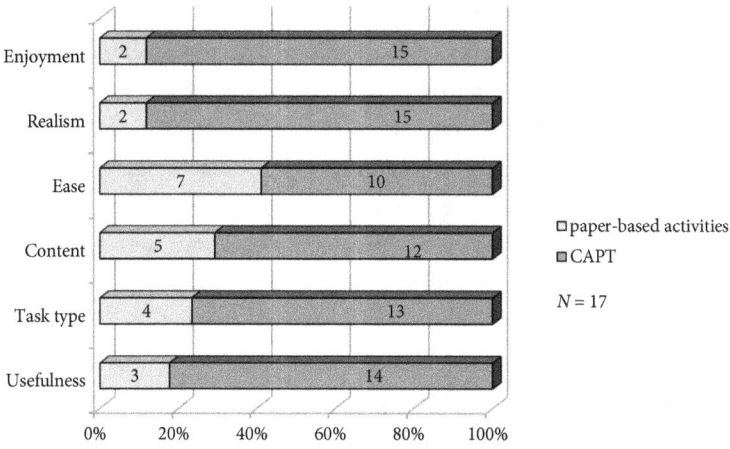

Figure 6.1 Results of the pilot perception questionnaire

6.2. Main study participants

The participants for the main study were three intact classes of sixty-one Chinese undergraduate year three students comprising two experimental groups and one control group, as illustrated in Table 6.1.

None of the learners in any of the three groups had previous study abroad experience but had been learning English between nine and eleven years in China ($M = 10.85$, $SD = .44$). For two years prior to this study, the participants had been students on a business-related degree programme at one of two partner institutions in China and had arrived in the UK to complete their final year at the British Higher Education Institute in the North West of England, where this study was located. The need for a control group to measure the true effectiveness of instruction is widely advocated (e.g. Cohen & Macaro 2010; Jeon & Kaya 2006; Norris & Ortega 2000).

Table 6.1 Main study participants

Group	Number of participants	Purpose	Instructional feature
CAPT	24	Experimental group Intact class	Explicit instruction. Use of CAPT materials for language practice
PAPER	20	Experimental group Intact class	Explicit instruction. Use of traditional paper-and-pencil activities for language practice
Control	17	Control group Intact class	Non-instructed group recruited for baseline data

All the participants ranged in age from nineteen to twenty-three years (M = 21.6, SD = 1.3) with a gender distribution of twenty-seven male and thirty-four female participants, conveniently distributed fairly evenly over the three groups. All learners had been in the UK for approximately one week at the time of the pretest (T1) to begin study on a summer pre-sessional English programme to improve their language level. The groups were randomly assigned for this research by the Director of Studies for the pre-sessional programme and then assigned to either an experimental or control group by the researcher, based on group totals; i.e. to provide a richer data set, the groups with the most participants were selected as the experimental groups. That all participant groups were intact classes meant results were more likely to represent pragmatic behaviour in natural settings so high ecological validity could be claimed with this approach (Bardovi-Harlig 2015).

The participants' overall IELTS score of 5.5 on arrival to the UK reflects an intermediate to upper intermediate proficiency level (CEFR B2 level). Due to challenges encouraging the experimental CAPT and PAPER groups to return voluntarily for the six-week delayed-posttest (T4) following the end of their course, the final sample totalled thirty-three learners (CAPT = 17, PAPER = 16) at this test stage.

The inclusion of the instructional period within the general English component of the study programme, and that the instructor volunteered to be responsible for the classes, beyond the treatment cycle, meant there were no adverse pedagogical implications of conducting the research in this way. These conditions satisfied the need for reciprocity in that both the researcher and participants profited from the investigation (Creswell 2009). Overall feedback was provided to the participants following the six-week delayed test (T4). This was also used as a strategy to incentivize the learners to return for this data collection stage. All participants voluntarily completed a consent form, detailing how the data would be used, assuring anonymity and confidentiality, and the ability to withdraw at any stage.

6.3. Main study instruments

The instruments employed to elicit data in the main study comprised:

- one CAPT (oral mode)
- one WDCT (written mode)
- one self-evaluation questionnaire of English contact during the study abroad stay.

Unlike in many L2 pragmatics studies, the CAPT and written production tasks had a multifunctional design as (i) testing tools to measure the effectiveness of the instruction (RQ 1), and (ii) classroom practice materials to examine long-term retention of the computer-animated format over paper-based class activities (RQ 2). At the testing stages, a total of six scenarios (three eliciting requests and three eliciting apologies) were presented to the learners in a combined format of the CAPT and WDCT. Similar computer-animated scenarios from the CAPT and written paper-based exercises were employed as in-class language practice activities during the instruction.

The interlocutors within the production tasks were characters whom the learners were likely to encounter in an academic context (a tutor, a librarian, a campus security guard), thereby increasing the external face validity of the instrument (Nureddeen 2008). DCT construction typically incorporates Brown and Levinson's (1987) power (P) – social distance (SD) – imposition (R) variables in order to determine learner sensitivity to these when formulating speech acts: the hypothesis being that status-unequal requests, for instance, would command more indirectness than a status-equal request. Interlocutor familiarity (social distance) and size of request (imposition) are also influential factors to consider when formulating appropriate utterances. In the present study, social distance (± SD) was the only variable differentiating the scenarios. Otherwise, status-unequal dyads (+P) were constant, given the study's focus on staff-student interactions. Equally, higher imposition (+R) requests and apologies were included in the scenarios, as led by staff members' descriptions of situations typifying interactions with international students. These situations were elicited during the design of the test and comprised non-congruent encounters where some effort to mitigate the interaction is expected given the status-challenging contexts. Participants were therefore placed in familiar roles and situations, according to the academic context within which they were currently studying, which are said to be key considerations to improve both the quality of response and construct validity of the tests (Bardovi-Harlig 1999; Schauer 2007). Table 6.2 provides an overview of the content within the CAPT and WDCT scenarios. The request and apology scenarios were alternated on the production tasks to avoid mechanical responses. In addition, the scenarios were reordered at the different test stages to reduce the effects of using identical testing material four times (pretest, posttest, two delayed tests) with the same experimental group participants.

The third instrument, the questionnaire of English use during the study abroad stay, aimed to measure the frequency learners engaged in a range of

Table 6.2 Content of the CAPT and WDCT scenarios

	Speech act (imposition)	Interlocutor (social distance, power)	Situation	Mode
Scenario 1 **Essay extension**	Request (+R)	Tutor (−SD, +P)	You need more time to finish your essay. You go to your tutor's office to ask for more time.	CAPT
Scenario 2 **Noisy party**	Apology (+R)	Security guard (+SD, +P)	You had a party at your flat with friends. Some students complained to this security guard about the noise and you want to apologize.	CAPT
Scenario 3 **Book a study room**	Request (+R)	Librarian (+SD, +P)	You want to find out how to book a study room. You ask a library assistant about it.	CAPT
Scenario 4 **Missed meeting**	Apology (+R)	Tutor (−SD, +P)	You missed a meeting with your tutor but you did not email him to explain. You go to your tutor's office to apologize.	WDCT
Scenario 5 **Classroom access**	Request (+R)	Security guard (+SD, +P)	You have left your mobile phone in a classroom but the building is now closed. It is very late but you go to the security office to ask if they can open the building for you.	WDCT
Scenario 6 **Lost library book**	Apology (+R)	Librarian (+SD, +P)	You have lost a book which you borrowed from the library. You go to apologize to a member of the library staff.	WDCT

Note: P = power, SD = social distance, R = imposition

English-medium activities to establish correlations between L2 interaction and 'natural' acquisition of request and apology language (RQ 3). Each instrument is described in detail in the following sections, beginning with the CAPT, the WDCT, and the study abroad language contact questionnaire.

6.3.1. The CAPT

For the purposes of this study, an innovative and unique set of computer-animated materials was devised. Virtual role-plays were employed for classroom language practice and embedded within a testing instrument to measure the effectiveness of instruction. The assessment tool is unique to L2 pragmatics studies and was named the CAPT due to the use of virtual role-plays to elicit oral responses.

One of several Internet-based animated movie sites (Xtranormal)[1] was selected to create the computer-animated scenarios for the CAPT. Movie-making sites such as this are increasingly available in the educational field, expanding the scope of incorporating technology into teaching. Computer-animated sites transform text scripts to animated movies using text-to-speech and animation technologies and generally follow a similar design procedure. Users choose from a series of pre-designed sets and characters and personalize the movie by adding movement, gesture and facial expressions to the characters, in addition to importing authentic voice recordings to further authenticate the interaction (see Chapter 3). Once designed, these virtual role-plays were embedded as short movie clips into a PowerPoint presentation and presented as an oral production task at the testing stages.

Figure 6.2 illustrates one of the scenarios on the CAPT, devised using this technology. The CAPT required learners to observe the PowerPoint presentation incorporating three scenarios: two calling for a request (scenario 1: essay extension, scenario 3: book a study room) and one calling for an apology (scenario 2: noisy party). The scenarios featured a range of animated interlocutors and problems which the learners had to address by engaging in a brief, single-turn interaction with each animated character. The original animated version of the CAPT can be located at the IRIS data research repository (Marsden et al. 2016) but an example can be found in Figure 6.2.

The procedure for completing the CAPT (Figure 6.3) begins with an initial instructional slide, directing learners through the main steps. In the remaining slides, learners are required to read the context of each scenario

You have not completed your essay.

You go to your tutor's office to ask for extra time. You know your tutor well

Figure 6.2 An example of a request scenario from the CAPT

Slide 1. Instructional slide
7 seconds delay to read instructions

Slide 2. Scenario: request for essay extension
7 seconds delay to read context
15 seconds delay to provide response

Slide 3. Scenario: apology for noisy party
7 seconds delay to read context
15 seconds delay to provide response

Slide 4. Scenario: request to book a study room
7 seconds delay to read context
15 seconds delay to provide response

Side 5. End of task slide

Figure 6.3 Procedure for completion of the CAPT

on the left of the screen, accompanied by a still of the animation on the right (Figure 6.2). Following a seven-second timed interval, the movie clip on each slide automatically begins with the interlocutor opening the conversation with a brief gambit such as '*Come in. You wanted to see me?*' Learners are then required to provide a single-turn oral response, including a suitable apology or request, as suggested by the context. A fifteen-second timed interval is provided for the response before the next scenario is automatically presented. Once complete, a final slide thanks the learners for their participation and asks them to alert the researcher. A decision on the optimum time intervals came from the two rounds of pilot testing.

6.3.2. The WDCT

The WDCT followed an archetypal construct as depicted in Figure 6.4. In a paper-based exercise containing three scenarios – one calling for a request (scenario 5: classroom access to retrieve a mobile phone) and two calling for an apology (scenario 4: missed meeting with tutor, scenario 6: lost library book) – participants were required to complete written responses to the interlocutor's opening line in the text dialogue. First, learners were presented with the setting of the scenario (e.g. '*At the tutor's office*'). A description of the context and problem followed. For comparability of both the written DCT and CAPT, it was necessary to include the interlocutor's gender and age as additional information in the WDCT rubric, as these were features discernible in the animated version but not clear in the written instrument. Learners were then invited to provide a written version of their oral response. As the pilot showed the participants completed the WDCT in approximately the same time as the CAPT, no strict timings were set for the written DCT.

At your tutor's office

You missed a meeting with your tutor but you did not email him to explain. You go to your tutor's office to apologize. He is 65 years old and you know him well.

Tutor: Thanks for coming. We had an appointment scheduled for last Tuesday but you didn't come.

You:

Figure 6.4 An example of an apology scenario from the WDCT

6.3.3. The study abroad language contact questionnaire

All sixty-one learners (CAPT = 24, PAPER = 20, control = 17) completed a two-part self-evaluation questionnaire on their extracurricular language use. Part A of the questionnaire elicited how frequently participants engaged in a variety of activities in English. Part B required learners to provide an overall skills assessment for listening, speaking, reading, writing and interaction. The participants had to rate statements presented on a five-point Likert scale. The questionnaire was a simplified, revised version of Freed et al.'s (2004) language contact profile. The original version was designed to focus on and assess oral performance (fluency and proficiency), as these features were seen to be 'sensitive to contextual variables' (Freed et al. 2004: 174). The original questionnaire, therefore, did not require learners to comment on their written performance – an approach since taken in other language contact investigations (Bardovi-Harlig & Bastos 2011; Taguchi 2008a). As the primary aim of this study was to improve oral communication and interaction between staff and students in a study abroad HE environment, the revised questionnaire for this study did not reference written communication either.

Part A of the questionnaire comprised twelve statements to be rated by the participants to self-evaluate the frequency of their English use on a five-point Likert scale (0 = never, 1 = a few times a year, 2 = monthly, 3 = weekly, 4 = daily). The first six statements focused on productive speaking skills, i.e. how often participants communicated in English with: tutor outside of class L1 English friends, classmates, English-speaking strangers, and service personnel. For instance, *'Since coming to the UK, I try to speak English to my tutor outside of class.'* The final six statements in Part A focused on receptive reading and listening skills, i.e. how often participants engaged in the following activities in English: watching English TV, watching English movies, reading English newspapers, reading English novels, reading English magazines and listening to English songs. For instance, *'Since coming to the UK, I watch English language television.'*

To avoid the limitation of Ranta and Meckelborg's (2013) examination of English use with people and activities from both inside and outside the participants' study programme, the questionnaire for this investigation focused only on contact variables outside of their study. This meant a learner in the present study would volunteer to use English in all of the questionnaire situations, leading to results reflecting personal choice for L2 interaction.

Part B was the shortest part of the questionnaire. Here, learners were asked to rate their English language ability on a five-point Likert scale from 'poor/beginner' (1 point) to 'L2-like/excellent' (5 points) across five skills: listening, speaking, reading, writing and interacting. Learners assigned a numeric score in a box under each relevant skill.

The first questionnaire administered at T1 also elicited data regarding the learners' personal details (e.g. age, gender, years of English study) to collect background information and confirm homogeneity of the participant groups. The T1 questionnaire elicited responses based on the learners' experience of using English in China, pre-arrival. The questionnaires administered at T2 (+ six weeks) and T4 (+ twelve weeks) were based on the learners' UK experience and can be found in Appendix 1.

6.4. Data collection procedure

This section details the two main data collection phases: the *instructional phase* (6.4.1) and the *testing phase* (6.4.2).

The instructional phase described in this first section begins with a broad outline of the overall six-week intervention to develop request and apology language. This is followed by an explanation of the teaching framework employed for each of the six sessions and example activities. A selection of the teaching resources utilized is also described. This section concludes with a description of a typical lesson sequence from the intervention.

6.4.1. Instructional phases

Ten hours of explicit pragmatic instruction on requests and apologies were delivered over a six-week period. The instructional delivery could be described as distributed practice (Miles 2014) since the lessons were spread evenly over that time. The researcher designed all of the classroom materials and provided the instruction. The concerns associated with the researcher-as-teacher approach (Bardovi-Harlig 2015), such as teaching to the test, were not considered to adversely affect the study since the input the experimental groups received was the same and the spotlight was on the differentiated training materials. The control group, an intact class enrolled in the same language programme, were test-only participants, providing non-instructed baseline data.

Instructional weeks 1, 4, 5 and 6 focused equally on both requests and apologies, whilst weeks 2 and 3 provided a more detailed overview of requests and apologies respectively. Weeks 1 and 6 also incorporated testing stages for approximately one hour of class time (see Figure 6.5). The sessions were delivered as part of a pre-sessional English for academic purposes (EAP) summer programme and were timetabled for two hours per week as 'communication skills' practice. The length of treatment was selected to maximize instructional effects. Meta-analyses of instructed pragmatic studies (Jeon & Kaya 2006; Plonsky & Zhuang 2019) suggest, in the main, longer treatments (over five hours) have proved more beneficial for learners. The effects of this explicit instruction would inform the outcome of RQ1.

Both experimental groups (CAPT and PAPER) participated in the six weeks of explicit pragmatic instruction on requests and apologies. The input the two experimental groups received was differentiated by 40 minutes of controlled and freer language practice in each of the six sessions (see Appendix 2) where the CAPT group used electronic tablets to work with computer-animated scenarios, in contrast to the PAPER group who completed more traditional paper-and-pencil activities. These stages constituted the longest, most focused section of independent practice for the students so knowledge/discussion could be developed and language practised. Otherwise, the instruction was the same for both experimental groups and covered pragmalinguistic and sociopragmatic aspects of request and apology behaviour. The effects of the differentiated training materials would inform

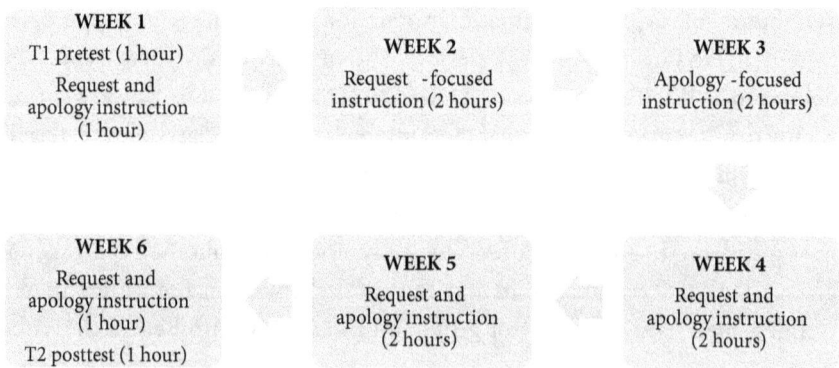

Figure 6.5 Six-week classroom-based instructional procedure

the outcome of RQ2. Appendix 2 details the six-week scheme of work for the intervention. Appendix 3 provides samples of the communicative scenarios employed.

The instructional framework employed in teaching weeks 2–5 (those not incorporating a testing phase) broadly followed Usó-Juan's (2010) five stages of awareness-raising and communicative practice activities: aspects of explicit instruction considered requisite for success (Bardovi-Harlig 2001). This is depicted in Figure 6.6. The organization of the input and activities each week did not always conform to the stages and timings illustrated in Figure 6.6; rather they were used as a guide for designing the training materials over the six-week period and ensuring some form of awareness-raising and language practice activities featured in the training sessions.

At *stage one*, learners were first invited to explore both the linguistic and cultural aspects of requests and apologies in their first language, for approximately twenty minutes, to raise awareness. For instance, this was achieved through highlighting pragmatic errors in scripted dialogues in weeks 2 and 4, explicit quiz questions in week 3, and the creation of mind maps and discussion in week 5. At *stage two*, cross-cultural differences were discussed from a second language perspective for approximately twenty minutes, and first and second language comparisons made, again utilizing discussion or *noticing* activities such as highlighting pragmatic errors in scripted dialogues. At this

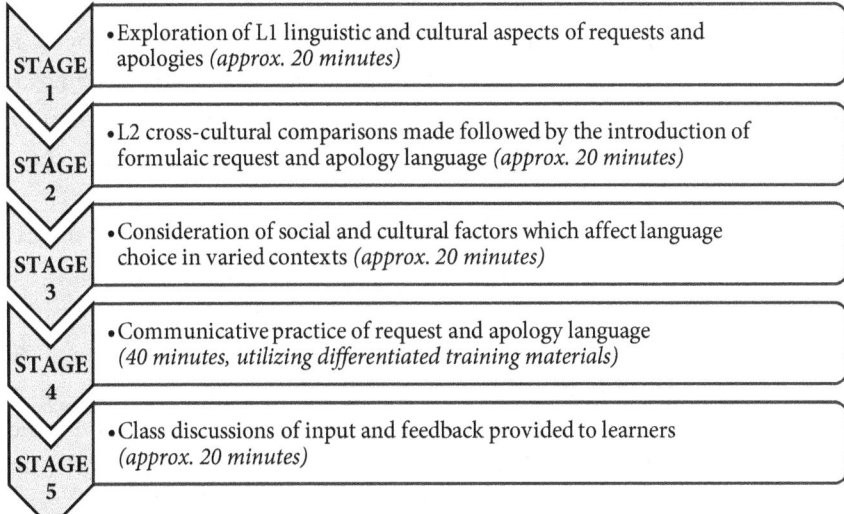

Figure 6.6 The instructional framework adopted for teaching request and apology speech acts

stage, guided input from the instructor is required, to introduce formulaic expressions used to realize L2 requests and apologies, for instance, as in weeks 2 and 3. *Stage three* was the application of this knowledge to consider social and cultural factors which may influence the learners' choice of how requests and apologies are realized in different contexts. For instance, in week 4, learners were provided with authentic contrasting scenarios involving a range of social and cultural features to encourage reflection on aspects associated with Brown and Levinson's theory of politeness (1987) such as power, distance and imposition, and how these variables may affect language choice. This stage typically lasted for around twenty minutes. At *stage four*, once these connections had been made, learners were provided with opportunities for communicative practice for around forty minutes. In this study, the CAPT group worked with other computer-animated scenarios on electronic tablets to extend opportunities for language practice. For example, one activity in week 3 involved being presented with a range of computer-animated scenarios, requiring learners to formulate appropriate apologies (paying attention to situation, context and interlocutor), before playing the animation to discover how well their suggestions matched. The final *stage five* (approximately twenty minutes) included teacher-learner discussions to summarize the input and provide feedback on the activities completed.

In terms of resources, learners were exposed to a range of oral and written materials in which the target pragmatic features could be observed such as excerpts from online videos, virtual role-plays, and fictional and non-fictional written material. Prior to the presentation of specific metapragmatic explanation, an inductive approach to the self-discovery of pragmalinguistic and sociopragmatic features from the materials was adopted to encourage observation skills and analysis (Schmidt 1993): techniques which could be transferred to day-to-day language practice. In the case of raising sociopragmatic awareness, for instance, learners had to remedy dialogues containing inappropriate requests or apologies by first deliberating what social aspects contribute to a successful or unsuccessful request or apology. Learners also offered their own examples of miscommunications over the instructional period which proved to be an effective resource for examples of challenging encounters. Where possible, this inductive learning approach was continued for all class activities to aid long-term retention of input and promote real-world learning and self-reflection strategies, as advocated by Shively's (2010) teaching framework.

Each lesson sequence typically included the following features:

1. Cross-cultural discussions of request and/or apology scenarios in academic contexts, considering power-social distance-imposition variables which may affect language choice.
2. Introduction of formulaic language sequences to realize requests and apologies.
3. Cross-cultural discussions of linguistic similarities and differences between first and target languages.
4. Controlled and freer language practice activities to consolidate learning.
5. Review and class feedback on input.

6.4.2. Testing phases

This section details the testing phases employed to measure both the effectiveness of the six-week intervention on requests and apologies and the amount of target language contact participants encountered during the same time period. First, an overview of the testing phases for both instruction and language contact is described. Next, specific details of the instructional testing followed by the language contact questionnaire are provided.

Participants were tested at four moments in time, as illustrated in Figure 6.7, a pretest (T1, week 1), followed by an immediate posttest (T2, week 6 immediately following treatment), and two delayed posttests (T3, 2 weeks after treatment; and T4, 6 weeks after treatment). Delayed tests were specifically employed to measure lasting instructional effects and longer-term language contact: an approach not frequently adopted in L2 pragmatics research, but highly recommended (Jeon & Kaya 2006). Although there is no exact consensus about the length of delay employed in a study of this kind, it has been suggested that a delay of more than a week is optimal and three weeks or longer ideal (Schmitt 2010: 157). In this study, the first delayed test (T3) was administered whilst access to all participants was still available and measured the short-term delayed treatment effects. A T3 language contact questionnaire was not administered at this time, however, as two weeks was not considered a sufficient time lapse for any changes to be observed. The second delayed test (T4) helped to ascertain longer-term instructional effects. The language contact questionnaire was also administered at T4. Practical constraints meant that T4 relied on voluntary contributions.

Each test was administered in a language laboratory in the same building as the pragmatics training, either directly before (T1) or directly after the instructional

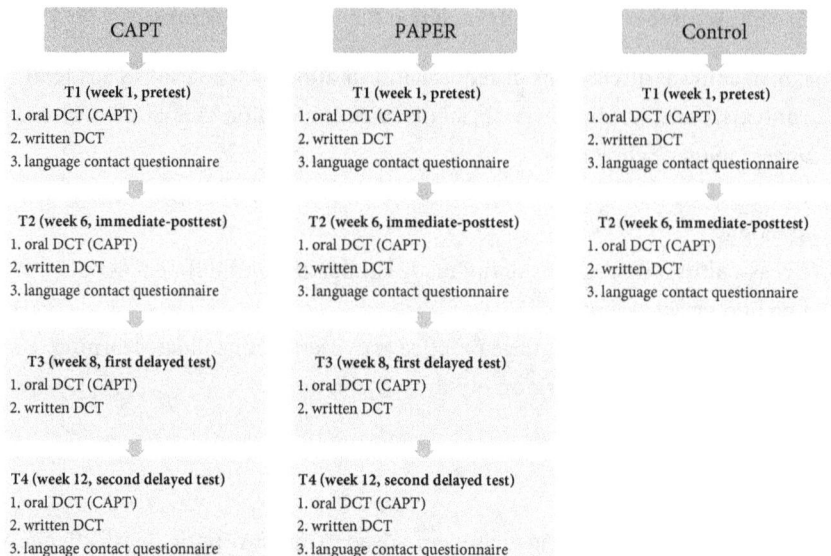

Figure 6.7 Testing procedure over the twelve-week period (T1-T4) for the experimental and control groups

period (T2) for the CAPT, PAPER and control groups. Regarding measurement of treatment effects, learners in the experimental groups (CAPT and PAPER) were contacted by email and invited to attend the same language laboratory setting for the T3-T4 posttests to ascertain short- and long-term retention of the classroom input. The tests were a combination of both the WDCT and CAPT for two reasons. First, this approach avoided the different modes of language practice in the instruction benefitting the CAPT or PAPER group at the four assessment stages. Second, in this way, transfer-appropriate processing (TAP), of the kind described by Dekeyser (2007), was accounted for by ensuring the learning and assessment tasks shared similarities so knowledge could be easily transferred from one situation to another without impeding assessment outcomes. Each group was divided into two halves: one half completed the CAPT, followed by the WDCT, whilst the other half began with the WDCT, followed by the CAPT. Learners completed both tests in approximately fifteen minutes.

The final aspect of the study, which sought to investigate the Chinese ESL learners' extracurricular engagement in the L2 environment, was measured via a self-reporting questionnaire, as described earlier. The aim of the questionnaire was for learners to evaluate their language contact and English language skills over specified periods of time in order for the researcher to ascertain frequency of engagement in the SA environment and to what extent this setting was influential in any language gains from the intervention. Following completion of the T1 and T2 tests, the experimental groups (CAPT and PAPER) and control group all completed the study abroad questionnaire, with a time lapse of six weeks between each test stage. The experimental groups also completed the questionnaire at T4.

6.5. Data treatment and analysis

Addressing calls to evaluate learner responses from multiple perspectives to gain a more holistic view of pragmatic performance beyond just an analysis of linguistic forms (e.g. Taguchi 2006), the findings from the instruction were analysed both qualitatively and quantitatively to enable a richer description of the data set. The procedure undertaken was as follows:

1. All the oral responses from the CAPT were recorded for analysis and assessment via Audacity software available at the research location.
2. Next, all 183 oral responses (61 learners × 3 scenarios) were transcribed verbatim. Together with the 183 responses transferred from the WDCT, the data were presented in a non-descript and randomized order at T1 and T2 (total = 366 responses) so the raters were unaware of which responses came from which group or which format (written or oral).
3. Two female L1 English ESL tutors[2] were recruited to rate the CAPT and WDCT responses from the experimental and control groups for overall effectiveness at T1 and T2. Tutors were selected over the use of corpus-based tools for two reasons: (i) the tutors' assessment provided a qualitative perspective to the data and their experience of using assessment scales to rate spoken and written performance qualified them for this task and (ii) the tutors represented the same higher status (+P) as the interlocutors described in the scenarios so they were in an excellent position to evaluate the participants' responses.
4. The raters were instructed to judge each request and apology independently. The request and apology responses were evaluated on a five-point Likert scale for pragmatic *appropriateness*, which determined to what extent the responses were successful in terms of levels of directness and politeness, as dictated by the scenarios. For the purposes of this study, appropriateness is defined as 'the knowledge of the conventions of communication in a society, as well as linguistic abilities that enable learners to communicate successfully in L2' (Taguchi 2006: 513). The rating scale employed in Table 6.3 was adapted from Shively and Cohen (2008) and Taguchi (2012).

Table 6.3 Rating scale to evaluate participant responses

Rating score	Description
5	I would feel completely satisfied with this response because the levels of directness, politeness and formality are almost entirely appropriate and effective for the situation. It is highly likely that the response would result in a positive outcome.
4	I would feel very satisfied with this response because the levels of directness, politeness and formality are appropriate and effective for the situation. Where there are non-L2-like features, these are minor and unlikely to affect a positive outcome.
3	I would feel satisfied with this response because the levels of directness, politeness and formality are generally appropriate and effective. The expressions may contain several non-L2-like features, but the expression would be regarded as achieving minimal levels of appropriateness for a positive outcome nevertheless.
2	I would not feel very satisfied with this response because the levels of directness, politeness or formality are not sufficiently appropriate or effective for the situation. Features are more inappropriate than appropriate and fail to achieve the satisfactory levels of indirectness or the expressions contain insufficient mitigation for a positive outcome.
1	I would not feel satisfied at all with this response because the levels of directness, politeness and formality are entirely inappropriate and ineffective for the situation. It is hard to imagine this response would result in a positive outcome.

Note: a positive outcome refers to compliance with the request or acceptance of the apology

The rating scale did not require attention to the grammatical accuracy of the responses, since the focus was on their overall effectiveness assessed in multidimensional way in terms of culture, medium and language, as described by Chen (2006). In this way, the success of the responses was evaluated from a sociopragmatic perspective.

5. Both raters attended a standardization meeting prior to the actual evaluation stage to explain the project, the instrument, the rating criteria and procedure. A number of practice items, followed by a comparison of ratings, were completed to achieve a final consensus. A rating of '3' was discussed as being 'of minimal satisfaction' and was included as the cut-off point for a response to be considered appropriate. Where queries were raised by the raters during the evaluation stage, these were resolved in follow-up meetings with the researcher.
6. From a pragmalinguistic perspective, the content of the responses was subsequently coded and analysed by the researcher to investigate the types

of request and apology strategies adopted over the twelve-week period. To understand which strategies were considered most effective for each scenario and which groups used these most successfully, at the different stages, all test responses awarded the highest scores of 4 (*highly appropriate*) or 5 (*completely appropriate*) by the raters were isolated from the rest of the responses and classified according to original coding schemes for requests (Table 6.4) and apologies (Table 6.5). The frequencies of the strategies used were then noted so that between-group comparisons could be investigated. Observing Cohen's (1988) guidelines, 20 per cent of the data were coded by another tutor of the same background as the researcher. A Pearson correlation coefficient yielded a high interrater reliability of .97.

7. The analysis of strategies employed for requests and apologies was followed by a frequency count of non-target-like features at each test stage.

Table 6.4 Coding scheme for request strategies

	Strategy	Definition	Example
1	*Direct*		
1a	Imperative	'directly signals that the utterance is an order' (Trosborg 1995: 204)	Give me an extension for my assignment
1b	Performative	'a performative verb conveys the requestive intent, explicitly marking the utterance as an order' (Trosborg 1995: 203)	I ask (request) that you give me an extension
1c	Obligation	'the speaker exerts his/her own authority or refers to some authority outside the speaker' (Trosborg 1995: 202)	I should (have to) have an extension
1d	Want statement	'the speaker expresses the desire that the event denoted in the proposition come about' (Zhang 1995: 44)	I want (need) an extension
2	*Conventionally indirect*		
2a	Ability	'questions the hearer's capacity to perform the desired act' (Trosborg 1995: 198)	Can (could) you give me/(I) have an extension
2b	Willingness	'questions the hearer's willingness to carry out the desired act which serves as a compliance-gaining strategy' (Trosborg 1995: 199)	Would you give me an extension?

Table 6.4 Coding scheme for request strategies *(continued)*

2c	Suggestory	'the hearer's cooperativeness is tested by inquiring whether any conditions exist that might prevent the action from being carried out' (Trosborg 1995: 201)	How about giving me an extension?
3	***Non-conventionally indirect***		
3a	Hints	'the requester can imply what he/she wants done. The desired action can be partially mentioned or left out altogether' (Trosborg 1995: 192)	I'm having trouble finding the book I need for my assignment …
4	***Internal modification devices***		
4a	Softeners (downtoners)	'modifiers used by a speaker to modulate the impact his/her request might have on the speaker' (Blum-Kulka et al. 1989: 284)	Could you <u>possibly/perhaps</u> give me an extension …
4b	Intensifiers	'adverbial intensifiers increase the impact of an utterance on the hearer' (Trosborg 1995: 214)	I'm sure, really
4c	Fillers (hesitators)	'the requester can convey he/she has certain qualms about asking' (Trosborg 1995: 213)	Could you… <u>erm/I wonder …</u> give me an extension?
4d	Attention-getters/Alerters	'to alert the hearer's attention to the ensuing speech act' (Zhang 1995: 32)	Excuse me; Sir, madam/lady, teacher; Sorry to bother you
4e	Politeness marker 'please'	'an optional element added to a request to bid for cooperative behaviour' (Blum-Kulka et al. 1989: 283)	Please
5	***External modification devices***		
5a	Preparators	'it is important in the first place that the requester prepares his/her request carefully' (Trosborg 1995: 216)	I have a problem…?
5b	Grounders	'allows the speaker to give reasons, explanations or justifications for his/her request' (Trosborg 1995: 218)	Could I have an extension? <u>I've had computer problems</u>
5c	Disarmers	'the speaker tries to remove any potential objections the hearer might raise upon being confronted with the request' (Blum-Kulka et al. 1989: 87)	I hate bothering you/If it's not too much trouble

5d	Self-criticism	'the speaker takes the blame by denigrating him/herself so as to put the hearer in a position where compliance appears to be a benevolent deed' (Zhang 1995: 63)	It's my fault./I made a mistake.
5e	Sweeteners	'paves the way for the request by establishing good feelings and cultivating an amiable atmosphere' (Zhang 1995: 60)	If you give me an extension, I promise to ….
5f	Apologizing	'the speaker apologises for the trouble the request will cause to the hearer' (Zhang 1995: 62)	I'm sorry
5g	Thanking	'expressions of gratitude offered for the anticipated compliance of the hearer' (Zhang 1995: 63)	Thank you/thanks

Note: The examples provided are fictitious in order to suit the appropriate strategy.

6.5.1. Coding scheme for request strategies

The complexities of designing a one-size-fits-all coding scheme are evidenced in the frequent modifications made to the content and number of strategies devised in the original CCSARP classifications for many speech act studies (Blum Kulka et al. 1989). This is perhaps no more apparent than with requests. The large volume of studies on request speech acts has resulted in a number of comprehensive variants of the CCSARP which imply requests are a complex speech act to perform. In fact, the opposite is true from an L1 English speaker perspective. Research reports L1 English requests are far from elaborate, relying on a small pool of moves and linguistic strategies (Aijmer 1996). The complexities of coding schemes for requests in fact arise as a result of research on multiple languages to capture the many L1/L2 variants of requests which exist. Unlike earlier studies which tend to dissect the request to analyse one element such as head acts (Lee-Wong 1994; Lin 2009; Yu 1999), or internal modification (Economidou-Kogetsidis 2013), this volume takes a holistic stance and investigates all the main components: head acts and internal/external modification strategies, as described in Chapter 4.

As the pilot data revealed no new emergent request strategies than those previously identified in earlier research, the request strategies chosen for the present study's coding scheme draw on several sources, using a top-down approach. First, a combination of the original CCSARP (Blum-Kulka et al. 1989) and Trosborg's (1995) early work provides the majority of categories in

Table 6.5 Coding scheme for apology strategies

	Strategy	Definition	Example
IFID			
A1	Offer of apology	'explicit expression of apology by means of a performative verb such as *apologise, excuse*' (Olshtain & Cohen 1983: 22)	I apologise
A2	Expression of regret	'an expression of attitude towards the offense' (Owen 1983: 71)	I'm sorry, I'm afraid
A3	Request for forgiveness	'a request for restoration of balance' (Owen 1983: 71)	Please forgive me
Adjunct			
B1	**Explanations**		
B1a*	Self-charge	the speaker acknowledges his personal behaviour, within his control, was the cause (new category)	I stayed up late watching TV
B1b	Self-deficiency	the speaker highlights personal weaknesses or neglectful behaviour as mitigating factors (Trosborg 1995)	I lost it
B1c*	Health reasons	the speaker cites that due to poor health, he/she was unable to fulfil his/her duties (new category)	I had a headache
B1d*	Third party	the speaker cites the moral duty to help someone in need as the mitigating factor (new category)	I had to help my friend move house
B2	**Blame strategies**		
B2a	Self-blame/ admission of responsibility	'offender's total acceptance and recognition of fault in causing the offence' (Kondo 2008: 147)	It's my fault
B2b	Blame-deflection	'he/she may blame a third party or even the complainer him/herself' (Trosborg 1995: 378)	I was told to do it
B3	Offer of repair	'apologiser makes a bid to do something about or pay for the damage caused by the offence' (Kondo 2010: 147)	I will buy a new one
B4	Promise of forbearance	'apologiser promises that the offence will not be repeated' (Kondo 2010: 147)	It won't happen again

B5	Intensifier	'adverbials intensifying part of the proposition such as an expression of regret or embarrassment' (Trosborg 1995: 386)	Very, really, so
B6	Alerter	'alert the hearer's attention to the ensuing speech act' (Zhang 1995: 32)	Teacher … excuse me …

Note: * indicates new categories for this study, based on responses from the pilot data. The examples provided are fictitious in order to suit the appropriate strategy.

the coding scheme. Second, the CCSARP list is further enhanced by strategies identified as common to L1 Chinese speakers in their L2 production of requests, e.g. 'want' statements (Chen 2006; Lin 2009; Wang 2011; Yu 1999). No categories from previous research were rejected at this stage in order to capture the largest possible range of strategies utilized, particularly during the pretests. The coding scheme in Table 6.4 was devised based on these considerations.

6.5.2. Coding scheme for apology strategies

The variations of coding schemes for apologies are typically directed by the need to appropriately categorize empirical data amassed from a wide range of languages, as seen with requests e.g. British-English, Canadian, Japanese (Tanaka et al. 2000), Chinese (Chang 2010), Hungarian and Polish (Susczcynska 1999); Russian (Shardakova 2005); Sudanese Arabic (Nurreddeen 2008), Thai (Bergman & Kasper 1993).

The present study also devised a unique coding scheme for apologies (Table 6.5). As with requests, a top-down approach was first adopted to categorize the strategies, drawing on early apology investigations (e.g. Bergman & Kasper 1993; Blum-Kulka et al. 1989; Holmes 1990; Olshtain & Cohen 1983; Trosborg 1987), in addition to more recent studies employing East Asian L2 learners of English (e.g. Chang 2010; Kim 2008; Rose 2000; Tanaka et al. 2000). Again, no categories from previous research were rejected at this stage either in order to capture the largest possible range of strategies utilized. The pilot data, however, also revealed emergent trends for particular types of *explanations* (highlighted as * in Table 6.5), so these were categorized and included as novel to the present data set. Table 6.5 was devised based on these considerations and findings.

Following Rose (2000), the apology strategies in Table 6.5 were grouped and divided into two main super-strategies: (A) the main apology strategy or illocutionary force indicating device (IFID) and (B) the subsequent supporting moves (adjuncts).

6.6. Statistical analyses

Following the manual data analysis by the raters and researcher, both the production task data and questionnaire data were statistically analysed using the Statistical Package for Social Sciences software (SPSS) version 22. Parametric tests were selected after establishing data were normally distributed through initial histogram checks. Data from the production tasks (before and after instruction) were partially analysed using one-way analyses of variance (ANOVA) and paired t-tests, in addition to a focus on frequencies of occurrence of specific request and apology formulae. Data from the questionnaires were analysed via a series of repeated measures and one-way ANOVA comparisons, in addition to post-hoc independent and paired t-tests. Normal distribution was again confirmed by non-significance found in Mauchley's tests in the repeated measures ANOVAs. The alpha level was set at .05. The proceeding findings are presented according to Norris et al.'s (2015) recommendations for the reporting of statistical analyses. The following chapters provide a detailed analysis of the findings from these instructional (Chapter 7) and environmental (Chapter 8) perspectives.

7

Request and apology findings

This chapter is organized according to each speech act under investigation. For the reader's convenience, the first half of the chapter reports on the results from the request data and the second half examines the apology data. For each speech act, the same reporting procedure is followed. First the raters' assessment of the appropriateness of the T1 (pretest) and T2 (immediate posttest) responses is reported. Second, findings from the linguistic analysis of the type and frequency of speech act strategies employed are presented. The concluding third section analyses language features reported to be culture- and language-specific to Chinese speakers which may affect their L2 production. These language features were specifically targeted in the intervention having been identified in existing research as under- or inappropriately utilized when formulating requests and apologies, so this section also investigates the extent to which the learners revise their use of these non-target-like features, post-instruction.

7.1. Raters' assessment of the request data

As a reminder, two female L1 English ESL tutors rated the CAPT and WDCT responses for 'appropriateness' from both experimental groups (CAPT and PAPER) and the control group at T1 (pretest) and T2 (immediate posttest) to determine their success from a sociopragmatic perspective. The mean scores given are out of a possible maximum of 30 points (3 scenarios, maximum of 5 Likert-scale points per scenario × 2 raters). The Pearson correlation coefficient found acceptable to moderately high interrater reliability between the raters' scores (T1 = .73; T2 = .89). The three request scenarios (classroom access, essay extension, book study room) are presented in the data analyses below, focusing on T1 to T2 results.

Table 7.1 summarizes descriptive statistics of the rater scores for the responses from the three participant groups (CAPT, PAPER, control). A one-way ANOVA

Table 7.1 Descriptive statistics: Raters' scores for request responses from the experimental and control groups T1-T2

Group	T1 (pretest) M (SD)	T2 (immediate posttest) M (SD)
CAPT (N=24)	16.29 (3.25)	19.96 (2.74)
PAPER (N=20)	16.60 (3.23)	17.55 (2.89)
Control (N=17)	17.47 (3.37)	15.47 (2.24)
Total (N=61)	16.72 (3.26)	17.91 (3.21)

Note: Maximum marks = 30.

reveals there were no significant differences and a small effect size between the groups at T1 with each group achieving slightly more than 50 per cent of the maximum possible scores: $F(2, 58) = .663$, $p = .519$, $\eta^2 = .02$. This indicates between-group comparability of request responses at the beginning of the study. In contrast, the T2 scores indicate there were statistically significant differences with a large effect size between groups: $F(2, 58) = 14.39$, $p < .001$, $\eta^2 = .33$.

Post hoc tests (Tukey HSD adjustment) reveal exactly where these T2 differences lie: CAPT-PAPER groups ($p = .01$); CAPT-control ($p < .001$); PAPER-control ($p = .06$). This firstly suggests the raters judged the CAPT group to have produced superior request utterances in comparison to both the PAPER and control groups at T2. It is notable, however, that the difference between the PAPER ($M = 17.55$) and control groups ($M = 15.47$) is approaching significance with the posttest mean score difference revealing a better performance from the PAPER group. This secondly indicates the experimental groups have both made gains on the control group's performance over the instructional period.

Further evidence of the CAPT group's success lies in a T1-T2 gain score analysis (Table 7.2).

A one-way ANOVA reveals statistically significant between-group differences with a large effect size: $F(2, 58) = 8.89$, $p < .001$, $\eta^2 = .23$. Post hoc comparisons

Table 7.2 Descriptive statistics: Gain scores for request responses from the experimental and control groups T1-T2

Group	Gain score M (SD)
CAPT (N=24)	3.67 (4.40)
PAPER (N=20)	.950 (4.90)
Control (N=17)	−2.00 (3.02)
Total (N=61)	1.20 (4.78)

Note: Gain scores calculated based on T2-T1 results.

(Tukey HSD adjustment) confirm the superiority of the CAPT vs control group's performance ($p < .001$) and the non-significant gain differences between the CAPT-PAPER ($p = .096$) and PAPER-control ($p = .098$) groups.

A final within-group paired sample t-test of the raters' T1 to T2 scores confirms that the CAPT group made the greatest improvements post-instruction, according to the raters. This is evidenced in the statistically significant T1-T2 differences and moderate effect size found only with the CAPT group: *CAPT:* $t(23) = -4.08$, $p < .001$, 95% CI [−5.52, −1.81], $r^2 = .42$. *PAPER:* $t(19) = -.866$, $p = .39$, 95% CI [−3.25, 1.35], $r^2 = .04$. *Control:* $t(16) = -1.16$, $p = .26$, 95% CI [−1.49,.435], $r^2 = .08$. In order to understand the reasons behind the success of the CAPT group's responses, the next step was to identify the specific request strategies and linguistic formulae employed by each group, which are presented in the following section.

7.2. Linguistic analysis of the request data

From a pragmalinguistic perspective, the content of the responses was analysed by the researcher to investigate the type and frequency of request strategy employed over the twelve-week period and what formulaic language was produced. The following procedure was adopted for this analysis:

1. All production task responses awarded the highest scores of 4 (very appropriate) or 5 (highly appropriate) by the raters were isolated from the original data set. The aim was to understand which strategies were considered most effective for each scenario and which groups used these most successfully,
2. The content of these high-scoring responses was analysed by the researcher according to the coding schemes presented in Chapter 6.
3. Following this, the strategies emerging as common to all the high-scoring responses for each scenario were identified and noted as being requisite for success. Exclusively analysing the responses considered highly successful by the raters helped to determine the minimum strategies considered requisite for each scenario. For instance, for the classroom access scenario, *alerter, request, self-criticism* and *apology* were common to all the high-scoring responses. This meant the raters considered all these strategies necessary for the request to be granted in this scenario. The aim was to analyse the frequency of these requisite strategies to determine if group differences could explain the raters' preference for the CAPT group responses.

Tables 7.3–7.5 highlight these requisite strategies for each request scenario and present the percentages and number of participants who utilized at least one of

Table 7.3 Frequency of requisite request strategies: Classroom access scenario

Request strategy	T1 (pretest)			T2 (immediate-posttest)			T3 (2-wk delayed)		T4 (6-wk delayed)	
	CAPT (N=24) *(%)	PAPER (N=20) *(%)	CTRL (N=17) *(%)	CAPT (N=24) *(%)	PAPER (N=20) *(%)	CTRL (N=17) *(%)	CAPT (N=24) *(%)	PAPER (N=20) *(%)	CAPT (N=17) *(%)	PAPER (N=16) *(%)
Request (2b-2d)	1 (4.17)	2 (10)	1 (5.88)	18 (75)	13 (65)	3 (17.65)	21 (87.5)	12 (60)	12 (70.59)	8 (50)
Alerter (4d)	17 (70.83)	16 (80)	11 (64.71)	13 (54.17)	15 (75)	11 (64.71)	19 (79.17)	13 (65)	10 (58.82)	6 (37.5)
Self-criticism (5d)	0	0	0	14 (58.33)	5 (25)	2 (11.76)	10 (41.67)	9 (45)	6 (35.29)	5 (31.25)
Apology (5f)	10 (41.67)	6 (30)	8 (47.06)	14 (58.33)	9 (45)	8 (47.06)	9 (37.5)	12 (60)	7 (41.18)	4 (25)

Note:
* = actual number of participants
% = percentage of group
2b-2d, 4d, 5d, 5f = strategy code (see Chapter 6 for coding scheme).

Table 7.4 Frequency of requisite request strategies: Essay extension scenario

Request strategy	T1 (pretest)			T2 (immediate-posttest)			T3 (2-wk delayed)		T4 (6-wk delayed)	
	CAPT (N=24) *(%)	PAPER (N=20) *(%)	CTRL (N=17) *(%)	CAPT (N=24) *(%)	PAPER (N=20) *(%)	CTRL (N=17) *(%)	CAPT (N=24) *(%)	PAPER (N=20) *(%)	CAPT (N=17) *(%)	PAPER (N=16) *(%)
Request (2b-2d)	0	2 (10)	0	16 (66.67)	4 (20)	1 (5.88)	16 (66.67)	0	9 (52.94)	9 (56.25)
Alerter (4d)	10 (41.67)	9 (45)	8 (47.06)	14 (58.33)	11 (55)	9 (52.94)	8 (33.34)	4 (20)	5 (29.41)	3 (18.75)
Explanation (5b)	10 (41.67)	8 (40)	6 (35.29)	19 (79.17)	11 (55)	5 (29.41)	22 (91.67)	18 (90)	13 (76.47)	11 (68.75)
Apology (5f)	22 (91.67)	18 (90)	14 (82.35)	22 (91.67)	18 (90)	12 (70.59)	16 (66.67)	17 (85)	10 (58.82)	11 (68.75)

Note:
* = actual number of participants
% = percentage of group
2b-2d, 4d, 5b, 5f = strategy code (see Chapter 6 for coding scheme).

Table 7.5 Frequency of requisite request strategies: Book a study room scenario

Request strategy	T1 (pretest)			T2 (immediate-posttest)			T3 (2-wk delayed)		T4 (6-wk delayed)	
	CAPT (N=24) *(%)	PAPER (N=20) *(%)	CTRL (N=17) *(%)	CAPT (N=24) *(%)	PAPER (N=20) *(%)	CTRL (N=17) *(%)	CAPT (N=24) *(%)	PAPER (N=20) *(%)	CAPT (N=17) *(%)	PAPER (N=16) *(%)
Request(2b-2d)	2 (8.33)	3 (15)	1 (5.88)	18 (75)	9 (45)	0	22 (91.67)	6 (30)	14 (82.35)	10 (62.5)
Alerter (4d)	14 (58.33)	10 (50)	9 (52.94)	18 (75)	11 (55)	10 (58.82)	19 (79.17)	8 (40)	15 (88.26)	10 (62.5)

Note:
* = actual number of participants
% = percentage of group
2b-2d, 4d = strategy code (see Chapter 6 for coding scheme).

7.2.1. Linguistic analysis of classroom access scenario

This scenario (interlocutor = campus security guard + social distance) required learners to request out-of-hours access to a building in order to retrieve a mobile phone left behind in a classroom (Table 7.3). An example of a successful response at T2 is: 'Excuse me. I'm sorry to disturb you (*alerter*) but would you mind helping me to find my mobile phone (*request*) please. I think I've left it in a classroom. It's my fault (*self-criticism*). I'm really sorry (*apology*)' (average rater score = 5).

The raters considered four strategies from the taxonomy presented in Chapter 6 to be requisite for an appropriate request in this scenario: *alerter, request, self-criticism, apology*. Of the four requisite strategies, two strategies do not appear frequently at T1, whilst two are much more common. For the former less common strategies, the raters awarded the highest marks to learners who selected conventionally indirect core requests: strategy 2b – willingness (e.g. 'Would you mind …?'), strategy 2c – suggestory (e.g. 'I was wondering if …'), strategy 2d – possibility (e.g. 'Would it be possible to …'). The ability modals (strategy 2a), '*can*', '*could*' as the alternative conventionally indirect choice were not considered appropriate for this scenario. Responses including ability modals typically received low scores.

Reviewing the results in Table 7.3, only four learners from all three participant groups employed these sequences (2b-2d) in their requests at T1. The data reveal that, instead, learners relied most heavily on ability modals to convey the request (forty-seven learners), followed by direct strategies (nine learners) in the form of 'want' statements (e.g. 'I want …', 'I hope …', 'I need …') at T1. The request strategies considered least coercive are evident at T2 with around 75 per cent of the experimental group learners selecting these more regularly. This trend is generally maintained to T3 and T4, although a higher number of CAPT group participants employ these request strategies throughout – a difference which gradually increases between the two experimental groups to T4. In contrast, the control group showed little evidence of naturally acquiring these expressions from L2 interaction (total of three learners at T2), continuing to rely on inappropriate ability modals.

The second less common strategy at T1 is the admission of *self-criticism* as a means of further mitigating the request, appealing to the interlocutor's goodwill to comply. Learners demonstrated an awareness of this as an apology strategy in other areas of the data but fail to include it in this request scenario. The data show *self-criticism* is not a strategy chosen by any learner at T1 and only a small proportion of learners in the PAPER (five learners) and control (two learners) groups select this strategy at T2. In contrast, over 50 per cent of the CAPT group employ this strategy at T2 but with gradual decreases in numbers to the delayed test stages. At T4, only approximately one-third of the experimental groups continue to employ *self-criticism* so this strategy is not maintained to the same high levels as the change in requests.

Whilst the least coercive requests and self-criticism were employed more frequently at T2, the requisite *alerters* and *apologies* are already commonly employed at the beginning of the study. Of the two strategies, *alerters* are employed more successfully with over half of participants employing these at each testing stage. The choice of alerter does change over time, however, with greater instances of the formulaic expression, '*sorry to bother you*', evident from the instructed groups at the posttest stages. In contrast, the control group tend to adopt more generic expressions such as '*excuse me*' or basic greetings such as '*good morning*', as employed by all groups at T1. The strategy of including an *apology* within the request is utilized by just less than 50 per cent of participants from each group at T1, demonstrating some pre-instruction awareness. This is followed by a general slight T2 increase, followed by a small decrease in frequency at T4.

7.2.2. Linguistic analysis of essay extension scenario

The request for additional time to complete an assignment was selected as a highly relevant scenario for learners in a SA academic context (interlocutor = tutor – social distance). An example of a successful request from the learner data is: 'Sorry to bother you' (*alerter*). I'm sorry (*apology*) I have not complete my essay. I had a bad fever yesterday (*explanation*). Would it be possibly to give me some extra time to finish it? (*request*) (average rater score = 4).

From the raters' perspective, an expectation of similar requisite strategies to the classroom access scenario was identified, despite increased familiarity between interlocutors: *alerter, apology, explanation, request*. What differs here is the need to provide a reason behind the request, replacing the self-criticism strategy from the previous scenario.

Similar trends from the classroom access scenario are also evident here in terms of non-salient and salient strategies at T1 (Table 7.4). In this case, the only non-salient strategy appears to be the raters' preference for conventionally indirect requests (strategies 2b-2d), as seen in the previous scenario, instead of the more common conventionally indirect use of ability modals (strategy 2a), to formulate the core request. Again, the use of *'can'* and *'could'*, in addition to direct expressions using *'want'* and *'need'*, are the most common strategy choices at T1 with all learners. At T2, there are few changes for the control group (+6 per cent), small improvements for the PAPER group (+10 per cent) and much greater use of less forceful requests for the CAPT group (+67 per cent). The disparity between the experimental groups is maintained to T3 but not to T4. At this stage about 50 per cent of the CAPT and PAPER groups employ polite requests.

As for the remaining internal and external requisite strategies – *alerter, explanation, apology* – the data reveal variability of awareness at T1, with *apologies* utilized by the majority of learners (at least 82 per cent) in each group and just under 50 per cent utilizing *alerters* and *explanations*. With the exception of an increase in use of *explanations* at T3, experimental group behaviour tends to follow the pattern of T2 increases, followed by gradual decreases at T3 and T4. It is also generally the case that more CAPT group than PAPER group participants adopt these strategies. The control group, on the other hand, fail to reach the levels achieved by the instructed groups at T2, maintaining their low pretest measures.

7.2.3. Linguistic analysis of 'book a study room' scenario

This scenario required the librarian to help with the learner's request to book a study room, with only two internal device strategies appearing to be common to all the high-scoring responses: *request* and *alerter*. A successful example from the learner data is 'Excuse me (*alerter*). I was wondering if it will be OK to book a study room?' (*polite request*) (average rater score = 4).

According to the raters' assessment in Table 7.5, there is an expectation to employ the lengthier conventionally indirect strategies (2b-2d), perhaps attributed to the greater social distance between interlocutors. As seen previously, the ability modals were not sufficient in this case, though these were the preferred initial choice for all group participants. Low T1 frequency of the strategies 2b-2d is again evident, with only six learners across the groups producing appropriate core requests. The use of these requests increases sharply for the CAPT group post-instruction (+67 per cent), marginally for the PAPER group (+30 per cent), and the control group fail to use them at all at T2. These differences generally continue to T3 and T4, with some gradual decreases over time. Greater numbers of the CAPT group participants, however, adopt the requisite strategies throughout.

Table 7.6 Frequency of combined production of all key request strategies by scenario (T1-T4)

Scenario	T1 (pretest)			T2 (immediate-posttest)			T3 (2-wk delayed)		T4 (6-wk delayed)	
	CAPT (N=24) *(%)	PAPER (N=20) *(%)	CTRL (N=17) *(%)	CAPT (N=24) *(%)	PAPER (N=20) *(%)	CTRL (N=17) *(%)	CAPT (N=24) *(%)	PAPER (N=20) *(%)	CAPT (N=17) *(%)	PAPER (N=16) *(%)
Classroom access (2b-2d, 4d, 5d, 5f)	0 (0)	0 (0)	0 (0)	9 (37.5)	2 (10)	0 (0)	8 (33.34)	3 (15)	4 (23.53)	1 (6.25)
Essay extension (2b-2d, 4d, 5b, 5f)	0 (0)	0 (0)	0 (0)	12 (50)	2 (10)	0 (0)	10 (41.67)	3 (15)	8 (47.06)	2 (12.5)
Book study room (2b-2d, 4d)	2 (8.33)	3 (15)	1 (5.88)	15 (62.5)	7 (35)	1 (5.88)	16 (66.67)	8 (40)	12 (70.59)	11 (68.75)

Note:
* = actual number of participants
% = percentage of group.

7.2.4. Frequency of combined production of all key request strategies

The data thus far reveal the following main findings: (i) the control group fail to make any T1-T2 gains in producing appropriate request strategies for the scenarios presented. The data show that the control group produces repeated patterns of language considered inappropriate for these contexts, with little variability; and (ii) the participants in both experimental groups, on the other hand, show considerable gain in their production of appropriate request language; (iii) the CAPT group almost consistently outperform the PAPER group with higher numbers of participants adopting the requisite strategies. It is useful to view these findings together to provide a clearer overview of group differences. Table 7.6 presents the percentages and number of participants who simultaneously produced <u>all</u> of the requisite strategies in each scenario, in contrast to Tables 7.3–7.5 which presented the frequencies of producing individual strategies.

What Table 7.6 shows is that, perhaps unsurprisingly, few participants are able to produce the requisite language at T1, with no instances of appropriate strategy use for 'classroom access' or 'essay extension'. At the posttest stages, though a decline in use is evident with the lapse of each posttest period, at T2 the CAPT group are 28 per cent to 40 per cent more successful at combining all of the strategies considered appropriate for each scenario. Variability of group performance over time periods 1–4 is best illustrated in Figures 7.1–7.3. These figures track the positive trajectory of the experimental groups between T1-T2, followed by a general trend of decline in appropriate request language at T3-T4, with the exception of the PAPER group's performance in the 'book study room' scenario. The superiority of the CAPT group performance is clear with higher

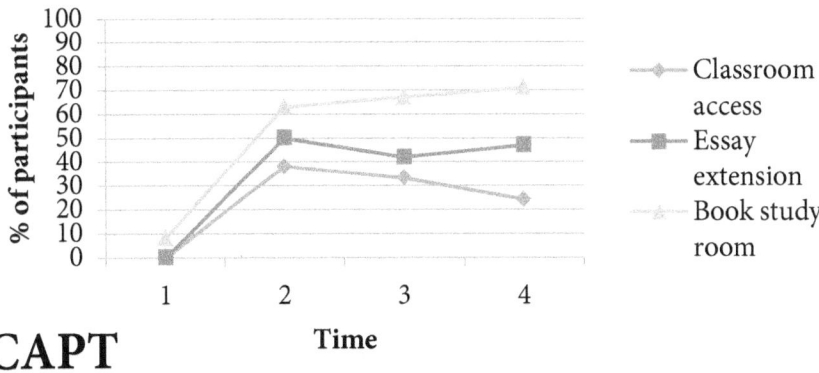

Figure 7.1 CAPT group performance of request production (T1-T4)

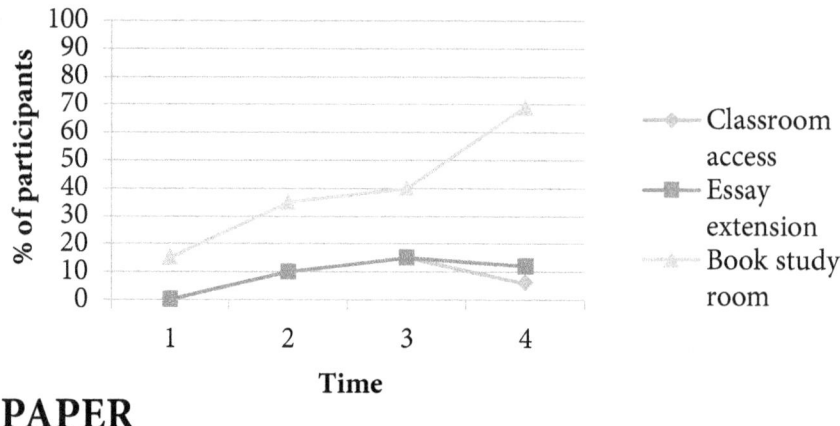

PAPER

Figure 7.2 PAPER group performance of request production (T1-T4)

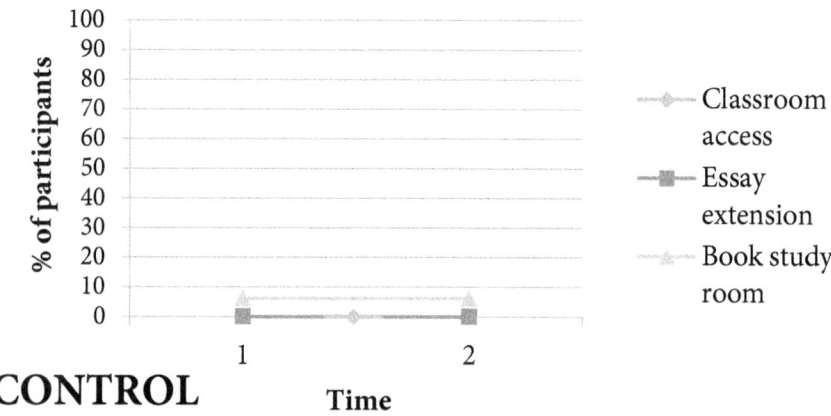

CONTROL

Figure 7.3 Control group performance of request production (T1-T4)

number of participants adopting the requisite strategies. In contrast, the control group fails to achieve any measurable success between T1-T2.

7.3. Non-target-like features of requests

As reported in Chapter 4, a range of non-target-like request features have been identified as common to Chinese L2 request production. Table 7.7 highlights the frequency of these features in the current study: (i) *ability modals*, (ii) direct *'want' statements*, (iii) *speaker-oriented requests*, (iv) *explicit apologies* and (v) *because-therefore patterns* in information sequencing of requests. The remaining non-target-like features of *verbosity*, and instances of *internal/ external modification*, are not conducive to frequency counts so are discussed separately in Chapter 9.

The frequency figures presented in Table 7.7 are the number of occurrences of each non-target-like feature across all three request scenarios. The percentage figures are calculated based on maximum frequency divided by the actual frequency figures found in the data. Maximum frequency is each participant per group using each strategy once, per scenario:

freq per cent = actual frequency in data ÷ (N × 3 [scenarios]) × 100

A worked example using *overuse of ability modals, 'can', 'could'*, taken from Table 7.7 is as follows: 47 ÷ (24 × 3) = 0.6528 (65.28 per cent).

From the frequencies presented in Table 7.7, an overall pattern of decline of non-target-like request features can be observed for the experimental groups between T1-T2, which is generally maintained to T3-T4. This decline is not matched by the control group who generally maintain their T1 performance levels, producing higher percentages of non-target-like features within their request language at T1-T2. For this reason, the data presented in the following paragraphs focus only on variability within the experimental groups' request behaviour.

The experimental groups' trends can be further subdivided to highlight non-target-like features which evidence (i) a considerable decline and (ii) features which appear more challenging to overcome, evidencing only minimal decline. First, the use of both *ability modals* and *speaker-oriented perspectives* when formulating requests decreases considerably post-instruction. At T1, 60–65 per cent of all participants select 'can' or 'could' for the core request, regardless of group. At T2, only 22 per cent of both experimental groups adopt this strategy which is generally maintained to T3 and T4. These ability modals are typically replaced with complex sequences such as 'Would it be possible to …', 'I was wondering if …'

The change of perspective from speaker to hearer within the request also evidences a similar level of decline with 67–68 per cent of all participant groups selecting the 'I' pronoun as part of the head act at T1 (e.g. 'Can *I* get in the building?', 'Can *I* have an extension?'), particularly for the classroom access and essay extension scenarios. T2 levels fall to 28 per cent (CAPT) and 30 per cent (PAPER), indicating a shift to the hearer-oriented perspective ('Would *you* mind opening the building?', 'Do *you* mind showing me how to book a study room?'). A decline is also evidenced in the use of direct request strategies such as '*I want* …', '*I need* …', although there are much lower levels of initial use in this case

Table 7.7 Non-target-like features of requests T1-T4

	T1 (pretest)		T2 (immediate-posttest)			T3 (2-wk delayed)		T4 (6-wk delayed)	
Language feature	CAPT (N=24) *(%)	PAPER (N=20) *(%)	CAPT (N=24) *(%)	PAPER (N=20) *(%)	CTRL (N=17) *(%)	CAPT (N=24) *(%)	PAPER (N=20) *(%)	CAPT (N=17) *(%)	PAPER (N=16) *(%)
Overuse of ability modals, 'can', 'could'	47 (65.28)	36 (60)	16 (22.22)	13 (21.67)	32 (62.75)	10 (13.89)	18 (30)	15 (29.41)	13 (27.08)
Overreliance on direct strategies	9 (12.5)	9 (15)	0	7 (11.67)	6 (11.76)	1 (1.39)	6 (10)	0	3 (6.25)
Overreliance on speaker-oriented perspective	49 (68.06)	40 (66.67)	20 (27.78)	18 (30)	35 (68.63)	25 (34.72)	26 (43.33)	26 (50.98)	30 (62.5)
Use of explicit apology to signal politeness	41 (56.94)	35 (58.33)	40 (55.56)	32 (53.33)	30 (58.82)	27 (37.5)	34 (56.67)	33 (64.71)	25 (52.08)
Because-therefore pattern in information-sequencing	54 (75)	54 (90)	38 (52.78)	47 (78.33)	45 (88.24)	48 (66.67)	48 (80)	46 (90.2)	48 (100)

Note:
* = actual number of participants
% = total usage of each feature as a percentage.

(CAPT = 13 per cent, PAPER = 15 per cent). Despite this, the CAPT group successfully remove this from their interlanguage completely, with the exception of one occurrence at T3. This is not the case for the PAPER and control groups who evidence similar T1 levels throughout. These low levels of direct strategies seem to contradict existing research highlighting high L2 levels of directness as a result of L1 transfer (e.g. Lin 2009; Yu 1999).

The second and final notable trend includes non-target-like features which also demonstrate a decline for the experimental groups, but to a lesser degree. This trend relates to the final two non-target-like features in Table 7.7; *explicit apology, because-therefore information sequencing*. At T1, over 57–59 per cent of all participants incorporate an *explicit apology* within the request which declines by a marginal 1–5 per cent at T2. For the CAPT group, a decline of around 20 per cent continues to T3 and T4 which is not matched by the PAPER group. High levels of *because-therefore information sequencing* can be seen at T1 with 75–90 per cent usage from all participants. Up to 22 per cent fewer instances of this pattern are observed at T2 but this is not sustained to the delayed-test stages. T3 and T4 show another increase, approximating T1 levels.

In sum, the data reveal improved request performance for the experimental groups following treatment, though some attrition is evident which seems to increase with the lapse of each time period. Generally, there is also evidence that the CAPT group outperform the PAPER group, particularly when analysing performance at the lexical level with the decline of non-target-like features of requests. In contrast, poor levels of request performance are maintained by the control group throughout.

7.4. Raters' assessment of the apology data

The procedure for the raters' assessment mirrored that conducted for the request data. Two female L1 English ESL tutors rated the oral and written production task responses for 'appropriateness' from both experimental groups (CAPT and PAPER) and the control group at the T1 and T2 to determine their success from a sociopragmatic perspective. The mean scores given are out of a possible maximum of 30 points (3 scenarios, maximum of 5 points per scenario × 2 raters). High interrater reliability using the Pearson correlation coefficient was calculated as .80 at T1 and .91 at T2. The three apology scenarios (lost library book, noisy party, missed appointment with tutor) are presented in the data analyses below, focusing on T1 to T2 results.

Table 7.8 summarizes descriptive statistics of the rater scores for the responses from the three participant groups (CAPT, PAPER and control). A one-way ANOVA reveals there were no significant differences or effect sizes between the groups at T1, with each group achieving about 50 per cent of the maximum possible scores: $F(2, 58) = 2.60$, $p = .083$, $\eta^2 = .08$. This indicates between-group comparability of appropriateness of responses at the beginning of the study. In contrast, the T2 scores indicate there were statistically significant differences between groups with a large effect size: $F(2, 58) = 30.84$, $p < .001$, $\eta^2 = .52$.

Post hoc tests (employing a Tukey HSD adjustment) reveal where these T2 differences lie: CAPT-PAPER groups ($p = .010$); CAPT-control ($p < .001$); PAPER-control ($p < .001$). As found in the request data, this suggests firstly the raters judged both experimental groups to have outperformed the control group at T2. Secondly, whilst the intervention seemed to have a positive effect on the experimental groups, the raters still considered the CAPT responses ($M = 21.46$) to be superior to the PAPER group responses ($M = 19.00$) with a statistically significant difference ($p = .010$).

Further evidence of the CAPT group's superior performance lies in a T1-T2 gain score analysis. A one-way ANOVA reveals statistically significant between-group differences with a large effect size: $F(2, 58) = 21.24$, $p < .001$, $\eta^2 = .42$. Post hoc comparisons (Tukey HSD adjustment) highlight the CAPT group responses to be more successful than the PAPER and control groups at the $p < .001$ level: CAPT-PAPER, $p < .001$; CAPT-control, $p < .001$; PAPER-control, $p = .110$.

A final within-group paired sample t-test of the raters' T1-T2 scores confirms that the CAPT group remained the highest performing group, according to the raters. This is evidenced in the statistically significant T1-T2 differences, with a large effect size, found only with the CAPT group: CAPT: $t(23) = -8.48$, $p = < .001$, 95% CI $[-6.69, -4.06]$, $r^2 = .76$. PAPER: $t(19) = -1.82$, $p = .09$, 95% CI

Table 7.8 Descriptive statistics: Raters' scores for apology responses from the experimental and control groups T1-T2

Group	T1 (pretest) M (SD)	T2 (immediate posttest) M (SD)
CAPT (*N*=24)	16.08 (3.45)	21.46 (2.64)
PAPER (*N*=20)	17.60 (2.44)	19.00 (1.97)
Control (*N*=17)	15.41 (3.02)	14.65 (3.55)
Total (*N*=61)	16.39 (3.11)	18.75 (3.87)

Note: Maximum marks = 30.

[−3.01,.21], r^2 = .15. *Control*: $t(16)$ = 1.24, p = .23, 95% CI [−.54, 2.07], r^2 = .08. In order to understand the reasons behind the success of the CAPT group responses, investigations turned to identifying the specific strategies and linguistic formulae employed by each group, which are presented in the following section.

7.5. Linguistic analysis of the apology data

Repeating the procedure conducted with the request data, the content of the responses was analysed by the researcher to investigate frequencies in the type of apology strategy employed over the twelve-week period and what formulaic language was adopted. As a reminder, all production task responses awarded the highest scores of 4 (*very appropriate*) or 5 (*highly appropriate*) by the raters were isolated and their content analysed according to the coding scheme presented in Chapter 6. As with the request data, the aim was to analyse the frequency of these requisite strategies to determine if group differences could explain the preference for the CAPT group responses. Tables 7.9–7.11 represent the percentages and number of participants who utilized at least one of the strategies considered key when constructing an apology. This analysis of formulae is also extended to cover T3-T4, beyond the raters' initial T1-T2 assessments to determine longer-term effects. The three apology scenarios are discussed in turn below: lost library book (7.5.1), noisy party at flat (7.5.2), missed appointment with tutor (7.5.3).

7.5.1. Linguistic analysis of lost library book scenario

From the apology taxonomy presented in Chapter 6, three strategies for the lost library book scenario (interlocutor = librarian + social distance) were identified as requisite to a successful response in the researcher's analysis: *expression of regret*, *offer of repair* and some form of *intensifier* (Table 7.9). An example of a successful apology from the post-instruction learner data is: 'I'm so sorry (*expression of regret + intensifier*). I have lost a book which I borrowed from the library. It's my fault. I'll pay for the book' (*offer of repair*) (average rater score = 4).

For 'expression of regret', the data show, even at T1, formulaic language such as *'I'm sorry'*, with accompanying intensifiers, is a common occurrence in the responses. This trend continues throughout the test stages, with the exception of a decrease in T1-T2 production for the control group. Of the three requisite strategies, *offer of repair* evidences the greatest increase in use for both

Table 7.9 Frequency of requisite apology strategies: Lost library book scenario

Apology strategy	T1 (pretest)			T2 (immediate-posttest)			T3 (2-wk delayed)		T4 (6-wk delayed)	
	CAPT (N=24) *(%)	PAPER (N=20) *(%)	CTRL (N=17) *(%)	CAPT (N=24) *(%)	PAPER (N=20) *(%)	CTRL (N=17) *(%)	CAPT (N=24) *(%)	PAPER (N=20) *(%)	CAPT (N=17) *(%)	PAPER (N=16) *(%)
Expression of regret (A2)	22 (91.67)	20 (100)	15 (88.24)	22 (91.67)	20 (100)	13 (76.47)	22 (91.67)	18 (90)	17 (100)	16 (100)
Offer of repair (B3)	20 (83.33)	14 (70)	15 (88.24)	23 (95.83)	17 (85)	13 (76.47)	24 (100)	17 (85)	16 (94.12)	12 (75)
Intensifier (B5)	17 (70.83)	18 (90)	9 (52.94)	18 (75)	14 (70)	9 (52.94)	18 (75)	16 (80)	14 (82.35)	13 (81.25)

Note:
* = actual number of participants
% = percentage of group
A2, B3, B5 = strategy code (see Chapter 6 for coding scheme).

Table 7.10 Frequency of requisite apology strategies: Noisy party at flat scenario

Apology strategy	T1 (pretest)			T2 (immediate-posttest)			T3 (2-wk delayed)		T4 (6-wk delayed)	
	CAPT (N=24) *(%)	PAPER (N=20) *(%)	CTRL (N=17) *(%)	CAPT (N=24) *(%)	PAPER (N=20) *(%)	CTRL (N=17) *(%)	CAPT (N=24) *(%)	PAPER (N=20) *(%)	CAPT (N=17) *(%)	PAPER (N=16) *(%)
Expression of regret (A2)	19 (79.17)	16 (80)	13 (76.47)	22 (91.67)	19 (95)	14 (82.35)	23 (95.83)	20 (100)	15 (88.24)	15 (93.75)
Promise of forbearance (B4)	3 (12.5)	2 (10)	6 (35.29)	19 (79.17)	14 (70)	5 (29.41)	23 (95.83)	20 (100)	15 (88.24)	12 (75)

Note:
* = actual number of participants
% = percentage of group
A2, B4 = strategy code (see Chapter 6 for coding scheme).

Table 7.11 Frequency of requisite apology strategies: Missed appointment with tutor

Apology strategy	T1 (pretest)			T2 (immediate-posttest)			T3 (2-wk delayed)		T4 (6-wk delayed)	
	CAPT (N=24) *(%)	PAPER (N=20) *(%)	CTRL (N=17) *(%)	CAPT (N=24) *(%)	PAPER (N=20) *(%)	CTRL (N=17) *(%)	CAPT (N=24) *(%)	PAPER (N=20) *(%)	CAPT (N=17) *(%)	PAPER (N=16) *(%)
Expression of regret (A2)	21 (87.5)	20 (100)	16 (94.12)	23 (95.83)	18 (90)	13 (76.47)	18 (75)	18 (90)	12 (70.59)	16 (100)
Explanation (B1a-B1d)	19 (79.17)	16 (80)	6 (35.29)	20 (83.33)	18 (90)	8 (47.06)	22 (91.67)	16 (80)	16 (94.12)	14 (87.5)
Self-blame (B2a)	2 (8.33)	1 (5)	1 (5.88)	19 (79.17)	17 (85)	0 (0)	18 (75)	18 (90)	15 (88.24)	10 (62.5)
Promise of forbearance (B4)	4 (16.67)	0 (0)	5 (29.41)	20 (83.33)	20 (100)	5 (29.41)	21 (87.5)	17 (85)	17 (100)	12 (75)

Note:
* = actual number of participants
% = percentage of group
A2, B1a-B1d, B2a, B4 = strategy code (see Chapter 6 for coding scheme).

experimental groups, though these are still marginal as the majority of the participants in each group are already using this strategy at T1. The T3 posttest (+ two weeks) evidences that the T2 performance for the experimental groups is sustained. It is only at T4 (+ six weeks) where small decreases in frequency *offer of repair* and *intensifier* appear. In contrast, there is no observable change in the *offer of repair* strategy for the control group, which remains consistently low throughout the test stages.

7.5.2. Linguistic analysis of noisy party at flat scenario

The raters considered scenario two (interlocutor = security guard + social distance) to need the fewest strategies: *expression of regret, promise of forbearance*. A successful example from the learner data is: 'I'm terribly sorry (*expression of regret*) about the noise. Because we have the party yesterday and it's all my fault. It will not happen again' (*promise of forbearance*) (average rater score = 4).

As seen previously, *expression of regret* was salient to most learners at T1 in this scenario too and was proceeded by a small rise in the number of experimental group participants using this language at T2, following instruction (Table 7.10). The control group's performance remained static across test stages.

In terms of the *promise of forbearance* strategy and its formulaic sequence, '*it won't happen again*', or other variations of this, both experimental groups evidenced a sharp post-instruction increase of around 60 per cent in production of this strategy, though more participants in the CAPT group than the PAPER group produced this language in two of the three posttests (T2 and T4). Little T1-T2 change is evident for the control group with production remaining consistently low (less than half of the control group produced the *promise of forbearance* strategy at T2).

7.5.3. Linguistic analysis of missed appointment with tutor scenario

From the raters' perspectives, the final scenario (interlocutor = tutor, - social distance) required the most strategies for a successful response, as presented in Table 7.11. The highest marks were awarded to responses containing all of the following four strategies: *expression of regret, explanation, admission of responsibility, promise of forbearance*. A successful example from the learner data representing this is: 'I'm really sorry (*expression of regret*) for missing the meeting. That day my friend got ill and I need to go to hospital (*explanation*). It's my fault (*admission of responsibility*). I promise that will not happen next time' (*promise of forbearance*) (average rater score = 5).

In this scenario, the need for an *expression of regret* supported by an *explanation* were salient to the learners at T1 for this scenario and were strategies which they maintained successfully throughout the investigation. Observable improvements in the use of the 'explanation' strategy for the experimental groups was also evident. This trend, however, is accompanied by the control group under-performing (particularly in the production of an *explanation*) at all test stages.

All learner groups at T1 were the least successful at producing an *admission of responsibility* such as '*It's my fault*' and a *promise not to repeat the offence* (e.g. '*I promise it won't happen again*') – both of which are considered to be key mitigators in this scenario. Less than one-third of participants from each group produced these strategies. At least two-thirds of participants in the experimental groups adopted these strategies much more successfully at the posttest stages. Again, the CAPT group still outperformed the PAPER group in three out of the four delayed-posttest measures at T3 and T4 for strategies (B2a – self-blame; 6-wk = +25 per cent) and (B4 – promise of forbearance; 2-wk = +3 per cent, 6-wk = +25 per cent). The control group's T1 scores remained static to T2.

7.5.4. Frequency of combined production of all key apology strategies

So far, the data reveal the following three main findings: (i) the control group did not acquire the appropriate apology behaviour as evidenced in the experimental groups, (ii) the participants in the experimental groups produced more of the key mitigating strategies post-instruction and (iii) the CAPT group generally outperformed the PAPER group in the production of appropriate apologies at the majority of test stages. These findings are highlighted more clearly in Table 7.12 which represents the percentage and number of participants who utilized *all* of the strategies considered requisite for each scenario in contrast to Tables 7.9–7.11 which captured instances of employing at least one. In all of the T2-T4 stages, more participants in the CAPT group than the PAPER group produced responses including all of the 'essential' strategies for each scenario.

The findings presented so far indicate the experimental groups (CAPT and PAPER) follow a positive trajectory throughout the twelve-week period, with the CAPT group outperforming the PAPER group for the majority of the time. Conversely, no clear patterns of development are observed for the control group, other than low T1 scores remaining static or decreases in

Table 7.12 Frequency of combined production of all key apology strategies by scenario

	T1 (pretest)			T2 (immediate-posttest)			T3 (2-wk delayed)		T4 (6-wk delayed)	
	CAPT (N=24) *(%)	PAPER (N=20) *(%)	CTRL (N=17) *(%)	CAPT (N=24) *(%)	PAPER (N=20) *(%)	CTRL (N=17) *(%)	CAPT (N=24) *(%)	PAPER (N=20) *(%)	CAPT (N=17) *(%)	PAPER (N=16) *(%)
Lost library book (A2, B3, B5)	15 (62.5)	12 (60)	9 (52.94)	18 (75)	13 (65)	7 (41.18)	20 (83.33)	13 (65)	14 (82.35)	9 (56.25)
Noisy party at flat (A2, B4)	3 (12.5)	2 (10)	4 (23.53)	21 (87.5)	13 (65)	5 (29.41)	22 (91.67)	14 (70)	16 (94.12)	9 (56.25)
Missed meeting with tutor (A2, B1a-B1d, B2a, B4)	4 (16.67)	1 (5)	2 (11.76)	21 (87.5)	15 (75)	1 (5.88)	22 (91.67)	12 (60)	11 (64.71)	11 (68.75)

Note:
* = actual number of participants
% = percentage of group.

production of apology strategies and associated formulaic language. These group features are best illustrated in Figures 7.4 and 7.5 which display the PAPER and CAPT groups' improved performance over T1-T4, in comparison to Figure 7.6, which tracks the more erratic performance of the control group over T1-T2.

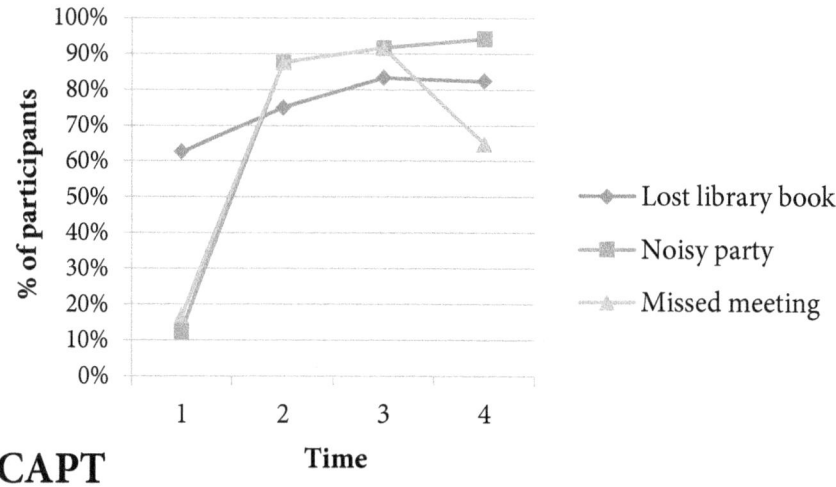

Figure 7.4 CAPT group performance of apology production (T1-T4)

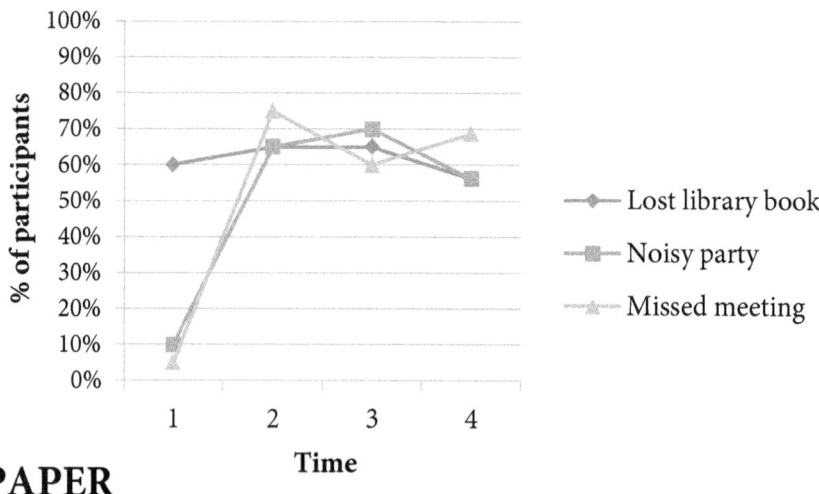

Figure 7.5 PAPER group performance of apology production (T1-T4)

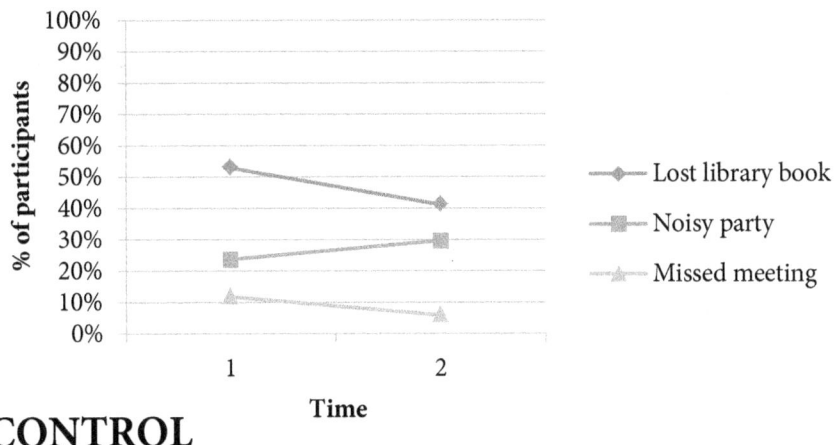

CONTROL

Figure 7.6 Control group performance of apology production (T1-T4)

7.6. Non-target-like features of apologies

Regarding findings from the apology data in the present study, Table 7.13 reveals a series of trends for the non-target-like language features before and after instruction. The frequency figures presented in Table 7.13 are the number of occurrences of each non-target-like feature across all three apology scenarios. The percentage figures are calculated based on maximum frequency divided by the actual frequency figures found in the data. Maximum frequency is each participant per group using each apology strategy once, per scenario:

freq per cent = actual frequency in data ÷ (N × 3 [scenarios]) × 100

A worked example using *'inappropriate request for forgiveness'*, taken from Table 7.13 is as follows: 9 ÷ (24 × 3) = 0.125 (12.5 per cent).

Firstly, at least 50 per cent of participants, regardless of group, exhibited *inappropriate requests for forgiveness* across the three scenarios at T1. Each group was inclined to use the majority of these in the 'tutor' scenario, followed by 'library' and 'party'. The experimental groups opted to use none or very few requests for forgiveness at T2 – a trend maintained to T3 and T4. This decline in use for the experimental groups is accompanied by sustained production (and slight increase) of *inappropriate requests for forgiveness* by the control group. These trends of T1 group comparability, followed by posttest decreases in inappropriate language use for the experimental groups, matched by sustained/ increased control group production, can be seen with a number of other

Table 7.13 Non-target-like features of apologies T1–T4

Language feature	T1 (pretest)			T2 (immediate-posttest)			T3 (2wk-delayed)		T4 (6wk-delayed)	
	CAPT (N=24) *(%)	PAPER (N=20) *(%)	CTRL (N=17) *(%)	CAPT (N=24) *(%)	PAPER (N=20) *(%)	CTRL (N=17) *(%)	CAPT (N=24) *(%)	PAPER (N=20) *(%)	CAPT (N=17) *(%)	PAPER (N=16) *(%)
Inappropriate use of 'I apologize'	0	0	0	0	0	0	0	0	0	0
Inappropriate request for forgiveness	9 (12.5)	7 (11.67)	7 (13.73)	0	1 (1.67)	8 (15.69)	0	1 (1.67)	0	0
Inappropriate use of phrase for context	0	0	0	0	0	0	0	1 (1.67)	0	0
Excessive offer of repair	1 (1.39)	0	0	1 (1.39)	0	2 (3.92)	0	0	0	0
Use of an imperative	0	0	0	0	0	1 (1.96)	0	0	0	0
Because-therefore pattern	5 (6.94)	4 (6.67)	4 (7.84)	2 (2.78)	0	4 (7.84)	0	1 (1.67)	1 (1.96)	1 (2.08)
Inappropriate address terms (sir, madam)	19 (26.39)	17 (28.33)	10 (19.61)	3 (4.17)	1 (1.67)	14 (27.45)	1 (1.39)	0	3 (5.89)	3 (6.25)
Use of multiple apologies	31 (43.06)	34 (56.67)	26 (50.98)	17 (23.61)	13 (21.67)	24 (47.06)	12 (16.67)	10 (16.67)	13 (25.49)	14 (29.17)
Undersupply of admission of responsibility**	2 (2.78)	2 (3.33)	1 (1.96)	40 (55.55)	29 (48.33)	2 (3.92)	43 (59.72)	37 (61.67)	23 (45.1)	19 (39.58)
'Explanation' strategy uncommon	15 (20.83)	10 (50)	8 (15.69)	28 (38.89)	22 (36.67)	4 (7.84)	31 (43.06)	26 (43.33)	16 (31.37)	16 (33.33)
'Promise of forbearance' strategy uncommon	5 (6.94)	3 (5)	5 (9.8)	42 (58.33)	32 (53.33)	6 (11.76)	47 (65.28)	34 (56.67)	22 (43.14)	20 (41.67)

Note: * = actual number of participants % = total usage of each feature as a percentage ** Explicit formulaic expressions containing the words 'fault', 'mistake', 'wrong' were scored as an admission of responsibility.

language features: the *'because-therefore' pattern* in the information sequencing of apologies and use of *inappropriate address terms*.

Reverse patterns of behaviour are evident when analysing the underproduction of particular apology strategies across the three participant groups. In this case, low T1 production is observed for all groups, followed by considerable experimental group increases, accompanied by no change in control group production. This trend is applicable to all three strategies highlighted as problematic in this study: *'admission of responsibility', 'explanation'* and *'promise of forbearance'*. The experimental groups' post-instruction increases for each of these strategies are 72 per cent, 28.5 per cent and 75 per cent, respectively, which are maintained to T3, but evidence a slight decrease at T4.

In sum, the experimental groups appear to have profited from the intervention, producing more target-like apology strategies considered appropriate for each of the contexts. In addition, there are fewer instances of non-target-like features of apology, post-instruction. The CAPT group outperform the PAPER group as a rule, whilst the control group fail to improve its performance levels.

8

Study abroad language contact findings

All sixty-one learners (CAPT = 24, PAPER = 20, control = 17) completed a two-part self-evaluation questionnaire on English language use during their SA stay, as described in Chapter 6. The questionnaire was a simplified, revised version of Freed et al.'s (2004b) language contact profile. The overall aim of the questionnaire was for learners to (i) evaluate the frequency of their productive and receptive English use and (ii) evaluate their overall language skills over the specified time periods. The outcome would identify to what extent the L2 environment was influential in any gains evident from the intervention.

As a reminder, part A of the questionnaire elicited how frequently the learners engaged in a variety of activities in English. Part B required learners to provide an overall skills assessment for listening, speaking, reading, writing and interaction in English. The questionnaire was administered at T1 (based on their experiences of using English in China), T2 (UK-based experience, six weeks post-arrival) and T4 (UK-based experience, twelve weeks post-arrival). This equated to a time lapse of six weeks between each test. The experimental groups (CAPT and PAPER) were the only groups to complete the questionnaire at T4 as the focus was to measure retention of the instructional input over time and identify any links with L2 contact. A questionnaire was not administered at T3 as the time lapse of two weeks was not considered long enough to result in any change for the self-reporting questionnaire. The results of parts A and B of the questionnaire are presented in the following sections.

8.1. Questionnaire part A (engagement in English)

The first part of the questionnaire required the learners to choose from a five-point Likert scale in order to self-evaluate the frequency of their English usage (0 = never, 1 = a few times a year, 2 = monthly, 3 = weekly, 4 = daily) whilst engaging in specific speaking activities (productive use) or listening/

reading activities (receptive use). Learners evaluated their own productive use of English (speaking to teachers, friends, classmates, strangers, service personnel) and receptive use of English (watching TV, watching films, listening to songs, reading newspapers, reading novels, reading magazines), at the three time periods (T1, T2 and T4). The *mean* scores are calculated out of maximum total of forty-eight points (six questions on productive activities, six questions on receptive activities, max four points per question). Due to challenges encouraging the CAPT and PAPER groups' participants to return voluntarily following the end of their course, the final sample for T4 totalled thirty-six learners (CAPT = 17, PAPER = 16).

The questionnaire findings are reported as follows. Firstly, the results are presented according to the participants' self-reported overall English use, combining both productive and receptive skills, to provide an initial overview. The two skills are subsequently divided to investigate differences within and between these two areas. The next section extends the results of the experimental groups to T4 to measure long-term environmental influences. This is followed by a focus on the frequency of the individual productive and receptive activities undertaken by the participants. The final section provides an overview of within- and between-group differences to investigate group variability.

The findings within each section are initially presented according to repeated measures ANOVAs, followed by subsequent post hoc tests. Where appropriate, relevant paired and independent t-tests are then presented at the end of each section to test for further differences within the data. A summary of the main findings concludes each section.

8.1.1. CAPT, PAPER and control groups' self-evaluations of overall English use (productive and receptive combined)

Table 8.1 summarizes the descriptive statistics of the CAPT, PAPER and control groups' self-evaluations of their combined productive and receptive English use at stages T1 (China-based experience) and T2 (UK-based experience, six weeks post-arrival). The *mean* frequencies were calculated based on a cumulative total of both productive and receptive scores, divided by the number of participants in each group. Considering the maximum possible score of 48, all three groups evaluate the frequency of both productive and receptive English use at T1 to be low, with most participants reporting using these skills only 'a *few times a year*'. By T2 (+ six weeks of UK-based experience), the frequency of engaging with English shows a marked increase for each group at comparable levels of between

Table 8.1 Descriptive statistics: CAPT, PAPER and control groups' self-evaluations of combined productive and receptive English use at T1 and T2

Group	T1 (China-based) M (SD)	T2 (UK-based, + 6 weeks) M (SD)
CAPT (N=24)	13.0 (5.62)	33.6 (5.38)
PAPER (N=20)	12.7 (4.62)	33.5 (5.05)
Control (N=17)	11.6 (2.50)	31.6 (2.59)
Total (N=61)	12.5 (4.57)	33.0 (4.67)

Note: Maximum marks = 48

+20 and +21 marks, in comparison to their T1 scores. By this stage, productive and receptive English use has become at least a *'weekly'* activity.

A 2 (time) × 3 (group) repeated measures ANOVA at T1 and T2 confirms the mean differences. In terms of the learners' self-evaluation of conducting activities in spoken English, there was a significant effect for time, with a very large effect size: $F(1, 58) = 782.4$, $p < .001$, partial $\eta^2 = .93$. There were no significant differences or effect sizes between the groups overall: $F(2, 58) = 1.21$, $p = .305$, partial $\eta^2 = .04$, nor any interaction of time × group: $F(2, 58) = .11$, $p = .900$, partial $\eta^2 = .004$. These results indicate that all three groups self-report to have increased the frequency of their overall English use between T1 and T2 and at parallel rates.

To detect where these significant differences in *time* might lie, the above analysis was subsequently broken down by skill (productive and receptive). Table 8.2 summarizes the descriptive statistics for T1 and T2 comparisons by productive and receptive activities.

Table 8.2 Descriptive statistics: CAPT, PAPER and control groups' self-evaluations of separate productive and receptive English use at T1 and T2

Group	T1 productive M (SD)	T2 productive M (SD)	T1 receptive M (SD)	T2 receptive M (SD)
CAPT (N=24)	3.54 (2.28)	16.9 (2.25)	9.50 (4.00)	16.7 (3.47)
PAPER (N=20)	3.05 (2.19)	16.3 (2.72)	9.60 (3.60)	17.2 (3.27)
Control (N=17)	3.18 (1.19)	15.6 (1.18)	8.41 (2.24)	16.0 (1.94)
Total (N=61)	3.28 (1.98)	16.3 (2.21)	9.23 (3.44)	16.7 (3.04)

Note: Maximum marks = 24 for either productive or receptive use.

In terms of productive English use, all three groups are comparable in their low self-assessment of this skill at T1, awarding themselves no more than

15 per cent of the total 24 marks available. These mean scores increase around fivefold at T2 which, again, is evident across all three groups. A 2 (time) × 3 (group) repeated measures ANOVA T1 to T2 reveals a significant main effect of time and a very large effect size: $F(1, 58) = 1048.02, p < .001$, partial $\eta^2 = .95$. There were no significant differences or effect sizes between the groups overall: $F(2, 58) = 1.81, p = .172$, partial $\eta^2 = .05$, nor for the interaction of time × group: $F(2, 58) = .50, p = .609$, partial $\eta^2 = .02$. These results indicate that all three groups show a parallel pattern across 'time' variables for productive English use.

Receptive English use revealed a smaller T1 to T2 difference between the mean scores than was evident with productive English use, though all three learner groups began T1 with around a 5–6 point gain on the productive English scores. This reveals receptive skills in English were employed more frequently than productive skills at T1. At T2, however, only marginal differences between productive and receptive skills were evident, demonstrating productive skills increased much more and were generally used as frequently as receptive skills, six weeks beyond the initial pretest. This is corroborated by a paired samples t-test which reveals a significant difference and very large effect size between productive and receptive gain scores T1 to T2: $t(60) = 11.4, p < .001$, 95% CI [4.62, 6.60], $r^2 = .68$.

As expected from the mean score data, a 2 (time) × 3 (group) ANOVA (T1 to T2) on receptive English use reveals a significant main effect of time with a very large effect size: $F(1, 58) = 239.6, p < .001$, partial $\eta^2 = .805$. There was no significant main effect of group: $F(2, 58) = .98, p = .382$, partial $\eta^2 = .03$, nor group × time interaction: $F(2, 58) = .078, p = .925$, partial $\eta^2 = .003$. These results indicate that all three groups evidenced comparable gains between T1 and T2 for self-reported receptive English use.

In summary, during the six-week period between T1 and T2, the CAPT, PAPER and control groups all increased the frequency of both their productive and receptive English which was found to be statistically significant with large to very large effect sizes. Productive English use increased to a higher degree T1-T2 for all groups which was also found to be statistically significant with a very large effect size. Receptive English use remained higher than productive use at every test stage, for all groups. There were no statistically significant differences or observable effect sizes between the groups at any of the stages, suggesting all three groups increased the frequency of English use at parallel rates.

The next section presents findings from T4 (UK-based, +12 weeks) for the experimental groups (CAPT and PAPER) productive and receptive use of English. The T4 findings are presented alongside T1-T2 not only for the reader's convenience, but due to statistical variation in the descriptive statistics where outputs have been calculated with listwise deletion due to missing data at T4. Comparisons between listwise and pairwise results reveal no significant differences, however: $p = .346$ (T1), $p = .794$ (T2). The *mean* and *standard deviations* for the whole population can be found in Table 8.2, as presented earlier.

8.1.2. Experimental groups' T1-T4 self-evaluations of productive and receptive English use

The descriptive statistics in Table 8.3 reveal that the increased frequency of the CAPT and PAPER groups' productive skills at T2 is generally maintained to T4 (+six weeks' difference). However, at this point, both groups evidence a marginal decrease of around −1 point overall. This represents a decrease in frequency from '*daily*' to '*weekly*' use on the original questionnaire.

A 3 (time) × 2 (group) repeated measures ANOVA reveals, in terms of the learners' self-evaluation of conducting productive activities in spoken English, there was a significant main effect of time T1-T4 with a very large effect size: $F(2, 62) = 294.6$, $p < .001$, partial $\eta^2 = .905$. There were no significant main effects of group though a small effect size was revealed: $F(1, 31) = 3.43$, $p = .073$, partial $\eta^2 = .10$, nor evidence of group × time interaction: $F(2, 62) = .205$, $p = .815$, partial $\eta^2 = .007$. These results indicate that both groups' reports of increasing their productive use of English between all three stages were generally comparable.

Focusing on T2-T4, a 2 (time) × 2 (group) repeated measures ANOVA reveals no significant main effect of time or effect size: $F(1, 31) = 2.761$, $p = .107$, partial

Table 8.3 Descriptive statistics: Experimental groups' self-evaluations of productive and receptive English use T1, T2 and T4

Productive	T1 M (SD)	T2 M (SD)	T4 M (SD)
CAPT (*N*=17)	3.53 (2.29)	17.1 (2.18)	15.9 (1.92)
PAPER (*N*=16)	3.00 (2.39)	15.8 (2.83)	15.1 (2.98)
Total (*N*=33)	3.27 (2.32)	16.5 (2.56)	15.5 (2.49)
Receptive			
CAPT (*N*=17)	9.47 (4.23)	16.4 (3.36)	17.1 (3.98)
PAPER (*N*=16)	8.94 (3.09)	16.7 (3.40)	16.1 (3.89)
Total (*N*=33)	9.21 (3.67)	16.6 (3.33)	16.6 (3.91)

Note: Maximum marks = 24 for either productive or receptive use.

$\eta^2 = .082$. Similarly, there is no main effect of group or effect size: $F(1, 31) = 2.816$, $p = .103$, partial $\eta^2 = .083$, nor interaction effect between time and group: $F(1, 31) = .135$, $p = .715$, partial $\eta^2 = .004$. Whilst both groups evidence a slight decrease in frequency of productive English use T2-T4, it is not therefore statistically relevant.

Supplementary post hoc comparisons of productive activities for the experimental groups within the three time periods (T1, T2 and T4), using a Tukey HSD adjustment, reveal that there were significant differences overall between T1-T2 ($p < .001$) and T1-T4 ($p < .001$). This was not the case at the T2-T4 phase ($p = .320$).

To detect the exact location of this significance, paired t-tests were selected to identify differences within the CAPT and PAPER groups. Results indicate that both groups were comparable in reporting increases in the frequency of their English usage between T1-T2 which was found to be statistically significant with very large effect sizes: *CAPT*: $t(23) = -19.23$, $p < .001$, 95% CI $[-14.77, -11.90]$, $r^2 = .94$. *PAPER*: $t(19) = -16.34$, $p < .001$, 95% CI $[-14.95, -11.55]$, $r^2 = .93$. This was also true for the T1-T4 phases: *CAPT*: $t(16) = -15.79$, $p < .001$, 95% CI $[-14.08, -10.75]$, $r^2 = .94$. *PAPER*: $t(15) = -13.25$, $p < .001$, 95% CI $[-14.00, -10.1]$, $r^2 = .92$. The T2-T4 phases revealed no significant differences for either group, though the CAPT group self-reported to use their productive skills more frequently with a large effect size: $t(16) = 2.06$, $p = .056$, 95% CI $[-.033, -2.39]$, $r^2 = .21$, in comparison to the PAPER group's self-report with a small effect size $t(15) = .728$, $p = .478$, 95% CI $[-1.45, 2.95]$, $r^2 = .03$.

The overall trend of increased frequency of learners' productive English, as reported above, is also evident with receptive English use (Table 8.3). Mixed results are evident at T4, with the CAPT group maintaining a positive trajectory in contrast to the PAPER group who evidence a slight decrease. As expected from the mean scores, a 3 (time) × 2 (group) repeated measures ANOVA illustrates a significant main effect of time on the learners' self-evaluation of their reading and listening activities in English with a very large effect size: $F(2, 62) = 69.71$, $p < .001$, partial $\eta^2 = .69$. The trend for comparability amongst both groups was also evident here with no significant main effect of group or effect size: $F(1, 31) = .182$, $p = .067$, partial $\eta^2 = .006$, nor group × time interaction: $F(2, 62) = .396$, $p = .675$, partial $\eta^2 = .013$. These results indicate that both groups increased the frequency of receptive English use between all three stages at comparable rates, as mirrored in their productive scores.

Focusing on the T2 to T4, a 2 (time) × 2 (group) repeated measures ANOVA reveals no significant main effect of time or effect size: $F(1, 31) = .010$,

$p = .920$, partial $\eta^2 = .0002$. Similarly, there is no main effect of group: $F(1, 31) = .114$, $p = .738$, partial $\eta^2 = .004$, nor interaction effect between time and group: $F(1, 31) = .794$, $p = .380$, partial $\eta^2 = .025$. Whilst there are contrasting T4 results for the CAPT and PAPER groups, as mentioned previously, these are not statistically relevant.

Comparable trends are evident between the learners' productive and receptive English use between the three test stages. Supplementary post hoc pairwise comparisons, with a Tukey HSD adjustment, reveal significant differences between T1 and T2 ($p < .001$) and T1-T4 phases ($p < .001$). There was no significant difference to be found between the T2 and T4 phases ($p = .899$). These results mirror those found with the productive skill.

To detect the exact location of the differences, subsequent post hoc paired samples t-tests revealed that both the CAPT and PAPER groups reported to significantly increase the frequency of receptive English use between T1 and T2 with very large effect sizes: CAPT = $t(23) = -8.90$, $p < .001$, 95% CI [−8.89, −5.53], $r^2 = .78$. PAPER = $t(19) = -8.07$, $p < .001$, 95% CI [−9.57, −5.63], $r^2 = .77$. This was also the case for differences between the T1 and T4 phases: CAPT = $t(16) = -7.05$, $p < .001$, 95% CI [−9.95, −5.35], $r^2 = .76$. PAPER = $t(15) = -8.03$, $p < .001$, 95% CI [−9.10, −5.26], $r^2 = .81$. Both groups consider themselves to have a greater receptive English use at T2 in comparison to their first arrival in the UK. This improvement is generally maintained to approximately the same level up to T4, though there is no evidence of increase or effect size as might be expected from the T1-T2 values: CAPT = $t(16) = -.731$, $p = .475$, 95% CI [−2.75, 1.34], $r^2 = .03$. PAPER = $t(15) = -.536$, $p = .600$, 95% CI [−1.67, 2.80], $r^2 = .02$. These increases again mirror productive English use, as reported earlier.

8.1.3. Experimental groups' T1-T4 self-evaluations of productive and receptive English use by activity

An investigation into changes in frequency of specific activities over the three time periods was also undertaken for both productive and receptive English use. The category 'productive use' (speaking) on the questionnaire was subdivided into interaction with five specific interlocutors whom the participants were likely to encounter in a SA setting: instructors, friends, classmates, strangers (e.g. members of the public) and service personnel (e.g. bank staff, supermarket staff). For receptive use, the focus was on three listening activities (watching TV, watching films, listening to songs) and three reading activities (reading newspapers, reading novels, reading magazines).

As previous analyses in this section have revealed both the CAPT and PAPER groups display parallel patterns of behaviour for productive and receptive use at each test stage, the following analysis does not separate the investigation by group but looks for overall trends in frequency of activities undertaken by the whole experimental group sample, based on the 'time' variable. Table 8.4 displays the descriptive statistics which reveal several key trends. These trends are explained in more detail in sections 8.1.3.1 and 8.1.3.2.

Table 8.4 Descriptive statistics: Experimental groups' self-evaluations of T1-T4 productive and receptive English use by activity

Productive activity	T1 (N= 44) M (SD)	T2 (N= 44) M (SD)	T4 (N= 33) M (SD)
Communicate with instructor	1.02 (.98)	3.23 (.80)	3.18 (.92)
Communicate with friends	.73 (.66)	2.89 (.87)	3.03 (.64)
Communicate with classmates	1.00 (.92)	3.84 (.43)	3.33 (.85)
Communicate with strangers	.45 (.63)	3.27 (.79)	3.06 (.66)
Communicate with service personnel	.09 (.29)	3.39 (.66)	2.91 (.77)
Receptive activity			
Watch TV	1.89 (.97)	2.82 (.92)	3.15 (.62)
Watch films	2.36 (.87)	3.14 (.73)	3.03 (.85)
Listen to songs	2.80 (.77)	3.70 (.46)	3.70 (.53)
Read newspapers	.95 (.86)	2.41 (.92)	2.24 (1.17)
Read novels	.68 (.83)	2.45 (.88)	2.18 (1.26)
Read magazines	.86 (.82)	2.41 (.99)	2.33 (1.21)

Note: Maximum score = 4 (0 = never, 1 = a few times a year, 2 = monthly, 3 = weekly, 4 = daily).

8.1.3.1. Experimental groups' T1-T4 self-evaluations of productive English use by activity

Reviewing the mean scores from a 3 (time) × 2 (group) repeated measures ANOVA, investigating trends in interaction with these interlocutors, T1-T2 changes in behaviour are noticeable.

First, as evidenced by the mean scores, there was a significant overall main effect of time for interaction with all of the five different interlocutors at the $p < .001$ level, with very large effect sizes: *communicate with instructor*, $F(2, 62) = 64.3$, $p < .001$, partial $\eta^2 = .68$; *communicate with friends*, $F(2, 62) = 96.2$,

$p < .001$, partial $\eta^2 = .76$; *communicate with classmates*, $F(2, 62) = 153.9$, $p < .001$, η^2_p partial $\eta^2 = .83$; *communicate with strangers*, $F(2, 62) = 160.3$, $p < .001$, partial $\eta^2 = .84$; *communicate with service personnel*, $F(2, 62) = 349.9$, $p < .001$, partial $\eta^2 = .92$. There was no evidence of group × time interaction for any of the interlocutors ($p = .332, p = .785, p = .242, p = .387, p = .145$), nor significant main effect of group ($p = .054, p = .624, p = .076, p = .635, p = .10$). These results indicate both the CAPT and PAPER groups increased their interaction with all five interlocutors at parallel rates.

Second, when scrutinizing the mean scores by activity, T1-T2 trends are evident. At T1, the groups self-report not to engage with any of the specific interlocutors more than '*a few times a year*'. In fact, for communicating with service personnel, this is borderline '*never*'. The activities can be ranked from least to most frequent at T1 as follows: *service personnel > stranger > friends > classmates > instructor.*

Third, at T2 (+ six weeks), frequency of engagement with all of the interlocutors increases from '*a few times a year*' to at least '*weekly*' (with the exception of '*friends*') with the following ranking from least to most frequent: *friends > instructors > strangers > service personnel > classmates*. Communicating with '*service personnel*' and '*strangers*' increases and moves up the ranking six weeks after T1. At T2, participants interact with these two interlocutors slightly more frequently than '*friends*' and '*instructor*', in contrast to T1. Using English with '*classmates*' still remains one of the most frequent activities but, at this stage, has moved from '*a few times a year*' to an almost '*daily*' activity, in comparison to T1.

Finally, interaction with all five interlocutors on a '*weekly*' basis at T2 is maintained to T4 which equates to a 12-week L2 stay by this point. That said, with the exception of *communicating with 'classmates'*, the mean scores do illustrate a slight decrease (< 1.0). Overall, the increases evident for productive skill (speaking) at the T1 and T2 stages are generally maintained to the T4 stage. Both experimental groups show parallel increases in English usage throughout, but these differences are found to be statistically significant at the T1 to T2, and T1 to T4 stages only. When investigating the interaction with the specific interlocutors presented on the questionnaire, participants reported to rarely interact with any of them in English at T1. Learners' interaction with the interlocutors increased to a '*weekly*' activity in most cases at T2 (+ six weeks SA stay) which was generally sustained to T4 (+ twelve weeks SA stay).

8.3.1.2. *Experimental groups' T1-T4 self-evaluations of receptive English use by activity*

The findings in Table 8.4 confirm that learners engage in receptive activities more frequently than productive ones. At T1, frequencies range from a *'few times a year'* to almost *'weekly'* but these are activity-dependent. The activities at T1 can be ranked as follows from least to most frequent: *read newspapers > read novels > read magazines > watch TV > watch films > listen to songs*, and illustrate that *'reading'* activities are less popular than *'listening'* activities in English. At T1, learners are engaging in listening activities on a *'monthly'* (TV and films) to *'weekly'* (songs) basis which is a direct contrast to all T1 productive skills which are used *'a few times a year'* at best. The preference for *'listening'* over *'reading'* is continued to T2 where the overall rankings remain fairly similar: *read magazines = read newspapers > read novels > watch TV > watch films > listen to songs*. Frequencies for both listening and reading activities increase further on similar trajectories to T2 (+ six weeks). Learners self-report using reading skills on a *'monthly'* basis and listening skills increase to *'weekly'* use, in general. At T4, however, the pattern shifts. Though still in use on a *'monthly'* basis, the mean scores for reading activities decrease slightly, whilst all activities involving *'listening'* continue to be used more and more frequently with *'listening to songs'* almost becoming a *'daily'* habit.

In summary, the experimental groups (CAPT and PAPER) T1-T2 comparability in their patterns of reported productive and receptive English use continues to T4. At T4, the CAPT and PAPER groups generally maintain this higher engagement, though a slight decrease is evident overall but is not found to be statistically significant. At most stages, receptive skills generally remain higher than productive for both groups. A breakdown of individual activities reveals an increase in frequency of use across the time variables. *'Speaking'* increases in frequency from *'a few times a year'* at T1 to *'weekly'* at both T2 and T4. As for receptive skills, *'listening'* appears to be the most practised skill, increasing in frequency from *'monthly'* to *'weekly'* throughout the time periods. *'Reading'*, on the other hand, is the least common, increasing from *'a few times a year'* to *'monthly'* by T4.

8.1.4. Experimental within-group and between-group comparisons for productive and receptive English use T1-T4

Having established comparability *between* the experimental groups in Sections 8.1.2 and 8.1.3, it is useful to conclude this analysis of part A of the questionnaire with a brief look at *within* and *between* group trends for speaking (productive) activities and listening/reading (receptive) activities.

Beginning with within-group trends, paired sample t-test investigations into differences between productive and receptive use within each experimental group (Table 8.5) reveal all participant self-evaluations of their productive use of English at the beginning of their SA experience (T1) are noticeably small with much higher receptive engagement in English which is significantly different (around +6 points) with a very large effect size. This is the case for both groups: CAPT = $t(23) = -8.87, p < .001$, 95% CI $[-7.35, -4.57]$, $r^2 = .77$. PAPER = $t(19) = -7.79$, $p < .001$, 95% CI $[-8.31, -4.79]$, $r^2 = .76$.

T1-T2 activity sharply increases for both productive and receptive use as previously noted although, at this stage, there is a marginal difference between skills: CAPT = $t(23) = .36, p = .725$, 95% CI $[-.803, 1.14]$, $r^2 = .00$. PAPER = $t(19) = -1.24, p = .232$, 95% CI $[-2.43, .63]$, $r^2 = .07$. Learners significantly increase their productive English use to the point where there is greater parity (evidenced by no statistical significance) between speaking (productive) and listening/reading (receptive) activities in English. This is in direct contrast to the T1 phase. At T4, group behaviour differs. For the CAPT group, receptive activities continue to increase, in contrast to a decrease in productive activities. This difference is found to be statistically significant with a small effect size: $t(23) = -2.19, p < .005$, 95% CI $[-2.84, -.08]$, $r^2 = .17$. As for the PAPER group, both productive and receptive skills marginally decrease at T4 with the difference between the skills approaching statistical significance with a small effect size: $t(19) = -1.85, p = .08$, 95% CI $[-3.30, .20]$, $r^2 = .15$.

Independent t-tests reveal no significant difference between the CAPT or PAPER groups' productive or receptive self-evaluations at any of the T1-T4 phases which confirms earlier analyses reporting comparability between

Table 8.5 Descriptive statistics: Paired sample t-tests analysing experimental within-group comparisons for productive and receptive English use T1-T4

	T1 M (SD)		T2 M (SD)		T4 (M, SD)	
	CAPT (N=24)	PAPER (N=20)	CAPT (N=24)	PAPER (N=20)	CAPT (N=17)	PAPER (N=16)
Productive	3.54 (2.28)	3.05 (2.19)	16.8 (2.25)	16.3 (2.72)	15.8 (1.46)	14.9 (2.91)
Receptive	9.50 (4.00)	9.60 (3.60)	16.7 (3.47)	17.2 (3.27)	17.3 (3.30)	16.5 (3.55)

Note: Maximum marks = 24.

the groups at all test phases: T1: $t(42) = .725$, $p = .473$, 95% CI [−.878, 1.86], $r^2 = .01$ (productive); $t(42) = −.086$, $p = .932$, 95% CI [−2.44, 2.24], $r^2 = 0$ (receptive). T2: $t(42) = .768$, $p = .447$, 95% CI [−.936, 2.09], $r^2 = .01$ (productive); $t(42) = −.480$, $p = .634$, 95% CI [−2.56, 1.57], $r^2 = 0$ (receptive). T4: $t(31) = 1.01$, $p = .31$, 95% CI [−.89, 2.65], $r^2 = .03$ (productive); $t(31) = .723$, $p = .475$, 95% CI [−1.81, 3.79], $r^2 = .02$ (receptive). The time periods between these phases are T1-T2 (+ six weeks), T2-T4 (+ six weeks), T1-T4 (+ twelve weeks).

This indicates that both groups were comparable in terms of their self-reported use at each of these stages with the mean scores revealing an almost identical pattern of behaviour for the two groups at each of the test stages. Any differences from the ANOVA results between the groups in their productive and receptive use of English at any of the stages are, therefore, not statistically relevant.

In summary, as evidenced by the absence of statistical significance on independent t-test measures, the CAPT and PAPER groups display comparable group behaviour in the following ways: (i) infrequent use of productive skills but much higher receptive activity at T1, (ii) a sharp increase of both skills at T2 (+ six weeks) with little difference now evident between productive and receptive use, and (iii) significant decreases in use of both skills at T4, with the exception of the receptive skills within the CAPT group which continue to increase.

8.2. Questionnaire part B (skills evaluation)

The second and final part of the questionnaire required participants to evaluate a specified set of skills to give an overall assessment of English use at each time period (T1, T2 and T4). As a reminder, the control group did not participate in the T4 stage.

On a Likert scale, learners were required to make a numeric selection between 1 (poor/beginner) and 5 (excellent/L1-like) to self-assess their skills for the following five categories: listening, speaking, reading, writing and interaction. The mean scores presented in this section are therefore calculated out of a maximum of 5. Section 8.2.1 presents the data for the CAPT, PAPER and control groups at the T1 to T2 stages. Section 8.2.2 focuses on the experimental groups only (CAPT and PAPER) and includes T4. This section concludes with an overview of within- and between-group differences for the five skills.

8.2.1. Experimental and control group comparisons of listening, speaking, reading, writing and interaction skills T1-T2

To identify differences between the evaluations of the five skills (listening, speaking, reading, writing, interaction) at T1 and T2, the data were first submitted to a 2 (time) × 3 (group) repeated measures ANOVA. A summary of the descriptive statistics for all five skills can be found in Table 8.6.

Similar trends between the skills and groups are evident throughout. All of the five skills show a significant main effect of time (T1-T2) with moderate to large effect sizes: *listening*, $F(1, 58) = 28.2, p < .001$, partial $\eta^2 = .33$; *speaking*, $F(1, 58) = 18.7, p < .001$, partial $\eta^2 = .24$; *reading*, $F(1, 58) = 13.2, p = .001$, partial $\eta^2 = .19$; *writing*, $F(1, 58) = 21.5, p < .001$, partial $\eta^2 = .27$; *interaction*, $F(1, 58) = 11.1, p = .002$, partial $\eta^2 = .16$. The mean scores in Table 8.6 indicate learners showed an improvement in each of the skills between the first two test phases.

In addition, given no significance or effect size was found within group × time interaction for any of the skills, it can be concluded that the improvement was comparable between all three groups: *listening*, $F(2, 58) = .568, p = .570$, partial $\eta^2 = .02$; *speaking*, $F(2, 58) = .308, p = .736$, partial $\eta^2 = .01$; *reading*, $F(2, 58) = 2.40, p = .10$, partial $\eta^2 = .07$; *writing*, $F(2, 58) = 2.04, p = .139$, partial $\eta^2 = .06$; *interaction*, $F(2, 58) = 1.74, p = .184$, partial $\eta^2 = .05$.

Table 8.6 Descriptive statistics: Experimental and control groups' T1-T2 self-evaluations of listening, speaking, reading, writing and interaction skills

Skill	Stage	M (SD)			
		CAPT (n=24)	PAPER (n=20)	Control (n=17)	Total (N=61)
Listening	T1	2.88 (.74)	3.10 (.55)	2.76 (.66)	2.92 (.67)
	T2	3.33 (.57)	3.45 (.61)	3.35 (.61)	3.38 (.58)
Speaking	T1	2.96 (.75)	2.70 (.73)	2.65 (.61)	2.79 (.71)
	T2	3.33 (.48)	3.05 (.61)	3.18 (.53)	3.20 (.54)
Reading	T1	2.71 (.75)	2.75 (.72)	2.06 (.75)	2.54 (.79)
	T2	2.83 (.57)	3.10 (.64)	2.76 (.56)	2.90 (.60)
Writing	T1	2.54 (.78)	2.30 (.80)	2.06 (.66)	2.33 (.77)
	T2	2.75 (.53)	2.85 (.67)	2.76 (.56)	2.79 (.58)
Interaction	T1	3.04 (.70)	2.65 (.75)	2.94 (.66)	2.89 (.71)
	T2	3.25 (.44)	3.30 (.66)	3.18 (.53)	3.25 (.54)

Note: Maximum score = 5.

Finally, no statistically significant main effect of group or effect size was found for *listening*, $F(1, 58) = .904$, $p = .411$, partial $\eta^2 = .03$; *speaking*, $F(1, 58) = 1.86$, $p = .16$, partial $\eta^2 = .06$; *writing*, $F(1, 58) = .946$, $p = .394$, partial $\eta^2 = .03$; *interaction*, $F(1, 58) = .746$, $p = .479$, partial $\eta^2 = .02$. For *reading*, however, a significant main effect of group was evident, $F(1, 58) = 4.64$, $p = .014$, with a small effect (partial $\eta^2 = .14$).

The *mean* scores in Table 8.6 suggest the control group made consistently lower evaluations than the CAPT and PAPER groups at T1 and T2. This is confirmed in post hoc comparisons (Tukey HSD adjustment) which reveal a significant difference between the control and PAPER group ($p = .011$) and a difference which approaches significance between the control and CAPT groups ($p = .084$). Reviewing the mean scores, however, the differences evident at each stage are minimal, with less than one point separating each group, so the above significance does not appear meaningful. The following section focuses on the experimental groups only (CAPT and PAPER) and includes the T4 phase. For the reader's convenience and due to descriptive statistics being calculated with listwise deletion because of missing data at T4, the T1-T2 results are also presented in the tables which follow. The *mean* and *standard deviation* scores for the whole population can be found in Table 8.6, as presented earlier. Comparisons between listwise and pairwise results reveal no significant differences; $p = .913$ (T1), $p = .666$ (T2).

8.2.2. Experimental group comparisons of listening, speaking, reading, writing and interaction skills T1-T4

The data were submitted to a 3 (time) × 2 (group) repeated measures ANOVA to identify any differences in the skills between the three time periods (T1, T2 and T4). The descriptive statistics are summarized in Table 8.7.

The analyses yielded a significant main effect of time for all five skills with very large effect sizes: *listening*, $F(2, 62) = 26.74$, $p < .001$, partial $\eta^2 = .46$; *speaking*, $F(2, 62) = 12.90$, $p < .001$, partial $\eta^2 = .29$; *reading*, $F(1.71, 53.13) = 10.86$, $p < .001$ partial $\eta^2 = .26$; *writing*, $F(2, 62) = 17.74$, $p < .001$ partial $\eta^2 = .36$; *interaction*, $F(1.77, 54.97) = 18.31$, $p < .001$ partial $\eta^2 = .37$.

With the exception of speaking, ($F(1, 31) = 5.79$, $p = .022$, small effect; partial $\eta^2 = .16$), group comparability was generally evident as the analyses did not highlight a significant main effect of group for the other skills or reveal any effect sizes: *listening*, $F(1, 31) = 1.39$, $p = .248$, partial $\eta^2 = .04$; *reading*, $F(1, 31) =$

Table 8.7 Descriptive statistics: Experimental groups' T1-T4 self-evaluations by skill

		M (SD)		
Skill	Stage	CAPT (*n*=17)	PAPER (*n*=16)	Total (*N*=33)
Listening	T1	2.82 (.81)	3.00 (.52)	2.91 (.68)
	T2	3.24 (.56)	3.38 (.62)	3.30 (.59)
	T4	3.59 (.62)	3.88 (.50)	3.73 (.57)
Speaking	T1	3.06 (.75)	2.56 (.63)	2.82 (.73)
	T2	3.41 (.51)	3.00 (.63)	3.20 (.60)
	T4	3.53 (.51)	3.19 (.66)	3.36 (.60)
Reading	T1	2.59 (.80)	2.75 (.78)	2.67 (.78)
	T2	2.76 (.66)	3.06 (.68)	2.91 (.68)
	T4	3.00 (.79)	3.50 (.63)	3.24 (.75)
Writing	T1	2.59 (.87)	2.19 (.83)	2.39 (.86)
	T2	2.71 (.59)	2.87 (.72)	2.79 (.65)
	T4	3.06 (.66)	3.31 (.48)	3.18 (.58)
Interaction	T1	3.06 (.75)	2.50 (.63)	2.79 (.74)
	T2	3.24 (.44)	3.25 (.68)	3.24 (.56)
	T4	3.47 (.51)	3.62 (.62)	3.55 (.56)

Note: Maximum score = 5.

2.37, $p = .134$, partial $\eta^2 = .07$; *writing*, $F(1, 31) = .001$, $p = .969$, partial $\eta^2 = .00$; *interaction*, $F(1, 31) = .708$, $p = .407$, partial $\eta^2 = .02$.

Group × time interaction was found for two skills with small effect sizes: *writing*, $F(2, 62) = 3.53$, $p = .035$, η^2_p partial $\eta^2 = .10$ and *interaction*, $F(1.77, 54.97) = 4.37$, $p = .021$, partial $\eta^2 = .12$, but absent for the three remaining skills with no to small effect sizes: *listening*, $F(2, 62) = .233$, $p = .793$, partial $\eta^2 = .01$; *speaking*, $F(2, 62) = .241$, $p = .786$, partial $\eta^2 = .01$; *reading* $F(1.71, 53.13) = .925$, $p = .390$, partial $\eta^2 = .02$.

Given the somewhat complex picture of the above analyses, it is helpful to draw on subsequent post hoc findings for further clarification (Table 8.8). Paired sample t-tests focusing on skill (T1-T2, T2-T4, T1-T4) reveal significant differences at each time period, for each skill, as illustrated and summarized in Table 8.8: *listening* ($p < .001$; $p = .001$; $p < .001$); *speaking* ($p = .001$; $p = .169$; $p < .001$); *reading* ($p = .040$; $p = .001$; $p = .001$); *writing* ($p = .002$; $p = .002$; $p = < .001$); *interaction* ($p = .004$; $p = .023$; $p < .001$). With the exception of T2-T4

Table 8.8 Paired sample t-test results for experimental groups by skill

	Stage	M (SD)	t	df	CI lower	CI upper	r^2
Listening	T1-T2	.41*** (.58)	−4.65	43	−.59	−.23	0.33
	T1-T4	.82*** (.64)	−7.40	32	−1.04	−.59	0.63
	T2-T4	.42** (.66)	−3.68	32	−.66	−.19	0.30
Speaking	T1-T2	.36** (.69)	−3.52	43	−.57	−.16	0.22
	T1-T4	.55*** (.56)	−5.56	32	−.75	−.33	0.49
	T2-T4	.15 (.62)	−1.41	32	−.37	.07	0.58
Reading	T1-T2	.23* (.71)	−2.12	43	−.44	−.01	0.94
	T1-T4	.58** (.87)	−3.81	32	−.88	−.27	0.31
	T2-T4	.33** (.54)	−3.55	32	−.53	−.14	0.28
Writing	T1-T2	.36* (.75)	−3.22	43	−.59	−.14	0.19
	T1-T4	.79*** (.89)	−5.07	32	−1.11	−.47	0.45
	T2-T4	.39* (.66)	−3.44	32	−.63	−.16	0.27
Interaction	T1-T2	.41* (.90)	−3.02	43	−.68	−.14	0.16
	T1-T4	.76*** (.66)	−6.57	32	−.99	−.52	0.57
	T2-T4	.30* (.73)	−2.39	32	−.56	−.46	0.15

Note: *p < .05, **p < .01, ***p < .001.

Table 8.9 Independent t-test results for experimental groups by skill

	Stage	M (SD) CAPT	M (SD) PAPER	t	df	CI lower	CI upper	r^2
Listening	T1	2.88 (.741)	3.10 (.553)	−1.12	42	−.630	.180	.03
	T2	3.33 (.565)	3.45 (.605)	−.661	42	−.473	.240	.01
	T4	3.59 (.618)	3.88 (.500)	−1.46	31	−.688	.114	.06
Speaking	T1	2.96 (.751)	2.70 (.733)	1.15	42	−.195	.712	.03
	T2	3.33 (.482)	3.05 (.605)	1.73	42	−.047	.617	.06
	T4	3.53 (.514)	3.19 (.655)	1.67	31	−.075	.759	.08
Reading	T1	2.71 (.751)	2.75 (.716)	−.187	42	−.491	.408	.08
	T2	2.83 (.565)	3.10 (.641)	−1.47	42	−.633	.100	.05
	T4	3.00 (.791)	3.50 (.632)	−1.99	31	−1.01	.01	.11
Writing	T1	2.54 (.799)	2.30 (.801)	1.01	42	−.241	.724	.02
	T2	2.75 (.532)	2.85 (.671)	−.552	42	−.466	.266	0
	T4	3.06 (.659)	3.31 (.479)	−1.26	31	−.665	.157	.05
Interaction	T1	3.04 (.690)	2.65 (.745)	1.81	42	−.046	.829	.07
	T2	3.25 (.442)	3.30 (.657)	−.30	42	−.386	.286	0
	T4	3.47 (.514)	3.63 (.619)	−.781	31	−.558	.249	.02

Note: Maximum score = 5.

speaking as italicized above, this indicates an overall picture of improvement for each skill with the lapse of each six-week period.

This reported positive trajectory of gains at each stage is not consistent across groups, however. First, both groups make significance gains at the $p < .005$ level with large to very large effect sizes for (i) T1-T2, T1-T4 *listening and speaking* (T2-T4 *listening only*) and (ii) T1-T4 *writing and interaction*. Though these gains differ in degree of significance, these are less noteworthy as no statistical significance is found on independent t-test analyses and all confidence intervals cross 0 in Table 8.9. This result confirms overall homogeneity between the CAPT and PAPER groups for each of these skills, at each stage.

Second, in contrast, the remaining skills and time variables reveal distinct group differences. No statistical significance is found with the CAPT group other than T2-T4 *interaction* where significance is noted ($p = .041$). In contrast, the PAPER group make significant gains on all skills, over all time periods (with the exception of T2-T4 interaction): *reading*, $p = .031$, $p = .004$, $p = .002$; *writing*, $p = .001$, $p = .014$, $p = .000$; *interaction*, $p = .019$, $p = .000$. Despite this, referring back to the independent t-test results noted in Table 8.9, there is no statistical between-group significance which suggests any differences found between the groups are not noteworthy. The *mean* scores in Table 8.7 confirm

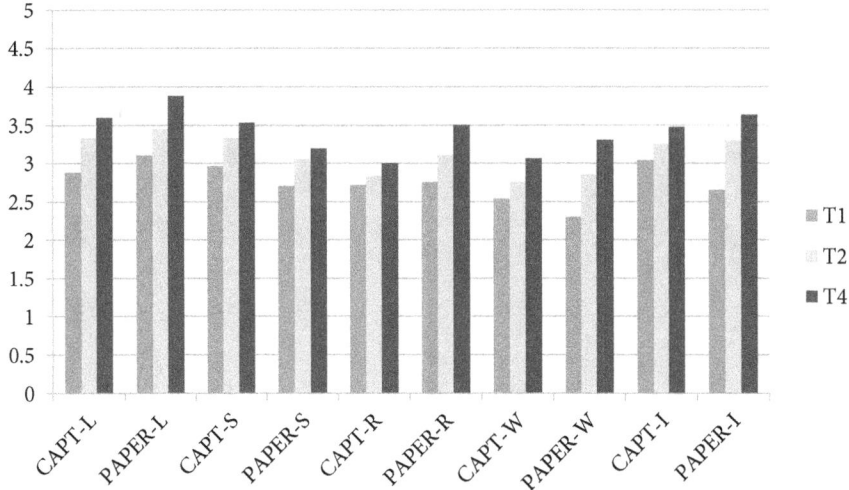

Note.
L = listening, S = speaking, R = reading, W = writing, I = interaction
T1 = pretest, T2 = posttest, T4 = six-week delayed test
1 = poor/beginner, 5 = excellent/native-like

Figure 8.1 Evolution of skills assessment by the experimental groups T1, T2 and T4

that there is < 1.0 difference in the between group scores for each skill, at each test stage, and that the PAPER group are not necessarily weaker at any stage. This suggests the groups' overall skills were comparable at the start of each stage and the PAPER group made only marginally greater advances between stages (though this was almost 50 per cent of the time periods analysed) according to their self-reporting.

Third, a basic pattern emerges between groups in terms of individual skills (Figure 8.1). Without exception, all groups report a small to moderate increase in competence for each skill, within the twelve-week test period. For the CAPT and PAPER groups, *'writing'* is consistently awarded the lowest scores within the five skills, across all three test stages. This suggests, for these learner groups, *writing* is the most difficult skill to improve, or there were fewer opportunities to practise, or a combination of both. In comparison, firstly *'listening'* and then *'interaction'* generally receive the highest scores overall for these two groups.

In summary, the CAPT, PAPER and control groups self-report small to moderate increases in competence for each skill with the lapse of each six-week time period. Disparity in the CAPT and PAPER groups' evaluations at T1, T2 and T4 is observed but given the small margins in *mean* score differences, supported by no between-group statistical significance, these differences are not considered statistically meaningful. All three learner groups consistently report *'writing'* to be their weakest skill at each test stage, whilst *'listening'* and *'interaction'* generally receive higher scores across the test phases. Interestingly, no maximum scores (5) were awarded for any skill, at any test phase. The highest score is generally, but not exclusively, awarded at T4 though this fails to reach '5' (excellent) for any skill.

Discussion

This chapter returns to discuss the original research questions guiding the study. The chapter begins with analysing the effectiveness of the explicit instructional intervention which is the main focus of this investigation (RQ1). This includes observations specific to the request and apology data regarding strategies and formulaic language employed T1-T4. The variability exhibited in the production of non-target-like requests and apologies concludes each of these sections. Next, the chapter examines the effectiveness of the differentiated training materials (RQ2). Finally, the results from the two-part self-evaluation questionnaire on English language use are considered in relation to frequency of language use, prolonged L2 stay and pragmatic development (RQ3).

9.1. Research question 1

How effective is explicit instruction in developing the pragmatic competence of requests and apologies in Chinese learners of English at a British Higher Education institution during a study abroad stay?

Several key findings are noticeable from the analyses in Chapter 7. First, regarding instruction, the study appears to show the positive outcomes of teaching speech acts in the classroom, providing a link between the explicit teaching of requests and apologies, and the improved performance of the experimental groups over the twelve-week period. This finding lends support to previous research on the value of explicit instruction (e.g. Taguchi 2015), sustained length of treatment (Jeon & Kaya 2006; Plonsky & Zhuang 2019), inclusion of awareness-raising and focused classroom practice (e.g. Shively 2008), and the need for learners' attention to be drawn to 'notice' language features for intake and production (Schmidt 1993).

When considering the reasons behind the experimental groups' post-intruction advances in request and apology production, raising awareness of the local cultural expectations for what constitutes successful and appropriate language was highly effective. The claims that politeness is realized in different ways in different cultures (e.g. Leech 2014; Ogiermann 2009), and that the misapplication of L1 rules to L2 language use is a main source of pragmatic miscommunication (e.g. Sabaté i Dalmau & Curell i Gotor 2007; Sifianou 1992), appear to hold true for the present investigation at the pre-instruction stage. For instance, whereas politeness is said to be marked by indirectness in Western cultures (Leech 2014), Chinese speakers often value directness as a key politeness principle (Lee-Wong 1994; Yu 1999). This feature was evident in many of the pretest request responses. Furthermore, the pretest request and apology responses revealed substantial negative L1 transfer, most likely influenced by positive politeness systems in Chinese culture where group values are said to dominate. The intervention appears to have enhanced L2 sociopragmatic awareness and reduced negative L1 transfer. The regularity of the cross-cultural discussions included in the intervention may have heightened the participants' cross-cultural sensitivity, whilst the introduction of a formulaic-based approach for request and apology language appears to have been a highly effective language learning strategy to also increase the learners' range of expressions.

9.1.1. Request language

Given the specific academic context presented and the high status interlocutors featured in the scenarios at the test stages, learners did not need a varied repertoire of request strategies to provide satisfactory responses and could successfully rely on a limited range of polite core requests and alerters, with additional external moves for more sensitive requests. Whilst this is welcome news in terms of where focused instruction needs to be, learners clearly did not either initially possess this requisite language or lacked the sociopragmatic knowledge to be able to apply status-preserving strategies within a particular scenario. This finding suggests that upon arrival in the UK, learners are not fully prepared for basic staff-student communication in a SA stay. Only those participants exposed to instruction benefitted and exhibited more target-like request behaviour.

Improvements in request production are most notable in strategies which were underdeveloped at T1: *polite core request* (internal modifier) and *self-criticism* (external modifier). Whilst the use of conventionally indirect strategies by the majority of learners in this study supports literature that this is the preferred universal feature for realizing requests (Blum-Kulka et al. 1989; Trosborg 1995; Wang 2011; Yu 1999), the data show that, above all, ability modals were the preferred strategy choice at T1 and, consequently, few instances of the more complex core requests (bi-clausals) – '*Would you mind ...* ', '*Would it be possible to ...* ', '*I (was) wonder(ing) if ...* ' – are apparent. Research suggests L1 English speakers draw on a much richer and varied set of polite requests, such as those illustrated above, whilst L2 users have a more limited range and are challenged by adopting the most appropriate expression for different social contexts (Lin 2009; Wang 2011; Yu 1999). Two possible explanations are offered for this cross-cultural variability. First, Yu's (1999) research shows Chinese EFL learners rarely use conditionals as a mitigating device as a result of L1 interference. Chinese language is described as a non-inflectional language which does not differentiate tense, case and person with different verb forms. This unfamiliarity with using past-tense modals as conditionals such as '*Would*', as a politeness device, means they are seldom used in Chinese request language. Furthermore, as reported previously, bi-clausal structures do not exist in Chinese which pose further challenges when these are adopted frequently by English L1 users.

The complexity of bi-clausal structures may also account for their low frequency in Chinese learner data (Wang 2011). For L1 users of English, bi-clausals provide an important syntactic device for polite situations or where imposition is high. Bi-clausal structures are typically longer, more elaborate and, therefore, syntactically challenging for learners of English. In contrast, and as exhibited in this present study at T1, Chinese participants typically opt for syntactically simpler and shorter requests, as can be effectively realized with ability modals. The fact that ability modals are also one of the earliest features learned (Chang 2010) suggests a reason for its continued overuse. The learners in this study have yet to achieve an advanced stage of proficiency which may also be symptomatic of the reliance on ability modals. That the learners in the experimental groups were able to substitute their use of ability modals with more appropriate sequences such as the more challenging bi-clausals at T2 and beyond supports the case for introducing these as formulaic wholes during input.

Direct strategies in the form of '*I want*', '*I need*' also offer a way to formulate a request in an economical way, with much less processing effort (Lee-Wong 1994). Nevertheless, direct strategies occur infrequently in the present data set, failing to corroborate earlier research. It is plausible that Brown and Levinson's imposition variables may account for this trend. According to Lee-Wong (1994), it would not be appropriate for Chinese speakers to use direct strategies in high imposition contexts, as presented in the test scenarios. Infrequent occurrence of direct strategy use is not entirely unexpected then in this study given the high-status interlocutors. This gives the impression that Brown and Levinson's variables are indeed important considerations for Chinese speakers, mirroring previous observations (Yu 1999).

The examples which follow to illustrate these points are labelled according to scenario/time (T)/group (CAPT, PAPER, control)/participant number (P) in Tables 9.1 and 9.2. The data set in Table 9.1 reveals all responses employing direct strategies, independent of time period, received the lowest scores of 1 or 2. This is likely to be attributed to the inappropriate use of directness (Sc3/T1/CAPT/P3; Sc1/T1/PAPER/P1), even when all other requisite conditions are satisfied (Sc2/T2/PAPER/P12). The latter case of Chinese L1 transfer dictates directness is commonly softened with the use of 'please' (Wang 2011), as demonstrated in the first example in Table 9.1.

The second main request device to benefit considerably from instruction concerns the external modifier, *self-criticism* (see Table 9.2 reporting T1-T2 changes for participants P9 and P1). Unlike the polite core requests which featured in all scenarios, self-criticism featured only in the 'classroom access' scenario so this was likely to be a contextually sensitive device to mitigate the high imposition and social distance. Whether participants were not sensitive to or perhaps had a different perception of the situation is unclear, but self-criticism as a mitigating device has not been reported as a feature of Chinese requests in earlier work (see Chapter 4). This example is illustrative of the necessity to have cross-cultural awareness to inform linguistic choices.

Table 9.1 Examples of direct strategy use in the request data

Scenario 1: Classroom access		
T1	PAPER: P1	'Excuse me sir. I left my mobile phone in the classroom but the building is closed. So **I want you to open the door** please.' (average rater score = 1)
Scenario 2: Essay extension		
T2	PAPER: P12	'I'm sorry to bother you. I didn't complete the essay. I'm sick and bad coughing last week so it's my fault. **I want another time for my essay**. It won't happen again.' (average rater score = 2)
Scenario 3: Book a study room		
T1	CAPT: P3	'Excuse me lady. **I want to find out** how to book a study room.' (average rater score = 1)

Table 9.2 Comparisons of self-criticism strategy use in the request data T1-T2

Scenario 1: Classroom access		
T1	CAPT: P9	'Sorry. My mobile phone has been left in a classroom. Can I go to the classroom to take my phone?' (average rater score = 2)
T2	CAPT P9	'I'm very sorry. I left my mobile phone in a classroom. **It's my fault**. I was wondering if you can open the building for me?' (average rater score = 5)
T1	PAPER: P1	'Hi. I have something wrong. My mobile phone was left in a classroom. But I cannot enter because now is too late to come in. So I want to go to classroom to find my phone.' (average rater score = 1)
T2	PAPER: P1	'Excuse me. Would it be possible to open the building for me? I am so sorry for asking you to do that. I have left my phone in the classroom. **It's my fault.**' (average rater score = 4)

Moderate improvements in request production can be observed with *alerters* (internal modifier), *explicit apologies* and *grounders* (both external modifiers). All appear to be moderately salient for participants, pre-instruction. The social expectation to use appropriate address terms in Chinese culture (Lee-Wong 1994) seems to have been transferred to the participants' requests in this data, though a shift to more formulaic expressions at T2 may have been deemed more appropriate. In terms of external modification devices, both *explicit apologies* and *grounders* (explanations) have been reported as common devices used to mitigate the imposition of a request and to mark politeness (Lin 2009; Yu 1999). The data in the present study support this claim with around 50 per cent of all learners employing grounders and at least 50 per cent of participants employing explicit apologies at T1 in the relevant scenarios.

Another trend within the data is the variability of changes in non-target-like features of request language. Whilst all the features evidence some post-instruction decline for the experimental groups, this was achieved with varying degrees of success. Specifically, participants were able to revise their use of (i) ability modals, (ii) direct strategies, (iii) speaker-oriented perspective, (iv) explicit apologies and (v) because-therefore pattern of information sequencing. It is likely that the former group of language features evidenced a greater decline as a direct result of the formulaic polite request expressions which were explicitly introduced as part of the instruction. These expressions typically comprised past-tense modals and bi-clausal structures, as described earlier. Specifically, the instruction introduced the phrases '*Would you mind*', '*Do you mind*', '*I was wondering if*', '*Would it be possible to*' (high power-distance-imposition variables) and '*Is it OK if*, '*Can I*', '*Could I*' (low power-distance-imposition variables). Consequently, ability modals, direct strategies and speaker-oriented perspectives decrease post-instruction or are completely removed from the interlanguage, as learners adopt the relevant pre-fabricated chunks. In contrast, instances of *apologies* and *because-therefore information sequencing* remain high, although there is no evidence to suggest this reflected in lower scores.

The success of adopting these formulaic expressions lends support to research claims concerning their importance for effective communication (Pawley & Syder 1983; Schmitt 2004; Wray 2008) and underlines how much formulaic language can, in fact, be found in speech acts such as requests (Wang 2011). That the learners did not always have L1-like command of these formulaic expressions post-instruction (see Table 9.3) but were still successful based on the raters' scores raises two interesting points. Firstly, there does appear to be a social expectation that conventionalized expressions are used, as outlined in Chapter 3. The influence of formulaic expressions is further underlined in that simply attempting to employ them, though not always syntactically or grammatically correct, was still considered positive, as reflected in the high raters' scores.

The second point concerns the perception of pragmatic competence versus grammatical competence for successful communication. As highlighted by Bardovi-Harlig and Dörnyei (1998), ESL tutors in the host community overwhelmingly favoured pragmatic ability over grammatical ability, whilst the reverse was true for EFL tutors in the at-home environment. This perception of the importance of pragmatic awareness seems true for this data and the examples presented above. Thomas's (1983: 96–7) seminal paper, seen as a driver of pragmatic studies, provides an emphatic distinction between the consequences of pragmatic and grammatical errors: '[W]hile grammatical error may reveal a speaker to be a less than proficient language user, pragmatic failure reflects badly on him/her as a person.' Academic contexts where regular staff-student contact takes place may be particularly sensitive to personal impressions, further highlighting the need to develop sufficient competency to produce pragmatically appropriate requests.

The non-target-like request features which evidence a much smaller decline in frequency may be attributed to implicit as opposed to explicit learning. Neither *apologies* nor *information sequencing* was explicitly targeted during the

Table 9.3 Examples of non-target-like conventional expressions in the request data

Scenario 1: Classroom access		
T2	PAPER: P4	'Excuse me sir. I'm a student here. I left my phone in a classroom. **Could you possible** open the door of the building for me? I'm very thank you for this.' (average rater score 4.5)
T2	CAPT: P18	'I'm so sorry that I left my mobile phone in the classroom. **I was wonder if I** can get my phone. It's my fault. It won't happen again.' (average rater score = 4)
Scenario 2: Essay extension		
T3	PAPER: P6	'Sorry to bother you. I'm very sorry about that not completed my essay because I was sick these days. **Would it be possibly to** give me some extra for me to do this?' (average rater score = 5)
T4	CAPT: P5	'I'm very sorry about that because I spend more time to get some information. It's my fault. **Would you mind to give me** extra time? Thank you.' (average rater score = 4)
Scenario 3: Book a study room		
T2	CAPT: P11	'I'm sorry. I don't know how to find out how to book a study room. **Do you mind to help me** find it?' (average rater score = 4)
T2	CAPT: P5	'Excuse me. **Could you mind tell me** how to book a study room. I'm a new student so I don't know how to do it.' (average rater score = 5)

intervention, but instead was there to be implicitly learned through the specific expressions introduced and discussions of appropriate request language. It is plausible that, as learners were not specifically guided to notice these features or when to use them, not every learner was able to adjust their existing practice. Consequently, these non-target-like features evidence a slower decline which further underlines the importance of explicit awareness-raising techniques, following Schmidt's (1993) noticing hypothesis, which appears to be best facilitated by explicit instruction.

The final features to be discussed here concern the *underuse of internal modification* and the associated *overuse of external modification*. Both features are found to be inextricably linked as studies report Chinese learners typically rely on external modification at the expense of internal modification, though the reverse pattern is evident in L1 speaker request production (Lin 2009; Wang

2011). Lee-Wong's (1994) findings that the majority of *internal modification* is realized through relatively few strategies such as *please* and *apologies*, and address terms is also confirmed in this study's data set. *Intensifiers* also feature to some degree as a means of increasing impact. The data yield no evidence, however, of *downtoners* or *hesitators*, as employed by English L1 users, suggesting these need specific instructional attention.

Regarding *external modification*, this has been shown to be the preferred way for Chinese learners to increase politeness and the chances of the request being carried out (Chen 2006; Wang 2011; Yu 1999). The first explanation offered relates to previous comments that internal modification typical of L1 users is too complex and challenging for L2 users. External supportive moves, on the other hand, are seen as an easier opportunity to achieve similar levels of mitigation and politeness: a strategy transferred from L1 culture where small talk and external modifiers preceding the request are the norm. Consequently, Wang (2011) notes that when making requests, the frequency of supportive moves such as 'grounders' typically increases for Chinese learners. A reported drawback of this reliance on external modification is requests which exceed typical L1 speaker length and are often described as verbose (Chen 2006; Wang 2011). Multiple grounders, in particular, are often the cause of extraneous detail within non-target requests. In this data set, rather than frequency, it seems the *content of grounders* was more influential on the scores, according to the raters (Table 9.4). In general, with all other requisite strategies being equal, explanations which are out of the speaker's control appear more acceptable than those over which the speaker had a direct influence. For instance, explanations accredited to sickness were preferable to personal reasons such as being busy with friends, as the examples in Table 9.4 illustrate.

A further cause of verbosity is said to be attributed to L2 user insecurities concerning their language ability; repetition and lengthier utterances can be a compensatory strategy to ensure the message is communicated (Wang 2011), as shown in the examples in Table 9.5.

To sum up, the data mainly support existing request research in terms of the effectiveness of explicit instruction. This was particularly evident with the underdeveloped T1 request strategies and non-target-like forms, attributed to challenges with L1-L2 mapping. Exposure to the L2 did not appear to be influential in the acquisition of request language without intervention. Language features considered requisite for successful production of requests, in the academic scenarios presented, included observing politeness, use of formulaic language, quality of the *grounder*, use of internal modification and the need to

Table 9.4 Examples of grounders in the request data

		Scenario 1: Classroom access
T2	CAPT: P8	'Sorry to bother you. I haven't complete my essay. I'm sorry **because I was sick**. Could you mind give me extra time to do it?' (average rater score = 4)
T3	PAPER: P10	'Yes, I'm very sorry I didn't complete my essay **because I have some troubles of my bank**. This is my fault. Would it be possible to have extra time? Thank you.' (average rater score = 4)
T2	CAPT: P4	'Excuse me. Sorry to bother you professor but I'm really sorry for my essay **because yesterday it's my best friend's party and I have to celebrate with her.** It's my fault. Do you mind giving me extra time?' (average rater score = 2)
T2	PAPER: P16	'I'm so sorry I not complete my essay. **Yesterday I go out and play with my friend** so I can't complete the essay. It's my fault and would you mind giving me extra time? I promise it won't happen again.' (average rater score = 2)

Table 9.5 Examples of strategy repetition in the request data

		Scenario 2: Book a study room
T2	CAPT: P4	'Yes, **I was wondering if you could help me to find out how to book a study room** and I want to study in the library and use the School's internet services but I don't know how to do it so **could you please help me to book a study room?**' (average rater score = 2)
T3	PAPER: P19	'Yes, hello. **I wonder if you can help me book a room for study** because I didn't have a living room at home so I just asking **could you help me book a study room.** Thank you.' (average rater score = 2)

avoid verbosity. In contrast, despite the data showing production of explicit apologies, information sequencing and the grammatical accuracy of formulaic language were at times non-target-like, these appeared to have less relevance and did not impact on the overall evaluation of the request responses.

9.1.2. Apology language

In terms of the apology strategies produced by the participants, a general pattern of performance was observable evidencing both cultural convergence and divergence in the use of apology strategies. Firstly, where requisite production of strategies was salient to the learners at T1, all participants, regardless of group, continued to produce this language throughout the test stages. Slight improvements were evident for the experimental groups who had received instruction at the posttest stages, however. Areas which were already part of the groups' knowledge base include '*offer of repair*' and '*expressions of regret*': both of which are reported as being a universal feature across a number of languages (e.g. Blum-Kulka et al. 1989; Trosborg 1995).

Formulaic expressions such as '*I'm sorry*' are further reported as being one of the earliest chunks acquired by L2 users, even at beginner level (Chang 2010) which may also account for its high frequency in this data. In fact, several studies have reported the preference for Japanese learners of English (Barnlund & Yoshioka 1990; Kondo 1997; Maeshiba et al. 1996), Korean learners of English (Byon 2006) and Catalan learners of English (Sabaté i Dalmau & Curell i Gotor 2007) to produce multiple explicit apologies, or IFIDs, to humble the speaker and appeal to the hearer in an apology situation. Apologies produced in this way signal '*I'm sorry*' to be substantive rather than ritualistic (Goffman 1971) and ensure genuine regret is emphasized.

In addition, this use of more than one IFID is reported to be the preferred way to intensify an apology in positive-face language systems in comparison to British English which typically incorporate internal IFID adverbials such as '*really*' and '*terribly*' to signal intensification, due to their 'highly routinised' nature (Aijmer 1996; Nureddeen 2008; Olshtain & Cohen 1983; Sabaté i Dalmau & Curell i Gotor 2007; Trosborg 1995). High levels of these features of multiple IFIDs to intensify the apology also appear in the Chinese participants' data from the present study, though these reduce by at least 50 per cent following instruction. In this case, it is plausible that the raters considered multiple apologies to be excessive rather than a means of conveying apologetic sincerity, and this may have had a negative effect on overall assessments of the responses at the T1 phases. The frequency of adverbial use to intensify the IFID was generally constant throughout each time period for all groups. Most adverbials appeared in the missed meeting with tutor scenario > noisy party > lost library book, and learners tended to opt for the following adverbials, in the order '*so*', '*very*', '*really*' – a preference mirrored in Chang's (2010) Chinese learners of English. What changed is the introduction of the adverbial '*terribly*', following instruction, though this failed to reach the same increased levels with no more than 20 per cent of the learners employing this.

Secondly, where learners failed to produce the requisite language at T1, marked improvements were evident in the experimental groups' performance, highlighting the success of the treatment. Trosborg (1987) notes that a single routinized formula is inadequate when the offence goes beyond a certain level and other strategies are needed for redressive action. This is true of the production task contexts in this study where there appeared to be an expectation from the raters that the explicit apology would be enhanced with other strategies in each scenario. This seems to have become salient to the participants through instruction. As a general observation, this improved performance was sustained to T3 but slightly decreased at T4. The 'most improved' strategies following treatment included '*admission of responsibility*' and '*promise of forbearance*'. Both the former and the latter are said to inherently threaten positive face (Nureddeen 2008), so it is plausible this is the reason for initial avoidance, given the positive politeness culture associated with China. Conversely, the control group failed to match the experimental groups' performance, maintaining consistently low production of the requisite language.

Interestingly, both experimental groups almost consistently adopted the sequencing of strategies as introduced in the intervention when producing their apologies at the posttest stages (Table 9.6), regardless of the number of strategies chosen to realize it: *explicit apology › explanation › admission of responsibility › offer of repair › promise of forbearance*. The examples presented below are labelled according to scenario/time (T)/group (CAPT, PAPER, control)/participant number (P).

This five-step sequencing of expression of apology > explanation > acknowledgement of responsibility > offer of repair > promise of forbearance appears to have been an accessible formula for the participants to adopt, memorize and reproduce. The results are that their utterances are successfully

Table 9.6 Sequencing pattern of strategy use in the apology data

Scenario: Lost library book		
T2	CAPT: P4	'Excuse me. I'm very sorry (*explicit apology*). I have lost a book that I borrowed in the library. I think I left it some place but I couldn't find it (*explanation*). It's my fault. (*admission of responsibility*) I'll pay for it. (*offer of repair*). It won't happen again (*promise of forbearance*).' (average rater score = 5)
Scenario: Missed meeting with tutor		
T2	PAPER: P10	'I'm so sorry for missing a meeting with you (*explicit apology*). Last Tuesday I suddenly had an important thing about my family but I forgot told you about it (*explanation*). It's my fault (*admission of responsibility*). I should send an email to you next time (*offer of repair*). It won't happen again (*promise of forbearance*).' (average rater score = 4)

organized and their messages clear. Regarding language choices within these strategies, when formulaic expressions were taught such as *'It's my fault'* and *'It won't happen again'*, these are reproduced most frequently and successfully within the apology utterances of the experimental groups, although at times the participants do not have complete command of them: *'It won't be to happen again'*, *'It won't be happened again'*. Even early research has shown English apologies to be extremely formulaic, governed by relatively few lexical items and syntactic patterns (e.g. Aijmer & Aijmer 1996; Holmes 1990; Trosborg 1995). This may account for the success with which the instructed participants were able to master and reproduce these expressions successfully in a short period of time. Sykes (2009, 2013) also reported that simplicity of formula facilitates learning at the lexical level but is not always found at the form level with accuracy (Johnson & De Haan 2013). These findings also offer further support to the positive benefits behind learning language as self-contained wholes, rather than individual items (Bardovi-Harlig 2009; Kecskes 2000b; Schmitt 2004; Wray 2008).

By comparison, the control group is less successful at achieving organization and clarity of message, without the benefit of instruction. The control group responses also mostly begin the remedial action with an IFID such as 'I'm sorry'. Beyond this, there is no obvious pattern of strategy choice and order, which in itself is not necessarily a problem. However, supporting previous research (Chang 2010; Olshtain & Cohen 1983; Trosborg 1995), the data reveal the apologies produced by the control group on many occasions are verbose. The messages are often impeded by disorganization and structured with inappropriate piecemeal items of grammar and lexis extracted from their existing knowledge. The example in Table 9.7 is representative of these features.

Table 9.7 Non-target-like pattern of strategy use in the apology data

Scenario: Noisy party		
T2	Control: P6	'Excuse me sir. I'm here to apologize to you because I had a party at my flat with my friend and there were students complaining to you about the noise and I think it's true that it's my mistake and I promise it won't again. I hope you can excuse me and I hope you can accept my sincere apology. Words can't describe how sorry I am. I wonder if there's anything I can do to make up for my mistake.' (average rater score = 2)

Table 9.8 Non-target-like linguistic forms in the apology data

Scenario: Lost library book		
T2	Control: P14	'Yes madam. I lost a book. I am so sorry about that (*explicit apology*). Maybe I will try and find this book and if I still cannot find it, I will make compensation to this (*offer of repair*). It won't happen this thing again (*promise of forbearance*).' (average rater score = 3)

In addition, mirroring Linnell et al.'s (1992) findings, the control group often produced functionally adequate but syntactically inadequate forms, as represented by the example in Table 9.8.

Regarding the non-target-like language features included in the instruction, two main findings are evident. Firstly, the instruction appears to have triggered a declining effect of inappropriate language use for the experimental groups by making the participants consciously aware of L1/L2 differences and the effects of negative L1 transfer. The CAPT and PAPER groups' production of *'inappropriate requests for forgiveness'*, *'inappropriate address terms'* and the *'because-therefore' pattern* have all but disappeared at the posttest stages after these interlanguage features were targeted as infelicitous during treatment. *'Inappropriate address forms'* within the alerter, in particular, have been replaced by suitable alternative fixed expressions, serving the same purpose of gaining the interlocutor's attention. Phrases such as *'Sorry to bother you'* and *'Excuse me'* were included in the instruction and successfully adopted as more appropriate alternatives by the experimental groups.

Secondly, apology strategies reported to be under-represented in L2 utterances have greatly increased as these become more salient for the experimental groups as key strategies to producing successful utterances. Research suggests that producing *'explanations'* is linguistically and cognitively demanding for learners (Chang 2010; Trosborg 1987). The data here show an increase of around 50 per cent following instruction but, interestingly, the participants only rely on a limited range of explanations such as *'having something important to deal with'* or *'being sick'*, perhaps indicating this is a more complex strategy to master. From a cultural perspective, explanations and making excuses for an offence are reported to be uncommon in Asian cultures as these strategies conflict with the need to be deferent in a face-threatening situation (Kim 2008; Kondo 1997). This could further account for the low T1 production. Contrary to these positive outcomes, the control group continue to exhibit non-target-like behaviour throughout the twelve-week period with little change to their strategy or languages choices.

This present study has found little or no evidence of other non-target-like language features reported in earlier apology research, particularly those identified in Linnel et al.'s (1992) study, namely *inappropriate use of 'I apologize'* or phrase for the context, or *excessive offers* of repair and *imperatives*. Contrasting the Linnel et al. (1992) study, given the high status interlocutors and contexts featured in this study, it is unsurprising that there are no instances of '*I apologize*' being used inappropriately as its production does not appear out of place in any of the situations presented in this study. In fact, the raters awarded high scores to many responses containing this expression. Similarly, as shown in Table 9.9, there was only one occurrence of an inappropriate phrase (T2 PAPER group participant) and two instances of the use of an imperative as a directive (T2 control group participants).

In Table 9.10, six instances of excessive offers of repair (highlighted in bold) are found in the T1 (CAPT × 1) and T2 data (CAPT × 1, control × 3) but such infrequent occurrences (from two participants) are not noteworthy, aside from presenting these as socially awkward examples to add to existing corpora on this feature.

Table 9.9 Other non-target-like apology features

Inappropriate phrase		
Noisy party (T2)	PAPER: P15	'Hi **my mate**. I'm sorry do a lot of noise in the hall. I will tell to him to don't make the noise. Sorry.' (average rater score = 1)
Use of an imperative		
Missed tutor appointment (T2)	Control: P5	'That's why I'm here. I want to apologize for it. I should have emailed you for the miss but I forgot. **Please arrange** another one for me.' (average rater score = 2)
Missed tutor appointment (T2)	Control: P17	'First of all I'm sorry I missed the meeting from last Tuesday. I forgot to sent the email to you. **Please tell me** some information from it.' (average rater score = 2)

Table 9.10 Excessive offers of repair in the apology data

Excessive offer of repair		
Missed tutor appointment (T1)	CAPT: P24	'I'm very sorry. I missed a meeting with you. But I didn't email you to explain. Now I want to give you a formal apology. **And this is my gift for you, a potted plant.** I hope you'll like.' (average rater score = 2)

Excessive offer of repair			
Missed tutor appointment (T2)	CAPT: P24		'I'm very sorry I missed a meeting with you but I didn't email you to explain. It's my fault. Last Thursday I have to go to hospital and **this is my gift for you, a potted plant.** I hope you'll like and next time I'll tell you immediately.' (average rater score = 2)
Missed tutor appointment (T2)	Control: P6		'I'm awfully sorry about it and I feel bad about it. **I can do anything I can to make it up to you** and please accept my sincere apology.' (average rater score = 1.5)
Lost library book (T2)	Control: P6		'Excuse me madam. I'm sorry that I've lost a book I borrowed from the library. It's all my fault. **I will do anything I can to make it up for you.**' (average rater score = 2)
Noisy party (T2)	Control: P6		'Excuse me sir. I'm here to apologize to you because I had a party at my flat with my friend and there were students complaining to you about the noise and I think it's true that it's my mistake and I promise it won't again. I hope you can excuse me and I hope you can accept my sincere apology. **Words can't describe how sorry I am. I wonder if there's anything I can do to make up for my mistake.**' (average rater score = 2)
Noisy party (T1)	Control: P1		'Oh sir. I'm so sorry to have such a big noises to disturb my neighbours and disturb you. I appreciate that it's my fault and I don't do that anymore, if that's ok. **I think I should get punish and help you to do something to ease the pain.** Again I'm so sorry to do that and I hope you can forgive us.' (average rater score = 2)

The data have highlighted several key findings. Firstly, whilst the claims for universality of language can be attested to in this study to some extent (inclusion of '*explicit apologies*' and '*offers of repair*'), this is outweighed by evidence to suggest language use is culture-specific when analysing apology production for Chinese learners of English. Secondly, development of appropriate apology production may be excessively hindered by the inadequate application of first language positive-face value systems (e.g. China) to second language negative-politeness value systems (e.g. the UK) as a cause of miscommunication. The findings evidence that, at T1, most participants fall back on their first language pragmatic systems at some point, resulting in their utterances being negatively judged for appearing over-polite or impolite. Thirdly, this non-target-like behaviour largely continues for the control group during the twelve-week period who have not benefitted from the training received by the experimental groups.

Overall, explicit pragmatic instruction has been found to be highly effective for both experimental groups (CAPT and PAPER) for developing successful request and apology language. Specifically, the results demonstrate that underdeveloped pragmalinguistic strategies at T1 improved significantly post-instruction at T2. For requests, these include the improved use of bi-clausal structures such as '*I was wondering if*'. For apologies, these include expressions for not repeating an offence such as '*It won't happen again*'. Improved sociopragmatic competence is also evident with participants seemingly becoming more sensitized to the context-dependent nature of strategy choice following treatment. Instructed participants appear more aware of the importance of strategies such as *self-criticism* (requests), *admissions of responsibility* (apologies) and *promises not to repeat offences* (apologies) in particular situations where, pre-instruction, L1 interference may have been accountable for a disregard or avoidance of these strategies. Negative L1 transfer also seemed to be the main factor for the non-target-like features of requests and apologies as summarized in previous empirical investigations. Post-instruction, all the non-target language features identified at T1 evidenced some decrease, particularly at the lexical level.

Despite the improved experimental group performance T1-T2, marginal attrition in most language areas was evident over T3 and T4, though the results still indicated an improvement on T1 levels. This suggests sustained and distributed classroom practice (Miles 2014) may be more conducive for longer-term recall than intensive, isolated treatments which lack continued attention and practice. Alongside the recommendation that instruction and practice are regularly revisited to maximize learning potential, that the control group failed to make any observable gains in the absence of instruction supports the claims that pragmatic competence is indeed a difficult area to master (Cohen 2008; Taguchi 2015). In addition, sociopragmatic competence, in particular, may be more challenging and tends to develop at a much later stage in natural conditions (Fukuya & Zhang 2002; Sabaté i Dalmau & Curell i Gotor 2007; Shardakova 2005).

Whilst not a specific focus of this book, incorporating the instruction of multiple speech acts within one treatment has proved effective, and some insights have emerged into how some speech acts may be more amenable to either lesson design from a practitioner's perspective or to learning from a student's perspective. For instance, when researching and designing the instructional materials for both speech acts, the complexity of the number of request strategies, and positioning within and surrounding the head act, was more time-consuming to organize into a practical set of training materials. On the other hand, the set of five main apology strategies with accompanying formulaic expressions was easily fashioned into a convenient 'five-step plan' to present to the learners, within the relatively short instructional period. Indeed, the results show participants did appear more well disposed to the accessible way in which the pragmalinguistic and sociopragmatic features of apologies were packaged and delivered within the intervention than with requests. In addition, a reduction of non-target-like features of apologies was evident to a greater effect than with requests.

Linked to the issue of learnability, the success with which the experimental groups adopted request and apology formulaic expressions, and sustained their use, was an unexpected outcome of this study. The claims that formulaic language relieves pressure (Weinart 1995) and is easily recalled (Kecskes 2000a, 2000b) cannot be entirely verified in this study in the absence of any supporting qualitative data. However, suggestions that formulaic language is highly routinized (Pawley & Syder 1983) and saves time and effort (Wray 2000) seem to hold true in the findings presented. Most notably, the fact that the majority of formulaic expressions introduced were short, fixed strings of words seems to advantage the learners. The expressions appeared to be highly recognizable and required little processing to understand them. As a result, the learners expanded their repertoire of formulaic expressions at T2, in comparison to the T1 performance. T1 results evidenced a limited repertoire and were characterized by an overuse of a small number of basic formulaic expressions, as seen in previous studies (Wang 2011; Yu 1999). That the learners employed formulaic language but did not always use these expressions accurately is in line with earlier investigations (Bardovi-Harlig 2009; Johnson & De Haan 2013; Sabaté i Dalmau & Curell i Gotor 2007). What sets the results in this study apart is that the raters' assessments show that accuracy when producing formulaic expressions is *not* requisite to successful use. It appears the intention to employ appropriate expressions is adequately recognized, which placates the need for complete command of their grammatical forms, as long as the message is clear. This finding further acknowledges the importance of pragmatic competence over grammatical competence in the ESL setting, as reported previously (e.g. Bardovi-Harlig & Dörnyei 1998).

9.2. Research question 2

To what extent can computer-animated practice materials, eliciting an oral performance, contribute to the short- and long-term production of requests and apologies, in comparison to traditional paper-based activities, eliciting a written performance?

Within the explicit instructional framework, the two experimental groups (CAPT and PAPER) were subjected to the same treatment conditions but differentiated by practice materials. This allowed for a closer examination of different training approaches and any subsequent effects on request and apology production between the groups.

Whilst the intervention appears to have had a positive effect on the PAPER group's pragmatic development of apologies, the CAPT group intervention seems to have been more beneficial, based on both the raters' assessment of the responses and the higher number of CAPT participants producing requisite mitigating strategies for *requests* (+8.3 learners at T2, +6.6 learners at T3, +3.3 learners at T4) and *apologies* (+9.6 learners at T2, +7.6 learners at T3, +7.0 learners at T4).

Regarding short-term recall of requests and apologies, both groups benefitted from the instruction but the CAPT group, who used computer-animated practice materials, almost always outperformed the PAPER group at T2 in terms of the quality of response, according to the raters. Statistical analyses of the T1-T2 rater differences evidenced this in several ways, including gain score differences between the CAPT and PAPER groups which were found to be statistically significant.

In the case of long-term recall, results were less decisive as both groups evidenced declines in the production of requisite strategies at T3 and T4. Overall, however, the CAPT group still maintained some advantage with several more participants producing the appropriate request and apology language on each scenario. The decrease in sustainability of the input for both experimental groups suggests the need for regular attention and review beyond the treatment cycle.

When investigating the content of responses produced by the two groups, and the superior CAPT performance, the picture is clearer. This was a useful exercise to determine the reasons behind group variability and demonstrated that the CAPT group produced better quality responses in terms of appropriacy and on more occasions following treatment. For instance, the CAPT group produced at least 10 per cent more requisite request and apology strategies at T2 but, in some scenarios, production of requisite strategies improved as much as 40 per cent. In addition, non-target-like features of request and apology language evidenced a greater decline in comparison to the PAPER group. Given that both of these experimental groups were assessed as comparable at the start of the study, and experienced almost identical levels of L2 contact during the instructional period, suggests the CAPT group have been advantaged by the well-documented links between motivation and learning success when exposed to technology-enhanced instruction.

Six months beyond the treatment phase, anecdotal feedback from several participants, who cited examples of successful request or apology post-instruction encounters, suggests the intervention itself was effective and valuable. Feedback identified the cross-cultural discussions, the contextualized communicative focus and practice opportunities as most beneficial for raising their awareness and sensitivity to pragmatic issues. The participants also made reference to the innovative training materials used in class. These comments support the positive results from previous investigations using the CAPT instrument. Administered with the comparable participant pilot group, '*enjoyable*', '*realistic to real life*' and '*helpful for developing interactive skills with NS*' were the top three criteria for preferring the CAPT as a learning tool. These equate to the claims that CALL materials are more motivating (Taguchi 2015), provide authentic, meaningful interaction (Belz 2007), and offer low-risk, simulated opportunities for communicative practice (Sykes et al. 2008). Revisiting Erben et al's (2008) reference to contextualized learning, it is reasonable to suggest that in this study, the CAPT instrument seems to have acted as a scaffolding mechanism for learning by offering greater exposure to meaningful and highly contextualized input. As Cercone (2006: 306) states, '[L]earning and memory are context driven [and] learning should be meaningful for the student.' With these contributory factors in mind, *both* the mode of delivery, with the enhanced audiovisual cues, and the learners' positive experiences of the innovative computer-animated tool, may be the underlying reasons for the CAPT group's overall success.

9.3. Research question 3

What role does the study abroad environment play in the pragmatic development of requests and apologies in Chinese learners of English at a British Higher Education institution during a study abroad stay?

In addition to the intervention, the language contact questionnaire captured participant engagement in the L2 during the SA period. Acknowledging that the findings presented are based on participant self-reports, the limitations of which are discussed in Chapter 10, the data seem to evidence that increased engagement in English use, with individual variation, is concomitant with prolonged SA stay, at least for the participants in this study. These observations support findings in much SA research (e.g. Bardovi-Harlig 2013; Bardovi-Harlig & Bastos 2011; Bella 2011; Taguchi 2008a). Furthermore, whether the groups received instruction or not does not seem to have had an overall impact on these findings, as evidenced by the lack of statistically significant differences and negligible effect sizes between group behaviour at any of the test stages. The main findings from each test stage (T1-T4) are summarized below.

Given the participants are basing their T1 evaluations on their English use pre-arrival to the UK, it is not unexpected that '*service personnel*' and '*stranger*' are interlocutors with whom they have little need or opportunity to interact in English. Despite the participants reporting communication in English with '*instructors*' and '*classmates*' to be their most frequent activity at the pretest stage, the low marks awarded (equated to '*a few times a year*') is still somewhat surprising and suggests, at least from a spoken English perspective, learners are unlikely to have acquired the levels of experience of using English interactively needed for a SA stay. Traditional Chinese teaching and learning practices may account for these results. Firstly, according to Chen et al. (2005) the emphasis in the Chinese classroom is often reported to be on reading, writing and grammar to enhance exam performance, at the expense of oral skills. Gu and Maley (2008) posit Chinese learners can face an academically challenging transition from classroom-based, textbook-focused learning in China, to the student-centred, interactive demands of UK-based teaching and learning. Secondly, the different cultures of learning where high achievers in China can rely on memorization techniques are learning strategies not likely to prepare SA students for the benefits of learning through social interaction (Gao 2006). Thirdly, according to Wen and Clement (2003), a reluctance to communicate is inherent in Chinese cultural values, supporting the data from the present study which reveals, in contrast to speaking in English, listening and reading are more popular activities at T1. The findings further suggest watching English films and listening to English songs to be popular resources for English as at least a '*monthly*' activity on average for the participants at T1. This is a trend which could be exploited more in the Chinese classroom for the benefit of English language learning.

It is encouraging to witness much greater engagement, on at least a weekly basis, with the specific interlocutors at T2, six weeks beyond arrival. This does not support findings of a reluctance to engage in the host environment as documented in previous investigations (Barron 2006; Cheng & Fox 2008; Gao 2006; Myles & Cheng 2003). Increased engagement in English with *service personnel* and *instructors*, in particular, is typical in a SA stay which necessitates independent interaction in a wide range of academic and public encounters. Although institutional support is available for handling more complex tasks such as dealing with visa issues, and often SA participants look for support from their own strong L1 networks, learners must still interact with L1 users of English to some extent to get day-to-day tasks done. This is illustrated in the post-arrival (+ six weeks) findings demonstrating learners in this study self-report to frequently engage with all the interlocutors who might be considered key in a SA stay. The only exception to this increase is interacting in English with '*friends*'. Inside the classroom, the evidence suggests learners are encouraged to use English with their peers within that setting. Outside the classroom, however, findings from other SA studies confirm anecdotal evidence from the researcher's own institution that SA participants are most likely to interact with other users of the same L1 and cultural background, as noted by Ranta and Meckelborg (2013), Cheng and Fox (2008), amongst others. The popularity of watching English films and listening to English songs is maintained from T1 but increases in frequency to at least a '*weekly*' activity six weeks after arrival in the UK.

At T4, twelve weeks beyond arrival in the UK, interaction with '*friends*' does become a weekly activity, whilst interaction with service personnel decreases slightly. The former result may be explained by increased confidence in using English by this stage, the likelihood social connections have been made after three months, and encouragement from tutors to interact as much as possible outside the classroom. Using English as a lingua franca in interaction with other international students could also explain this as learners have had the opportunity to develop their friendship networks in class and within international student societies, for instance. The latter could be explained by the lack of need to engage with such a range of service personnel post-SA arrival. Certainly, in the first few weeks, there are a number of formalities such as opening a bank account which necessitate face-to-face interaction. Post-arrival, this is less so and, in fact, many typical service encounters can be facilitated online which, increasingly, even applies to shopping for food. This circumvents the need to interact face to face with service personnel on a regular basis. Contact with English via online interaction should not be underestimated as a rich source of input. Indeed, Bardovi-Harlig and Bastos (2011) call for extending the LCP domains of L2 contact to include online platforms and social media.

The findings from part A illustrating increased frequency of engagement in the SA environment with the lapse of each six-week period support the overall trend in part B for the participants to self-report improvement in their listening, speaking, reading, writing and interaction skills also across these time periods. Notwithstanding the results should be interpreted with the caveat that perceived levels of skill are not the same as measured levels of skill, the findings still illustrate a concomitant improvement in the participants' self-evaluations of their listening and interaction skills, which is likely to be the outcome of this greater engagement in the SA environment. Mirroring the findings in part A, the intervention does not seem to have affected the groups' self-assessments of these skills in part B, as comparability between the groups is generally evident with only marginal differences.

No observable change in group behaviour was evident for the control group at the end of the treatment period, contrasting the results found with the instructed groups. This finding corroborates the need for intervention for pragmatic development for several reasons. First, no link has been identified in this study between exposure to the second language environment and natural acquisition of the sociopragmatic and pragmalinguistic aspects of language needed to produce successful requests or apologies. This lack of development may be indicative of the short twelve-week period covered in this study. Félix-Brasdefer (2004) and Schauer (2009) also reported SA stays of at least nine months were needed for signs of pragmatic development. Specifically regarding apologies, Kondo (1997) reported Japanese learners needing a one-year US study abroad period to show signs of approximating aspects of target-like strategy choice and perceptions of contextual factors with apologies. Second, learners may not have been provided with the requisite feedback needed to change their language behaviours, particularly with sociopragmatic feedback which may require a more sensitive approach. Third, L2 contact, and pragmatic development, may have been impeded by issues of self-confidence and the preference to stay in L1 groups, as earlier studies with Chinese learners have reported (Cheng & Fox 2008; Myles & Cheng 2003; Ranta & Meckelborg 2013; Wen & Clement 2003).

In summary, and based on the findings of the self-reporting questionnaire, all three groups (CAPT, PAPER, control) significantly increased their L2 contact over the three months at comparable rates and assessed their reading, writing, speaking, listening and interaction skills as also developing concomitantly with the lapse of each time period. This demonstrates that far from isolating themselves and withdrawing to their own first language groups (Cheng & Fox 2008; Myles & Cheng 2003) this Chinese cohort reports to embrace the SA environment, interacting on a daily to weekly basis in English, depending on the activity. For this study, it is plausible that although a generally significant increase in English contact for all groups is observed, this contact may not have always linked directly to the type of scenarios captured in the tests, or learners did not always capitalize on the opportunities for practising requests and apologies which the environment may have provided. Communication in service encounters, for example, was significantly increased for both experimental groups but this can of course include a range of situations within and around the academic setting. It is also possible that a longitudinal study of longer duration may yield different results and that the three-month period may not have been sufficient for a positive correlation to be found for these particular speech acts, as noted in previous studies (Félix-Brasdefer 2004; Schauer 2009).

10

Conclusions and future directions

The main goal of this study was to explore the efficacy of explicit teaching methods for improving the request and apology performance of Chinese L1 speakers during an academic study abroad sojourn in the UK. Within this, the study further considered the role of differentiated teaching materials and the influence of the second language environment for improving pragmatic performance. This concluding chapter outlines the contributions this study has made to our understanding of pragmatic development from theoretical, methodological and pedagogical perspectives. Finally, the limitations and suggested future lines of research are presented.

10.1. Contributions to L2 pragmatics research

Chapter 1 outlined aspects of SLA theory which underpinned the present study, namely *instructed SLA*, Schmidt's (1993) *noticing hypothesis*, Swain's (1996) *output hypothesis* and Long's (1996) *interaction hypothesis*. This study has provided new empirical support for all of the above theories in a number of unique ways: the instructional training materials for both speech acts were designed to promote inductive learning whereby the participants undertook self-discovery tasks to *notice* linguistic features and worked out patterns which were regularly *communicatively practised*. Teaching two speech acts alongside one another is unique to interventional studies and has been shown to be highly effective. Applying knowledge to simulated, interactive language production tasks through the use of virtual role-plays is also a unique feature of this study. Combining these three theoretical stances, within the unique instructional design and resources, seems to have had a positive effect on the pragmatic performance of the instructed groups.

The study also provided specific ways of optimizing classroom learning in ISLA. That the participants were offered contextualized opportunities for language practice, simulating situations which they might encounter themselves in an academic environment, may have been effective. One of the features underpinning ISLA is, how can instructional effects be maximized in the classroom? One such way is to manipulate the learning conditions, as described in Chapter 1. To my knowledge, this is first study to incorporate differentiated practice materials to manipulate learner engagement and is also unique to the British academic SA setting. The findings indicated that the use of technology via the CAPT activities enhanced learning and recall of the request and apology input, but also provided clearer evidence that some speech acts may be more amenable to instruction than others.

This study also enhances our understanding of the role social interaction in the environment plays in pragmatic development. Tracking the participants' L2 contact at the pre-, post- and delayed-test phases, alongside the intervention, is a distinct design feature of this study. The claim that pragmatic development is not easily acquired in a natural environment seems to have been verified with the control group's inability to advance their request and apology pragmatic knowledge, despite reporting that their social interaction incrementally increased. The short three-month experimental period of this study may account for these results, or the quality or frequency of opportunities to use request and apology language. The data suggest that despite efforts to engage in the L2, these interactions may not necessarily supply what is needed to advance pragmatic knowledge: some aspects such as requests and apologies may need initial (and repeated) stimulation from instructional input. This finding makes an original contribution to the SA research and existing literature on instructed second language programmes.

This study also addressed a number of methodological gaps in L2 pragmatics research. First, the original design of the intervention, which included multiple experimental groups, successfully facilitated an analysis of not only explicit instruction, but comparisons of differentiated language practice materials to measure their effectiveness against one another. In addition, employing more than one group provided for a larger data set to also compare the two instructional targets side by side, and the ease with which requests and apologies could be taught and learned. To the researcher's knowledge, the use of multiple experimental groups for these ends has not been attempted so this study therefore provides a foundation on which to build our understanding of the effectiveness of pragmatics training materials and the amenability of different pragmatic targets to instruction.

Second, this study is only one of a few investigations comparing instruction versus exposure of requests and apologies in a SA setting. Furthermore, focusing on interlocutor perceptions when measuring the success of the request and apology responses, rather than comparing the learner data to their L1 counterparts, is also rarely employed and therefore a unique feature of this investigation. Measuring performance through ratings also suited the main aim of the study which was to improve staff-student communication in a SA academic context and avoided the assumption that total target-like convergence was either preferable or necessary for successful communication. In addition, a distinctive outcome of employing rating scales also diverted the focus to what pragmatic aspects were important to get right in order not to affect the outcomes of the request or apology and which pragmatic infelicities were overlooked as nonessential. To my knowledge, these areas have not been directly addressed in previous studies. Due to the changing face of how English is used internationally, the debates surrounding how pragmatics success is measured need to be considered more in L2 pragmatics research design.

Finally, the study introduced a methodological innovation in the form of the CAPT to train students and elicit learner data. Work is needed to refine the instrument, but it has gone some way to creating more authentic interactions through virtual interlocutors with L1 accents and dialects and who displayed prosodic language features and non-verbal signals to enhance the simulated interaction. At the same time, the CAPT still retained the benefits of being able to effectively capture large amounts of data in a controlled setting. That the virtual role-plays embedded within the tool were also adapted for classroom language practice materials demonstrated their flexibility to be used in multiple ways. There is additional scope for using the virtual role-plays as self-access materials and investigating the efficacy of this approach for developing pragmatic competence outside of classroom-based learning. For instance, Timpe-Laughlin et al. (2015), amongst others, provide detailed suggestions of how pragmatic training materials can be embedded within online platforms. Web-based self-access materials have also been implemented to good effect in other speech act studies (e.g. Cohen & Ishihara 2005; Cohen & Sykes 2010; Teng & Fei 2013).

From a pedagogical perspective, the intervention employed in this study has provided unique evidence for both the design of instructional interventions and ways of maximizing teaching and learning within it. This is important since it appears pragmatic knowledge of requests and apologies at least does need initiating through formal instruction. Several frameworks for classroom-based teaching of pragmatics now exist (e.g. Ishihara & Cohen 2010; Shively 2010; Usó-Juan 2010), and the one adopted for the present study (Usó-Juan 2010) was found to be successful. Practitioners might be more confident to pursue the inclusion of pragmatics on curricula as more studies such as this test the validity of instructional designs.

This study has contributed several distinctive insights into some of the specific ways L2 pragmatics training could be maximized within an instructional programme. This section concludes with some recommendations based on these insights.

i) *Identification of interlanguage gaps in learners' pragmatic knowledge.* Assessing aspects of pragmatic saliency and interlanguage gaps is useful at the beginning of the intervention to determine which pragmatic aspects need most instructional attention and are of most value. Future investigations could take a systematic approach to this through some form of (pragmatic) needs analysis of the kind traditionally implemented in ELT (see historical overview in West 1994). In this way, since not all L2 challenges covered in pragmatics literature will apply to all learner groups, pragmatic targets which meet learners' immediate communicative needs can be addressed.

ii) *Formulae-based input may be particularly effective.* As Schmitt and Carter (2004) claim, using one or more formulaic sequences is the preferred realization of many language functions such as requests and apologies. Taken together with the cognitive advantages of learning in this way (e.g. Wang 2011; Wray 2000), the introduction of formulaic language proved highly successful in this study. An original aspect of this study is also that teaching learners what *not* to say and when *not* to say it, when formulating requests and apologies, is equally as important as teaching learners how to get it right. This was addressed when non-target-like features of requests and apologies were highlighted within the instruction as potentially hearer-alienating (Sabaté i Dalmau & Currel i Gotor 2007).

iii) *Managing learners' intended communicative goal and interlocutor expectations.* Teacher-student discussions need to instil learner confidence about realistic (and preferred) communicative goals and how these might be best achieved inside and outside the classroom. This study also confirms interlocutor expectations favour pragmatic competence over grammatical competence, so this also needs to be a central feature of pragmatic input.

iv) *Technology can enhance pragmatic teaching materials and learning outcomes.* This study appeared to verify the benefits of technology-enhanced teaching and learning. For the first time, this study contributes empirical evidence that even short periods of engagement with technology such as the CAPT, as a medium for pragmatic development, can produce more beneficial results than working with traditional paper-based activities. Similar results have previously been reported in the wider contexts of language learning (e.g. Butler 2015; Sykes et al. 2008).

The findings of this study will be of interest to academics and practitioners who work with large numbers of international students from East Asia who currently study in UK Higher Education institutions. The findings may help shape the content of other instructed SA programmes, particularly those in positive-negative politeness contexts.

10.2. Limitations and directions for future research

In terms of the research design, the participant profile was restricted to a relatively small sample of undergraduate learners of one nationality, studying in intact groups in an academic, English-speaking SA setting. The findings may thus not be generalizable to other learner groups and contexts. Recent meta-analyses have recommended broadening the scope of L1 groups of different proficiency levels and ages, studying a range of foreign languages to avoid the high concentration of studies employing university-level participants studying English as a second language (Jeon & Kaya 2006; Taguchi 2015).

In addition, this study only captured pragmatic development and language contact over a short period of time (three months). Future research could measure either natural acquisition or maintenance of instructed pragmatic input over an extended period of time, particularly as previous reports have indicated pragmatic development is a gradual process in the absence of instruction (Kasper & Rose 2002; Sabaté i Dalmau & Curell i Gotor 2007). Where interventions do take place, participants should be monitored and tested more frequently, over a longer period. The results from this study indicate the onset of attrition two weeks beyond the posttest. A longitudinal study might identify whether there is a turning point at which learners start to naturally acquire target-like forms and production increases, and whether there is a turning point at which instructional benefits decrease. Furthermore, correlations between length of instructional periods and how long pragmatic knowledge/awareness is maintained have yet to be addressed. This may be resolved by the inclusion of multiple delayed tests or Jeon and Kaya's (2006) suggestion of a 'process test' which measures weekly or biweekly interim test results to provide information on developmental transitions.

Several questions remain unanswered in the study. For instance, why did learner contact with the L2 increase and were their motivations for engaging more in the L2 personal or necessary? What contributed to the ease with which formulaic language was learned during the instruction? Enhancing the study with retrospective verbal reports or post-instruction interviews may have provided the qualitative evidence to answer these questions: an approach which has yielded interesting findings to date. Taguchi (2002) employed simulated recall to investigate conversational implicature amongst eight Japanese learners of English and found the method revealed their mental processes and individual differences during task completion. In the event the research procedure limits the capacity to undertake post-instruction analyses of this kind, qualitative information could be gleaned by extending or replacing the language contact questionnaire with phased journal entries to also trace affective factors and individual differences, for instance, as undertaken in other studies (e.g. Cohen & Shively 2007; Winke & Teng 2010). This would shed further light on the complex interplay of factors contributing to the success, or failure, of SA experiences.

Related to data collection tools, it must be acknowledged that the language contact questionnaire was based on learner self-reports and that results should be indicative rather than conclusive, given the information is based on learner estimates which may be inaccurate or untruthful. Still, trends can be drawn upon to provide a clearer picture of the influence of environmental factors. Bardovi-Harlig and Bastos (2011) advocate future language contact questionnaires also elicit synchronous and asynchronous computer-mediated communication patterns in the SA context as online communication and social media now feature as an integral part of daily life and academia, providing an additional rich source of input for learners.

The limitations of operationalizing the CAPT as an instructional tool and data collection instrument must also be recognized, and work needs to continue to develop its design. Firstly, regarding the scenario content, whilst improved request and apology performance was established post-instruction, this was within the boundaries of high-status interlocutors and high imposition variables. What is not clear, however, is to what extent the participants would be equally sensitive to situations containing a range of power-distance-imposition variables and be able to appropriately self-select from request and apology strategies, according to the sociopragmatic context given. A different study would be needed to investigate this. Secondly, it was assumed the participants would perceive the power-social distance-imposition variables in the scenarios in the way they were intended. This cannot be verified, however. To avoid this possible mismatch in perceptions, other investigations have employed either 'situation assessment questionnaires' to determine if the scenarios presented are perceived and rated similarly by different language groups (e.g. Economidou-Kogetsidis 2010; Kim 2008; Maeshiba et al. 1996), or the content of the scenarios themselves is drawn from comparable participants' personal experiences (e.g. Chang 2010). Finally, as Su (2010) proposes, it may have been prudent to include another speech act such as refusals or complaints to act as a distractor within the collection of production tasks scenarios. This could have pre-empted any response sets resulting from exposure to requests and apologies alone.

10.3. Concluding remarks

The current study has expanded the scope of existing knowledge regarding the effects of explicit pragmatic instruction of requests and apologies to Chinese learners of English, specifically exploring the role of technology-enhanced practice materials and the study abroad environment for improving pragmatic competence. This study adopted an approach to isolate language features which both L1 Chinese users and L1 British-English users share, those which were considered requisite for successful requests and apologies, and those which were considered hearer-alienating, in the academic context presented. In this way, underdeveloped features of pragmalinguistic and sociopragmatic language, which might trigger negative reactions, could be identified to promote a more targeted approach to instructional programmes.

What this study has shown is that L2 learners need clear guidance and training to notice and explore interlanguage pragmatic differences, specifically regarding requests and apologies since access to, and exploitation of, this information is not guaranteed through L2 exposure alone. Furthermore, Chinese ESL learners are challenged by the pragmatic norms of an English-speaking environment and are not fully equipped with the necessary skills to engage as successfully as they could be in a SA setting in the absence of guided and targeted instruction. This volume has therefore attempted to outline several opportune ways pragmatic instruction can be facilitated in the language classroom. As in this study, researchers are encouraged to continue pushing the boundaries of existing second language pragmatics investigations, particularly from methodological and pedagogical perspectives, so outcomes may have a direct impact on learner experiences, whilst enhancing our understanding of pragmatic development a little further each time.

Notes

Chapter 1

1. Positive politeness is the use of strategies to redress the addressee's positive face wants by, for example, treating the hearer as a member of the same group. Output strategies include the use of group-identity markers such as expressing interest in the hearer, joking or being optimistic. It is the sugaring of the pill technique (Culpeper et al. 2018: 46).
2. Negative politeness is the use of strategies to redress the addressee's negative face wants. The speaker indicates respect for the hearer's face wants and the wish not to interfere with the hearer's freedom of action. Output strategies include mitigating techniques which soften the blow of a face threat (Culpeper et al. 2018: 46).

Chapter 2

1. Rapport management is a broad concept defined as 'the management of harmony-disharmony among people' (2000: 13) and promotes social interdependence rather than a focus on the self. 'It examines the way that language is used to construct, maintain and/or threaten social relationships' (2003: 12).
2. Politic behaviour is defined as 'linguistic behaviour which is perceived to be appropriate to the social constraints of the ongoing interaction' (2003: 19). It imagines politeness from the viewpoint of *expected* behaviour.
3. 'The number of foreign students enrolled in tertiary education programmes worldwide rose from 2 million in 1999 to 5 million in 2016, at an average annual rate of 5.1 per cent among OECD countries and 6.4 per cent among non-OECD countries' (OECD 2018).

Chapter 3

1. Ethnography is the practice of gaining an insider perspective on the sociocultural norms and behaviour of a community and its members (Roberts et al. 2001). Ishihara and Cohen (2010) are amongst those advocating a learner-as-ethnographer approach. Through field notes or use of diaries, for example, learners

can record their L2 interactions, cross-cultural misunderstandings, observe L2 behaviour or collect authentic L2 language samples. These findings can then be taken back to the classroom to create, test and possibly revise hypotheses about local practices. These awareness-raising activities act as guided simulations for future independent learning of pragmatics (Ishihara & Cohen 2010).

Chapter 6

1. This website no longer exists in its original format. It is now marketed under the name 'nawmal' and can be accessed at www.nawmal.com.
2. The raters were L1 British-English speakers of a similar age and were employed at the study location. Each rater had over twenty years of English language teaching experience and had contact with Chinese-speaking students as part of their teaching programmes.

References

Abrams, Z. (2013), 'Say What?! L2 Sociopragmatic Competence in CMC: Skill Transfer and Development', *CALICO Journal*, 30 (3): 423–45.

Aijmer, K. (1996), *Conversational Routines in English: Convention and Creativity*, New York: Longman.

Aijmer, K. and Aijmer, P. K. (1996), *Conversational Routines in English: Convention and Creativity*, New York: Longman.

Akikawa, K. and Ishihara, N. (2010), 'Requesting a Letter of Recommendation: Teaching Students to Write Email Requests', in D. H. Tatsuki and N. Houck (eds), *Pragmatics: Teaching Speech Acts*, 47–66, Virginia: TESOL Inc.

Alcón Soler, E. (2005), 'Does Instruction Work for Learning Pragmatics in the EFL Context?', *System*, 33: 417–35.

Alcón Soler, E. (2012), 'Teachability and Bilingualism Effects on Third Language Learners' Pragmatic Knowledge', *Intercultural Pragmatics*, 9: 511–41.

Alcón Soler, E. (2015), 'Pragmatic Learning and Study Abroad: Effects of Instruction and Length of Stay', *System*, 48: 62–74.

Alcón Soler, E. and Guzman Pitarch, J. (2010), 'The Effect of Instruction on Learners' Pragmatic Awareness: A Focus on Refusals', *International Journal of English Studies*, 10 (1): 65–80.

Alcón Soler, E. and Martinez-Flor, A. eds. (2008), *Investigating Pragmatics in Foreign Language Learning, Teaching and Testing*, New York: Multilingual Matters.

Anderson, J. R. (1993), *Rules of the Mind*, Hillsdale, NJ: Lawrence Erlbaum.

Austin, J. L. (1962), *How to Do Things with Words*, Oxford: Oxford University Press.

Bachman, L. F. (1990), *Fundamental Considerations in Language Testing (Oxford Applied Linguistics)* (5th ed.), Oxford: Oxford University Press.

Bachman, L. F. and Palmer, A. S. (1982), 'The Construct Validation of Some Components of Communicative Proficiency', *TESOL Quarterly*, 16 (4): 449–65.

Bachman, L. F. and Palmer, A. S. (1996), *Language Testing in Practice: Designing and Developing Useful Language Tests*, New York: Oxford University Press.

Bachman, L. F. and Palmer, A. S. (2010), *Language Assessment in Practice*, Oxford: Oxford University Press.

Bardovi-Harlig, K. (1999), 'Exploring the Interlanguage of Interlanguage Pragmatics: A Research Agenda for Acquisitional Pragmatics', *Language Learning*, 49 (4): 677–713.

Bardovi-Harlig, K. (2001), 'Evaluating the Empirical Evidence: Grounds for Instruction in Pragmatics', in K. R. Rose and G. Kasper (eds), *Pragmatics in Language Teaching*, 13–32, Cambridge: Cambridge University Press.

Bardovi-Harlig, K. (2009), 'Conventional Expressions as a Pragmalinguistic Resource: Recognition and Production of Conventional Expressions in L2 Pragmatics', *Language Learning*, 59 (4): 755–95.

Bardovi-Harlig, K. (2012), 'Formulas, Routines and Conversational Expressions in Pragmatics Research', *Annual Review of Applied Linguistics*, 32: 206–27.

Bardovi-Harlig, K. (2013), 'Developing L2 Pragmatics', *Language Learning*, 63: 68–86.

Bardovi-Harlig, K. (2014), 'Awareness of Meaning of Conventional Expressions in Second Language Pragmatics', *Language Awareness*, 23: 41–56.

Bardovi-Harlig, K. (2015), 'Designing Instructional Effect Studies for L2 Pragmatics: A Guide for Teachers and Researchers', in S. Gesuato, F. Bianchi and W. Cheng (eds), *Teaching, Learning and Investigating Pragmatics: Principles, Methods and Practices*, 135–64, Cambridge: Cambridge Scholars Publishing.

Bardovi-Harlig, K. (2018), 'Matching Modality in L2 Pragmatics Research Design', *System*, 75: 13–22.

Bardovi-Harlig, K. and Bastos, M. T. (2011), 'Proficiency, Length of Stay, and Intensity of Interaction and the Acquisition of Conventional Expressions in L2 Pragmatics', *Intercultural Pragmatics*, 8 (3): 347–84.

Bardovi-Harlig, K. and Dörnyei, Z. (1998), 'Do Language Learners Recognize Pragmatic Violations? Pragmatic versus Grammatical Awareness in Instructed L2 Learning', *TESOL Quarterly*, 32 (2): 233–59.

Bardovi-Harlig, K. and Hartford, B. (2005), *Interlanguage Pragmatics: Exploring Institutional Talk*, New York: Routledge.

Bardovi-Harlig, K. and Hartford, B. S. (1990), 'Congruence in Native and Nonnative Conversations: Status Balance in the Academic Advising Session', *Language Learning*, 40 (4): 467–501.

Bardovi-Harlig, K. and Hartford, B. S. (1993), 'Learning the Rules of Academic Talk: A Longitudinal Study of Pragmatic Development', *Studies in Second Language Acquisition*, 15 (3): 279–304.

Bardovi-Harlig, K. and Mahan-Taylor, R. (2003), 'Teaching Pragmatics', Available online: https://americanenglish.state.gov/files/ae/resource_files/intro.pdf (accessed 6 June 2018).

Bardovi-Harlig, K. and Vellenga, H. E. (2012), 'The Effect of Instruction on Conventional Expressions in L2 Pragmatics', *System*, 40 (1): 77–89.

Bardovi-Harlig, K., Mossman, S. and Vellenga, H. E. (2015), 'Developing Corpus-Based Materials to Teach Pragmatic Routines', *TESOL Journal*, 6: 499–526.

Barnlund, D. C. and Yoshioka, M. (1990), 'Apologies: Japanese and American Styles', *International Journal of Intercultural Relations*, 14 (2): 193–206.

Barron, A. (2003), *Acquisition in Interlanguage Pragmatics: Learning How to Do Things with Words in a Study Abroad Context*, Amsterdam: John Benjamins.

Barron, A. (2006), 'Learning to Say "You" in German: The Acquisition of Sociolinguistic Competence in a Study Abroad Context', in M. A. DuFon and E. Churchill (eds), *Language Learners in Study Abroad Contexts*, 59–88, Clevedon: Multilingual Matters.

Barron, A. (2007), '"Ah No Honestly We're Okay:" Learning to Upgrade in a Study Abroad Context', *Intercultural Pragmatics*, 4 (2): 129–66.

Barron, A. (2016), 'Developing Pragmatic Competence Using EFL Textbooks: Focus on Requests', *Literacy Information and Computer Education Journal (LICEJ)*, 7 (1): 2172–9.

Barron, A. (2019), 'Using Corpus-Linguistic Methods to Track Longitudinal Development: Routine Apologies in the Study Abroad Context', *Journal of Pragmatics*, 146: 87–105.

Bataller, R. (2010), 'Making a Request for a Service in Spanish: Pragmatic Development in the Study Abroad Setting', *Foreign Language Annals*, 43 (1): 160–75.

Beebe, L. M. and Cummings, M. C. (1996), 'Natural Speech Act Data versus Written Questionnaire Data: How Data Collection Method Affects Speech Act Performance', in S. M. Gass and J. Neu (eds), *Speech Acts across Cultures*, 65–86, Berlin: Mouton De Gruyter.

Bella, S. (2011), 'Mitigation and Politeness in Greek Invitation Refusals: Effects of Length of Residence in the Target Community and Intensity of Interaction on Non-Native Speakers' Performance', *Journal of Pragmatics*, 43 (6): 1718–40.

Belz, J. A. (2007), 'The Role of Computer Mediation in the Instruction and Development of L2 Pragmatic Competence', *Annual Review of Applied Linguistics*, 27: 45–75.

Bergman, M. L. and Kasper, G. (1993), 'Perception and Performance in Native and Non-Native Apology', in S. Blum-Kulka and G. Kasper (eds), *Interlanguage Pragmatics*, 82–108, Oxford: Oxford University Press.

Billmyer, K. (1990), '"I Really Like Your Lifestyle": ESL Learners Learning How to Compliment', *Penn Working Papers in Educational Linguistics*, 6 (2): 31–48.

Billmyer, K. and Varghese, M. (2000), 'Investigating Instrument-Based Pragmatic Variability: Effects of Enhancing Discourse Completion Tests', *Applied Linguistics*, 21 (4): 517–52.

Blum-Kulka, S. and Olshtain, E. (1984), 'Requests and Apologies: A Cross-Cultural Study of Speech Act Realization Patterns (CCSARP)', *Applied Linguistics*, 5 (3): 196–213.

Blum-Kulka, S. and Olshtain, E. (1986), 'Too Many Words: Length of Utterance and Pragmatic Failure', *Studies in Second Language Acquisition*, 8 (2): 165–80.

Blum-Kulka, S., House, J. and Kasper, G. (1989), *Cross-Cultural Pragmatics: Requests and Apologies*, Norwood, NJ: Ablex Pub. Corp.

Boers, F. and Lindstromberg, S. (2012), 'Experimental and Intervention Studies on Formulaic Sequences in a Second Language', *Annual Review of Applied Linguistics*, 32: 83–110.

Bouton, L. (1994), 'Can NNS Skill in Interpreting Implicature in American English Be Improved through Explicit Instruction? – A Pilot Study', in L. Bouton (ed.), *Pragmatics and Language Learning, Vol. 5*, 89–109, UrbanaChampaign, IL: Division of English as an International Language Intensive English Institute: University of Illinois at Urbana-Champaign.

Brown, L. (2013), 'Identity and Honorifics Use in Korean Study Abroad', in C. Kinginger (ed.), *Social and Cultural Aspects of Language Learning in Study Abroad*, 268–98, Philadelphia, PA: John Benjamins.

Brown, P. and Levinson, S. C. (1987), *Politeness: Some Universals in Language Usage*, New York: Cambridge University Press.

Butler, Y. G. (2015), 'The Use of Computer Games as Foreign Language Learning Tasks for Digital Natives', *System*, 54: 91–102.

Byon, A. S. (2004), 'Sociopragmatic Analysis of Korean Requests: Pedagogical Settings', *Journal of Pragmatics*, 36 (9): 1673–704.

Byon, A. S. (2006), 'Developing KFL Students' Pragmatic Awareness of Korean Speech Acts: The Use of Discourse Completion Tasks', *Language Awareness*, 15 (4): 244–63.

Byram, M. (1997), *Teaching and Assessing Intercultural Communicative Competence*, Clevedon: Multilingual Matters.

Byram, M. (2012), 'Conceptualizing Intercultural (Communicative) Competence and Intercultural Citizenship', in J. Jackson (ed.), *The Routledge Handbook of Language and Intercultural Communication*, 85–98, New York: Routledge.

Campbell, J. and Li, M. (2008), 'Asian Students' Voices: An Empirical Study of Asian Students' Learning Experiences at a New Zealand University', *Journal of Studies in International Education*, 12 (4): 375–96.

Canale, M. (1983), 'From Communicative Competence to Communicative Language Pedagogy', in J. C. Richards and R. W. Schmidt (eds), *Language and Communication*, 2–27, New York: Longman.

Canale, M. and Swain, M. (1980), 'Theoretical Bases of Communicative Approaches to Second Language Teaching and Testing', *Applied Linguistics*, 1 (1): 1–47.

Cercone, K. (2006), 'Brain-Based Learning', in S. E. Korsgaard and D. Omurchu (eds), *Enhancing Learning through Technology*, 292–322, Hershey, PA: Idea Group Inc.

Chang, M., Curran, J., Hsu, Y. K. and Hsu, C. C. (2016), 'Do Chinese Students Waffle in Their Apologies? An Exploration into EFL Learners' Emails', in Y. Chen, D. V. Rau and G. Rau (eds), *Email Discourse among Chinese Using English as a Lingua Franca*, 61–90, Singapore: Springer.

Chang, Y. F. (2010), '"I No Say You Say Is Boring": The Development of Pragmatic Competence in L2 Apology', *Language Sciences*, 32 (3): 408–24.

Chapelle, C. A. and Sauro, S. (2017), *The Handbook of Technology and Second Language Teaching and Learning*, New Jersy: John Wiley & Sons.

Chen, C. E. (2006), 'The Development of E-mail Literacy: From Writing to Peers to Writing to Authority Figures', *Language Learning & Technology*, 10 (2): 35–55.

Chen, J. F., Warden, C. A. and Chang, H. T. (2005), 'Motivators That Do Not Motivate: The Case of Chinese EFL Learners and the Influence of Culture on Motivation', *TESOL Quarterly*, 39 (4): 609–33.

Chen, R., He, L. and Hu, C. (2013), 'Chinese Requests: In Comparison to American and Japanese Requests and with Reference to the "East-West Divide"', *Journal of Pragmatics*, 55: 140–61.

Chen, Y. (2015a), 'Developing Chinese EFL Learners' Email Literacy through Requests to Faculty', *Journal of Pragmatics*, 75: 131–49.

Chen, Y. (2015b), 'Chinese Learners' Cognitive Processes in Writing Email Requests to Faculty', *System*, 52: 51–62.

Cheng, D. (2017a), 'Students' Self-Perceptions of Apologies to Instructors', *Language Awareness*, 26 (4): 261–81.

Cheng, D. (2017b), '"Communication Is a Two-way Street" Instructors' Perceptions of Student Apologies', *Pragmatics*, 27 (1): 1–32.

Cheng, L. and Fox, J. (2008), 'Towards a Better Understanding of Academic Acculturation: Second Language Students in Canadian Universities', *Canadian Modern Language Review*, 65 (2): 307–33.

Chomsky, N. (1965), *Aspects of the Theory of Syntax*, Cambridge: MIT Press.

Cole, S. and Anderson, A. (2001), 'Requests by Young Japanese: A Longitudinal Study', The Language Teacher Online, 25 (8). Available online: http://www.jalt-publications.org/tlt/articles/2001/08/anderson/ (accessed 21 September 2017).

Codina-Espurz, V. (2008), 'The Immediate vs. Delayed Effect of Instruction on Mitigators in Relation to Learner Language Proficiency in English', in E. Alcón-Soler (ed.), *Learning How to Request in an Instructed Language Learning Context*, 227–56, Bern: Peter Lang.

Cohen, A. D. (2005), 'Strategies for Learning and Performing L2 Speech Acts', *Intercultural Pragmatics*, 2 (3): 275–301.

Cohen, A. D. (2008), 'Teaching and Assessing L2 Pragmatics: What Can We Expect from Learners?', *Language Teaching*, 41 (2): 213–35.

Cohen, A. D. (2016), 'The Teaching of Pragmatics by Native and Nonnative Language Teachers: What They Know and What They Report Doing', *Studies in Second Language Learning and Teaching*, 6 (4): 561–85.

Cohen, A. D. (2018), *Learning Pragmatics from Native and Nonnative Language Teachers*, Bristol: Multilingual Matters.

Cohen, A. D. and Ishihara, N. (2005), 'A Web-Based Approach to Strategic Learning of Speech Acts', Minneapolis, MN: Center for Advanced Research on Language Acquisition (CARLA), University of Minnesota. Available online: http://carla.umn.edu/speechacts/Japanese%20Speech%20Act%20Report%20Rev.%20June05.pdf (accessed 18 September 2017).

Cohen, A. D. and Macaro, E. (2010), 'Research Methods in Second Language Acquisition', in E. Macaro (ed.), *Continuum Companion to Second Language Acquisition*, 107–33, London: Continuum.

Cohen, A. D. and Shively, R. L. (2007), 'Acquisition of Requests and Apologies in Spanish and French: Impact of Study Abroad and Strategy-Building Intervention', *The Modern Language Journal*, 91 (2): 189–212.

Cohen, A. D. and Sykes, J. M. (2010), 'Language Learner Strategies and Their Effect on Speech Act Performance', Applied Linguistics Forum 30 (1). Available online: file:///C:/Users/nikna/AppData/Local/Packages/Microsoft.

MicrosoftEdge_8wekyb3d8bbwe/TempState/Downloads/2010._Cohen_A._D._and_Sykes_J._M._Langua%20(1).pdf (accessed 17 June 2020).

Cohen, A. D. and Tarone, E. (1994), 'The Effects of Training on Written Speech Act Behavior: Stating and Changing an Opinion', *Minnetesol Journal*, 12: 39–62.

Cohen, J. (1988), *Statistical Power Analysis for the Behavioral Sciences* (2nd ed.), Hillsdale, NJ: Lawrence Erlbaum Associates.

Cook, V. (2002), 'Background to the L2 User', in V. Cook (ed.), *Portraits of the L2 User*, 1–28, Clevedon: Multilingual Matters.

Crandall, E. and Basturkmen, H. (2004), 'Evaluating Pragmatics-Focused Materials', *ELT Journal*, 58 (1): 38–49.

Creswell, J. W. (2009), *Research Design: Qualitative, Quantitative, and Mixed Methods Approaches* (3rd ed.), Thousand Oaks, CA: Sage Publications.

Creswell, J. W. and Plano Clark, V. L. (2010), *Designing and Conducting Mixed Methods Research* (2nd ed.), Thousand Oaks, CA: Sage Publications.

Crystal, D. (1997), *English as a Global Language*, Cambridge: Cambridge University Press.

Culpeper, J. and Haugh, M. (2014), *Pragmatics and the English Language*, Basingstoke: Palgrave Macmillan.

Culpeper, J., Mackey, A. and Taguchi, N. (2018), *Second Language Pragmatics from Theory to Research*, Abingdon: Routledge.

Cunningham, J. D. (2016), 'Request Modification in Synchronous Computer-Mediated Communication: The Role of Focussed Instruction', *Modern Language Journal*, 100 (2): 484–507.

Davis, J. (2007), 'Resistance to L2 Pragmatics in the Australian ESL Context', *Language Learning*, 57: 611–64.

De Freitas, S. (2006), 'Learning in Immersive Worlds: A Review of Game-Based Learning', JISC E-Learning Programme. Available online: http://www.webarchive.org.uk/wayback/archive/20140615100504/; http://www.jisc.ac.uk/media/documents/programmes/elearninginnovation/gamingreport_v3.pdf (accessed 2 February 2015).

Dekeyser, R. (2007), *Practice in a Second Language: Perspectives from Applied Linguistics and Cognitive Psychology*, Cambridge: Cambridge University Press.

Dewaele, J. M. (2018), 'Why the Dichotomy "L1 versus LX User" Is Better than "Native versus Non-Native Speaker"', *Applied Linguistics*, 39 (2): 236–40.

Dörnyei, Z., Durow, V. and Zahran, K. (2004), 'Individiual Differences and Their Effect on Formulaic Sequence Acquisition', in N. Schmitt (ed.), *Formulaic Sequences*, 87–106, Amsterdam: John Benjamins.

Drew, P. and Heritage, J. (1992), *Talk at Work: Interaction in Institutional Settings*, New York: Cambridge University Press.

Duff, P. (2007), 'Second Language Socialisation as Sociocultural Theory: Insights and Issues', *Language Teaching*, 40: 309–19.

Economidou-Kogetsidis, M. (2008), 'Internal and External Mitigation in Interlanguage Request Production: The Case of Greek Learners of English', *Journal of Politeness Research. Language, Behaviour, Culture*, 4 (1): 111–38.

Economidou-Kogetsidis, M. (2010), 'Cross-Cultural and Situational Variation in Requesting Behaviour: Perceptions of Social Situations and Strategic Usage of Request Patterns', *Journal of Pragmatics*, 42 (8): 2262–81.

Economidou-Kogetsidis, M. (2011), '"Please Answer Me as Soon as Possible": Pragmatic Failure in Non-Native Speakers' E-Mail Requests to Faculty', *Journal of Pragmatics*, 43 (13): 3193–215.

Economidou-Kogetsidis, M. (2012), 'Modifying Oral Requests in a Foreign Language: The Case of Greek Cypriot Learners of English', in M. Economidou-Kogetsidis and H. Woodfield (eds), *Interlanguage Request Modification*, 163–202, Amsterdam: John Benjamins.

Economidou-Kogetsidis, M. (2013), 'Strategies, Modification and Perspective in Native Speakers' Requests: A Comparison of WDCT and Naturally Occurring Requests', *Journal of Pragmatics*, 53: 21–38.

Eisenstein, M. and Bodman, J. (1993), 'Expressing Gratitude in American English', in G. Kasper and S. Blum-Kulka (eds), *Interlanguage Pragmatics*, 64–81, New York: Oxford University Press.

Erben, T., Bau, R., Jin, L., Summers, R. and Eisenhower, K. (2008), 'Using Technology for Foreign Language Instruction: Creative Innovations, Research and Applications', in T. Erben and I. Sarieva (eds), *Calling All Foreign Language Teachers: Computer Assisted Language Learning in the Classroom*, 13–35, Larchmont, NY: Eye on Education.

Eslami, Z. R. (2010), 'Refusals: How to Develop Appropriate Refusal Strategies', in A. Martínez-Flor and E. Usó Juan (eds), *Speech Act Performance. Theoretical, Empirical and Methodological Issues*, 217–36, Amsterdam: John Benjamins.

Eslami, Z. R. (2011), 'In Their Own Voices: Reflections of Native and Nonnative English Speaking TESOL Graduate Students on Online Pragmatic Instruction to EFL Learners', *The Electronic Journal for English as a Second Language*, 15 (2): 1–21.

Eslami, Z. R. and Eslami-Rasekh, A. (2008), 'Enhancing the Pragmatic Competence of Non-Native English Speaking Teacher Candidates (NNESTCs) in an EFL Context', in E. Alcón Soler and M. P. Safont (eds), *Intercultural Language Use and Language Learning*, 178–97, Netherlands: Springer.

Eslami, Z. R. and Liu, C. (2013), 'Learning Pragmatics through Computer-Mediated Communication in Taiwan', *Iranian Journal of Society, Culture, & Language*, 1 (1): 52–73.

Eslami, Z. R., Eslami-Rasekh, A. and Fatahi, A. (2004), 'The Effect of Explicit Metapragmatic Instruction on the Speech Act Awareness of Advanced EFL students', *TESL-EJ*, 8 (2): 1–12.

Eslami, Z. R., Mirzaei, A. and Dini, S. (2015), 'The Role of Asynchronous Computer Mediated Communication in the Instruction and Development of EFL Learners' Pragmatic Competence', *System*, 48: 99–111.

Fantini, A. and Tirmizi, A. (2006), 'Exploring and Assessing Intercultural Competence', *World Learning Publications*. Paper 1. Available online: https://digitalcollections.sit.edu/cgi/viewcontent.cgi?referer=; https://www.google.co.uk/&; httpsredir=1&article=1001&context=worldlearning_publications/ (accessed 27 October 2018).

Faerch, C and Kasper, G. (1989), 'Internal and External Modification in Interlanguage Request Realization', in S. Blum Kulka, J. House and G. Kasper (eds), *Cross-Cultural Pragmatics: Requests and Apologies*, 221–47, Norwood, NJ: Ablex

Félix-Brasdefer, J. C. (2004), 'Interlanguage Refusals: Linguistic Politeness and Length of Residence in the Target Community', *Language Learning*, 54 (4): 587–653.

Félix-Brasdefer, J. C. (2006), 'Linguistic Politeness in Mexico: Refusal Strategies among Male Speakers of Mexican Spanish', *Journal of Pragmatics*, 38 (12): 2158–87.

Félix-Brasdefer, J. C. (2007), 'Natural Speech vs. Elicited Data: A Comparison of Natural and Role Play Requests in Mexican Spanish', *Spanish in Context*, 4 (2): 159–85.

Félix-Brasdefer, J. C. (2008), 'Perceptions of Refusals to Invitations: Exploring the Minds of Foreign Language Learners', *Language Awareness*, 17 (3): 195–211.

Félix-Brasdefer, J. C. (2012), 'Email Requests to Faculty: E-politeness and Internal Modification', in M. Economidou-Kogetsidis and H. Woodfield (eds), *Interlanguage Request Modification*, 87–118, Amsterdam: John Benjamins.

Flores-Salgado, E. (2011), *The Pragmatics of Requests and Apologies: Developmental Patterns of Mexican Students*, Amsterdam: John Benjamins Publishing Co.

Fraser, B. (1981), 'On Apologizing', in F. Coulmas (ed.), *Conversational Routine*, 259–71, The Hague: Mouton.

Fraser, B. (1985), 'Pragmatic Formatives', in J. Verschueren and M. Bertuccelli-Papi (eds), *Proceeding of the International Pragmatics Conference*, Viagreggio, Italy.

Freed, B., Dewey, D., Segalowitz, N. and Halter, R. (2004), 'The Language Contact Profile', *Studies in Second Language Acquisition*, 26 (2): 349–56.

Fukushima, S. (2002), *Requests and Culture: Politeness in British English and Japanese*, Switzerland: Peter Lang AG.

Fukuya, Y. and Zhang, Y. (2002), 'Effects of Recasts on EFL Learners' Acquisition of Pragmalinguistic Conventions of Request', *Second Language Studies*, 21 (1): 1–47.

Fukuya, Y. J. (1998), 'Consciousness-Raising of Downgraders in Requests', Paper Presented at Second Language Research Forum '98, University of Hawai'i at Manoa *(ERIC document Reproduction Service No. ED466100)*.

Fukuya, Y. J. and Clark, M. K. (2001), 'A Comparison of Input Enhancement and Explicit Instruction of Mitigators', in L. Bouton (ed.), *Pragmatics and Language Learning, Vol. 10*, 111–30, Urbana, IL: Division of English as an International Language Intensive English Institute, University of Illinois at Urbana-Champaign.

Gao (Andy), X. (2006), 'Understanding Changes in Chinese Students' Uses of Learning Strategies in China and Britain: A Socio-Cultural Re-Interpretation', *System*, 34 (1): 55–67.

Garcia, C. (1989), 'Apologizing in English: Politeness Strategies Used by Native and Non-Native Speakers. Multilingua', *Journal of Cross-Cultural and Interlanguage Communication*, 8 (1): 3–20.

Gee, J. P. (2005), *Why Video Games Are Good for Your Soul*, Sydney, Australia: Common Ground.

Giles, H., Coupland, J., Coupland, N. and Coupl, J. eds. (1991), *Contexts of Accommodation: Developments in Applied Sociolinguistics*, Cambridge: Editions De La Maison Des Science De L'homme.

Glaser, K. (2018), 'Enhancing the Role of Pragmatics in Primary English Teacher Training', *Glottodidactica. An International Journal of Applied Linguistics*, 45 (2): 119–31.

Goffman, E. (1967), *Interaction Ritual: Essays on Face-to-Face Behavior*, New York: Knopf Doubleday Publishing Group.

Goffman, E. (1971), *Relations in Public: Microstudies of the Public Order*, New York: Basic Books.

Golato, A. (2003), 'Studying Compliment Responses: A Comparison of DCTs and Recordings of Naturally Occurring Talk', *Applied Linguistics*, 24 (1): 90–121.

Gomez-Laich, M. P. (2016), 'Second Language Learners' Divergence from Target Language Pragmatic Norms', *Studies in Second Language Learning and Teaching*, 6 (2): 249–69.

Gu, Q. and Maley, A. (2008), 'Changing Places: A Study of Chinese Students in the UK', *Language and Intercultural Communication*, 8 (4): 224–45.

Gu, Y. (1990), 'Politeness Phenomena in Modern Chinese', *Journal of Pragmatics*, 14 (2): 237–57.

Halenko, N. (2013), 'Using Computer-Animation to Assess and Improve Spoken Language Skills'. Conference Proceedings: ICT for Language Learning, 286. Florence: Liberiauniversitaria.

Halenko, N. (2018), 'Using Computer-Assisted Language Learning (CALL) Tools to Enhance Output Practice', in C. Jones (ed.), *Practice in Second Language Learning*, 137–63, Cambridge: Cambridge University Press.

Halenko, N. and Aslan, E. (forthcoming), Surveying Pragmatics in UK-based university TESOL courses.

Halenko, N. and Flores-Salgado, E. (2019), 'Embedding ICT to Teach and Assess the Pragmatic Targets of Refusals and Disagreements in Spoken English', British Council ELT Research Papers 19 (3). Available online: https://www.teachingenglish.org.uk/sites/teacheng/files/K058_Embedding%20ICT.pdf (accessed 2 February 2020).

Halenko, N. and Jones, C. (2011), 'Teaching Pragmatic Awareness of Spoken Requests to Chinese EAP Learners in the UK: Is Explicit Instruction Effective?', *System*, 39 (2): 240–50.

Halenko, N. and Jones, C. (2017), 'Explicit Instruction of Spoken Requests: An Examination of Pre-Departure Instruction and the Study Abroad Context', *System*, 68: 26–37.

Halenko, N., Jones, C., Davies, L. and Davies, J. (2019), 'Surveying Pragmatic Performance during a Study Abroad Stay: A Cross-Sectional Look at the Language of Spoken Requests', *Intercultural Communication Education*, 2 (2): 71–87.

Hall, E. T. (1977), *Beyond Culture*, New York: Anchor Books.

Hall, J. K., Hellerman, J. and Pekarek Doehler, S. eds. (2011), *L2 Interactional Competence and Development*, Bristol: Multilingual Matters.

Hartford, B. S. and Bardovi-Harlig, K. (1992), 'Experimental and Observational Data in the Study of Interlanguage Pragmatics', in L. F. Bouton and Y. Kachru (eds), *Pragmatics and Language Learning Monograph Series (Vol. 3)*, 33–52, Urbana, IL: Division of English as an International Language, University of Illinois at Urbana-Champaign.

Hassall, T. (2013), 'Pragmatic Development during Short-Term Study Abroad: The Case of Address Terms in Indonesian', *Journal of Pragmatics*, 55: 1–17.

Henery, A. (2015), 'On the Development of Metapragmatic Awareness Abroad: Two Case Studies Exploring the Role of Expert-Mediation', *Language Awareness*, 24 (4): 316–31.

Hernández, T. A. and Boero, P. (2018), 'Explicit Instruction for Request Strategy Development during Short-Term Study Abroad', *Journal of Spanish Language Teaching*, 5: 1–15.

Hill, B., Ide, S., Ikuta, S., Kawasaki, A. and Ogino, T. (1986), 'Universals of Linguistic Politeness: Quantitative Evidence from Japanese and American English for Specific Purposes', *Journal of Pragmatics*, 10: 347–71.

Hill, T. (1997), 'The Development of Pragmatic Competence in an EFL Context', Unpublished Doctoral Dissertation, Temple University, Tokyo.

Hinkel, E. (2018), 'Teaching and Learning Formulaic Sequences and Prefabs', in J. I. Liontas (ed.), *The TESOL Encyclopedia of English Language Teaching*, 1–8, New York: John Wiley & Sons, Inc.

Hofstede, G. H. (2005), *Cultures and Organizations: Software of the Mind; [Intercultural Cooperation and Its Importance for Survival]* (2nd ed.), New York: Mcgraw-Hill Professional.

Holmes, J. (1990), 'Apologies in New Zealand English', *Language in Society*, 19 (2): 155–99.

Houck, N. R. and Tatsuki, D. H. (2011), *Pragmatics: Teaching Natural Conversation*, Virginia: Teachers of English to Speakers of Other Languages, Inc.

House, J. (1988), '"On Excuse Me Please …": Apologizing in a Foreign Language', in B. Ketterman, P. Bierbaumer, A. Fill and A. Karpf (eds), *English Als Zweitsprache*, 303–27, Tubingen: Narr.

House, J. (2008), 'What Is an "Intercultural Speaker"?', in E. Alcón Soler and M. P. Safont Jordá (eds), *Intercultural Language Use and Language Learning*, 7–22, Narr, Tübingen: Springer.

House, J. (2018), 'Authentic vs Elicited Data and Qualitative vs Quantitative Research Methods in Pragmatics', *System*, 75: 4–12.

House, J. and Kasper, G. (2000), 'How to Remain a Nonnative Speaker', in C. Riemer (ed.), *Kognitive aspekte Des Lehrens Und Lernens Von Fremdsprachen: Festschrift Fur Willis J. Edmondson Zum 60. Geburtstag = Cognitive Aspects of Foreign Language Learning and Teaching*, 101–18, Tubingen: Narr.

Hymes, D. (1972), 'Models of Interaction of Language and Social Life', in J. J. Gumperz and D. H. Hymes (eds), *Directions in Sociolinguistics: The Ethnography of Communication*, 35–71, New York: Holt, Rinehart and Winston.

Ide, S. (1993), 'Linguistic Politeness III: Linguistic Politeness and Universality', *Multilingua*, 12 (1): 223–48.

Ishida, M. (2009), 'Development of Interactional Competence: Changes in the Use of ne in L2 Japanese during Study Abroad', in H. Thi Nguyen and G. Kasper (eds), *Talk-in-Interaction: Multilingual Perspectives*, 351–85, Honolulu, HI: University of Hawai'i, National Foreign Language Resource Center.

Ishihara, N. (2010), 'Instructional Pragmatics: Bridging Teaching, Research, and Teacher Education', *Language and Linguistics Compass*, 4 (10): 938–53.

Ishihara, N. (2011), 'Co-Constructing Pragmatic Awareness: Instructional Pragmatics in EFL Teacher Development in Japan', *TESL-EJ*, 15 (2): 1–17.

Ishihara, N. and Cohen, A. D. (2010), *Teaching and Learning Pragmatics*, Malaysia: Pearson Education Limited.

Ishihara, N. and Tarone, E. (2009), 'Subjectivity and Pragmatic Choice in L2 Japanese: Emulating and Resisting Pragmatic Norms', in N. Taguchi (ed.), *Pragmatic Competence in Japanese as a Second Language*, 101–28, Berlin: Mouton De Gruyter.

Iwai, T. (2013), 'Using *n desu* in Small Talk: JFL Learners' Pragmatics Development', in K. Kondo-Brown, Y. Saito-Abbott, S. Satsutani, M. Tsutsui and A. Wehmeyer (eds), *New Perspectives on Japanese Language Learning, Linguistics and Culture*, 181–202, Honolulu, HI: University of Hawai'i, National Foreign Language Resource Center.

Iwasaki, N. (2011), 'Learning L2 Japanese "Politeness" and "Impoliteness": Young American Men's Dilemmas during Study Abroad', *Japanese Language and Literature*, 45: 67–106.

Jeon, E. H. and Kaya, T. (2006), 'Effects of L2 Instruction on Interlanguage Pragmatic Development: A Meta-Analysis', in J. M. Norris and L. Ortega (eds), *Synthesizing Research on Language Learning and Teaching*, 165–211, Amsterdam: John Benjamins.

Johnson, N. H. and De Haan, J. (2013), 'Strategic Interaction 2.0', *International Journal of Strategic Information Technology and Applications*, 4 (1): 49–62.

Jones, C. and Halenko, N. (2014), 'What Makes a Successful Spoken Request? Using Corpus Tools to Analyse Learner Language in a UK EAP Context'. *Apples- Journal of Applied Language Studies*, 8 (2): 23–41.

Kasper, G. (1989), 'Interactive Procedures in Interlanguage Discourse', in W. Oleksy (ed.), *Contrastive Pragmatics*, 189–229, Amsterdam: Benjamins.

Kasper, G. (1992), 'Pragmatic Transfer', *Second Language Research*, 8: 203–31.

Kasper, G. (1996), 'Developmental Issues in Interlanguage Pragmatics', *Studies in Second Language Acquisition*, 18 (2): 149–69.

Kasper, G. (1997), 'Can Pragmatic Competence Be Taught?', Honolulu, HI: University of Hawai'i at Manoa, Second Language Teaching and Curriculum Center. Available online: http://www.nflrc.hawaii.edu/networks/nw06/ (accessed 29 March 2009).

Kasper, G. and Blum Kulka, S. eds. (1993), *Interlanguage Pragmatics*, New York: Oxford University Press.

Kasper, G. and Rose, K. R. (2002), *Pragmatic Development in a Second Language*, Malden, MA: Blackwell Publishers.

Kasper, G. and Zhang, Y. (1995), *Pragmatics of Chinese as Native and Target Language*, Second Language Teaching and Curriculum Centre, University of Hawai'i at Manoa, Honolulu, HI: University of Hawai'i Press.

Kecskes, I. (2000a), 'Conceptual Fluency and the Use of Situation-Bound Utterances', *Links and Letters*, 7: 145–61.

Kecskes, I. (2000b), 'A Cognitive-Pragmatic Approach to Situation-Bound Utterances', *Journal of Pragmatics*, 32 (5): 605–25.

Kecskes, I. (2010), 'Situation-Bound Utterances as Pragmatic Acts', *Journal of Pragmatics*, 42 (11): 2889–97.

Kecskes, I. (2014), *Intercultural Pragmatics*, Oxford/New York: Oxford University Press.

Kecskes, I. (2015), 'Situation-Bound Utterances in Chinese', *East Asian Pragmatics*, 1 (1): 107–26.

Kecskes, I. and Assimakopoulos, S. (2017), *Current Issues in Intercultural Pragmatics*, Amsterdam: John Benjmains.

Kim, H. (2008), 'The Semantic and Pragmatic Analysis of South Korean and Australian English Apologetic Speech Acts', *Journal of Pragmatics*, 40 (2): 257–78.

Kim, H. Y. (2014), 'Learner Investment, Identity, and Resistance to Second Language Pragmatic Norms', *System*, 45: 95–102.

Kinginger, C. (2009), *Language Learning and Study Abroad: A Critical Reading of Research*, New York: Palgrave Macmillan.

Kinginger, C. (2013), *Social and Cultural Aspects of Language Learning in Study Abroad*, Netherlands: John Benjamins.

Kirkpatrick, A. (1991), 'Information Sequencing in Mandarin Letters of Request', *Anthropological Linguistics*, 33 (2): 183–203.

Kirkpatrick, A. (1992), 'Schemas, Authentic Texts and Cross-Cultural Communication', *Australian Review of Applied Linguistics*, Supplement 9: 101–19.

Kondo, S. (1997), 'The Development of Pragmatic Competence by Japanese Learners of English: Longitudinal Study on Interlanguage Apologies', *Sophia Linguistica*, 41: 265–84.

Kondo, S. (2008), 'Apologies: Raising Learners' Cross-Cultural Awareness', in A. Martinez-Flor and E. Uso-Juan (eds), *Speech Act Performance: Theoretical, Empirical and Methodological Issues*, 145–63, Amsterdam/Philadelphia, PA: John Benjamins.

Kondo, S. (2010), 'Apologies: Raising Learners' Cross-Cultural Awareness', in A. Martinez-Flor and E. Uso-Juan (eds), *Speech Act Performance: Theoretical, Empirical and Methodological Issues*, 145–62, Amsterdam: John Benjamins Publishing Co.

Kubota, M. (1995), 'Teachability of Conversational Implicature to Japanese EFL Learners', *The Institute for Research in Language Teaching Bulletin*, 9: 35–67.

Labben, A. (2016), 'Reconsidering the Development of the Discourse Completion Test in Interlanguage Pragmatics', *Pragmatics*, 26 (1): 61–91.

Lee, C. F. K. (2004), 'Written Requests in Emails Sent by Adult Chinese Learners of English', *Language, Culture and Curriculum*, 17 (1): 58–72.

Leech, G. (2014), *The Pragmatics of Politeness*, Oxford/New York: Oxford University Press.

Leech, G. N. (1983), *Principles of Pragmatics* (12th ed.), New York: Longman.

Lee-Wong, S. M. (1994), 'Imperatives in Requests: Direct or Impolite – Observations from Chinese', *Pragmatics Quarterly Publication of the International Pragmatics Association (IPRA)*, 4 (4): 491–515.

Le-Thi, D., Rodgers, M. P. H. and Pellicer-Sánchez, A. (2017), 'Teaching Formulaic Sequences in an English Language Class: The Effects of Explicit Instruction versus Coursebook Instruction', *TESL Canada Journal*, 34 (3): 111–39.

Lewis, M. (1993), *The Lexical Approach: The State of ELT and a Way Forward*. Hove, England: Language Teaching Publications.

Li, C. and Gao, X. (2017), 'Bridging "What I Said" and "Why I Said It": The Role of Metapragmatic Awareness in L2 Request Performance', *Language Awareness*, 26 (3): 170–90.

Li, S. (2012), 'The Effects of Input-Based Practice on Pragmatic Development of Requests in L2 Chinese', *Language Learning*, 62 (2): 403–38.

Li, S. (2013), 'Amount of Practice in Pragmatic Development of Request-Making in L2 Chinese', in N. Taguchi and J. M. Sykes (eds), *Technology in Interlanguage Pragmatics Research and Teaching*, 43–70, Amsterdam: John Benjamins.

Li, S. (2014), 'The Effects of Different Levels of Linguistic Proficiency on the Development of L2 Chinese Request Production during Study Abroad', *System*, 45: 103–16.

Li, S. and Taguchi, N. (2014), 'The Effects of Practice Modality on the Development of Pragmatic Performance in L2 Chinese', *Modern Language Journal*, 98: 794–812.

Liddicoat, A. and Crozet, C. (2001), 'Acquiring French Interactional Norms through Instruction', in K. R. Rose and G. Kasper (eds), *Pragmatics in Language Teaching*, 125–44, Cambridge: Cambridge University Press.

Liddicoat, A. J. (2011), 'Language Teaching and Learning from an Intercultural Perspective', in E. Hinkel (ed.), *Handbook of Research in Second Language Teaching and Learning*, 837–55, Abingdon: Routledge.

Liddicoat, A. J. and Scarino, A. (2013), *Intercultural language Teaching and Learning*, New York: Wiley-Blackwell.

Limberg, H. (2015), 'Principles for Pragmatics Teaching: "Apologies" in the EFL Classroom', *ELT Journal*, 69 (3): 275–85.

Limberg, H. (2016), 'Teaching How to Apologize: EFL Textbooks and Pragmatic Input', *Language Teaching Research*, 20 (6): 700–18.

Lin, Y. H. (2009), 'Query Preparatory Modals: Cross-Linguistic and Cross-Situational Variations in Request Modification', *Journal of Pragmatics*, 41 (8): 1636–56.

Linnell, J., Porter, F. L., Stone, H. and Chen, W. (1992), 'Can You Apologize Me? An Investigation of Speech Act Performance among Non-Native Speakers of English', *Educational Linguistics (University of Pennsylvania Graduate School of Education)*, 8: 33–53.

Llanes, À. (2011), 'The Many Faces of Study Abroad: An Update on the Research on L2 Gains Emerged during a Study Abroad Experience', *International Journal of Multilingualism*, 8 (3): 189–215.

LoCastro, V. (2001), 'Individual Differences in Second Language Acquisition: Attitudes, Learner Subjectivity, and L2 Pragmatic Norms', *System*, 29: 69–89.

Locastro, V. (2003), *An Introduction to Pragmatics: Social Action for Language Teachers*, Ann Arbor: The University of Michigan Press.

Locher, M. A. and Watts, R. J. (2005), 'Politeness Theory and Relational Work', *Journal of Politeness Research: Language, Behaviour, Culture*, 1: 9–33.

Loewen, S. (2015), *Introduction to Instructed Second Language Acquisition*, New York: Routledge.

Long, M. H. (1996), 'The Role of Linguistic Environment in Second Language Acquisition', in W. C. Ritchie and T. K. Bhatia (eds), *Handbook of Second Language Acquisition*, 413–68, San Diego, CA: Academic Press.

Lyster, R. (1994), 'The Effect of Functional-Analytic Teaching on Aspects of French Immersion Students' Sociolinguistic Competence', *Applied Linguistics*, 15 (3): 263–87.

Maeshiba, N., Yoshinaga, N., Kasper, G. and Ross, S. (1996), 'Transfer and Proficiency in Interlanguage Apologizing', in S. Gass and J. Neu (eds), *Speech Acts across Cultures: Challenges to Communication in a Second Language*, 155–87, Germany: Mouton De Gruyter.

Major, E. M. (2005), 'Co-National Support, Cultural Therapy, and the Adjustment of Asian Students to an English-Speaking University Culture', *International Education Journal*, 6: 84–95.

Mao, L. R. (1994), 'Beyond Politeness Theory: "Face" Revisited and Renewed', *Journal of Pragmatics*, 21 (5): 451–86.

Marquez-Reiter, R. (2000), *Linguistic Politeness in Britain and Uruguay: A Contrastive Study of Requests and Apologies*, Netherlands: Benjamins (John) North America Inc., US.

Marsden, E., Mackey, A. and Plonsky, L. (2016), 'The IRIS Repository: Advancing Research Practice and Methodology', in A. Mackey and E. Marsden (eds), *Advancing Methodology and Practice: The IRIS Repository of Instruments for Research into Second Languages*, 1–21, New York: Routledge.

Martinez-Flor, A. (2006), 'The Effectiveness of Explicit and Implicit Treatments on EFL Learners' Confidence in Recognising Appropriate Suggestions', in K. Bardovi-Harlig, C. Félix-Brasdefer and A. S. Omar (eds), *Pragmatics and Language Learning* (Vol. 11), 199–225, Honolulu, HI: University of Hawai'i at Manoa, National Foreign Language Resource Center.

Martínez-Flor, A. (2008a), *Investigating Pragmatics in Foreign Language Learning, Teaching and Testing*, Bristol: Multilingual Matters.

Martinez-Flor, A. (2008b), 'The Effect of Inductive-Deductive Teaching Approach to Develop Learners' Use', in E. Alcón Soler (ed.), *Learning How to Request in an Instructed Language Learning Context*, 191–226, Switzerland: Peter Lang Pub.

Martinez-Flor, A. (2012), 'Examining EFL Learners Long-Term Instructional Effects When Mitigating Requests', in M. Economidou-Kogetsidis and H. Woodfield (eds), *Interlanguage Request Modification*, 243–74, Amsterdam: John Benjamins.

Martínez-Flor, A. and Usó-Juan, E. (2006), 'Developing Communicative Competence through Listening', in E. Usó-Juan and A. Martínez-Flor (eds), *Current Trends in the Development and Teaching of the Four Language Skills*, 29–47, Berlin: Mouton De Gruyter.

Martinez-Flor, A. and Usó-Juan, E. (2010), 'The Teaching of Speech Acts in Second and Foreign Language Instructional Contexts', in A. Trosborg (ed.), *Pragmatics across Languages and Cultures* (7th ed.), 423–43, Berlin: Mouton De Gruyter.

Masuda, K. (2011), 'Acquiring Interactional Competence in a Study Abroad Context: Japanese Language Learners' Use of the Interactional Particle *ne*', *Modern Language Journal*, 95: 519–40.

Matsumoto, Y. (1988), 'Reexamination of the Universality of Face: Politeness Phenomena in Japanese', *Journal of Pragmatics*, 12: 403–26.

Matsumoto, Y. (1989), 'Politeness and Conversational Universals – Observations from Japanese', *Multilingua*, 8 (2/3): 207–21.

Matsumura, S. (2001), 'Learning the Rules for Offering Advice: A Quantitative Approach to Second Language Socialization', *Language Learning*, 51: 635–79.

Matsumura, S. (2003), 'Modelling the Relationships among Interlanguage Pragmatic Development, L2 Proficiency, and Exposure to L2', *Applied Linguistics*, 24 (4): 465–91.

McConachy, T. (2018), *Developing Intercultural Perspectives on Language Use*, Bristol: Multilingual Matters.

Morris, K. (2017), 'Learning by Doing: The Affordances of Task-Based Pragmatics Instruction for Beginning L2 Spanish Learners Studying Abroad', Unpublished doctoral dissertation. University of California, California.

Myles, J. and Cheng, L. (2003), 'The Social and Cultural Life of Non-Native English Speaking International Graduate Students at a Canadian University', *Journal of English for Academic Purposes*, 2 (3): 247–63.

Nattinger, J. and DeCarrico, J. (1992), *Lexical Phrases and Language Teaching*, Oxford: Oxford University Press.

Nguyen, M. (2011), 'Learning to Communicate in a Globalized World: To What Extent Do School Textbooks Facilitate the Development of Intercultural Pragmatic Competence?', *RELC Journal*, 42 (1): 17–30.

Nguyen, T. T. M., Pham, M. T. and Cao, T. H. (2013), 'The Effects of Explicit Metapragmatic Instruction on EFL Learners' Performance of Constructive Criticism in an Academic Setting', *Pragmatics and Language Learning*, 13: 213–44.

Norris, J. M. and Ortega, L. (2000), 'Effectiveness of L2 Instruction: A Research Synthesis and Quantitative Meta-Analysis', *Language Learning*, 50 (3): 417–528.

Norris, J. M., Plonsky, L., Ross, S. J. and Schoonen, R. (2015), 'Guidelines for Reporting Quantitative Methods and Results in Primary Research', *Language Learning*, 65 (2): 470–76.

Nureddeen, F. A. (2008), 'Cross Cultural Pragmatics: Apology Strategies in Sudanese Arabic', *Journal of Pragmatics*, 40 (2): 279–306.

O'Driscoll, J. (1996), 'About Face: A Defence and Elaboration of Universal Dualism', *Journal of Pragmatics*, 25 (1): 1–32.

Octu, B. and Zeyrek, D. (2008), 'Development of Requests: A Study on Turkish Learners of English', in M. Puetz and J. Neff Van Aertselaer (eds), *Developing Contrastive Pragmatics: Interlanguage and Cross-Cultural Perspectives*, 265–300, Berlin: Mouton De Gruyter.

OECD. (2018), 'Graph B6.3 – Change in the Outflow Compared to the Inflow of Mobile Students (2013 to 2016): Indices of Change of Inward and Outward Mobility (2013 = 100)', Access to Education, Participation and Progression, Paris: OECD Publishing. Available online: https://doi.org/10.1787/eag-2018-graph116-en (accessed 12 June 2020).

Ogiermann, E. (2009), *On Apologising in Negative and Positive Politeness Cultures*, Amsterdam: John Benjamins Publishing Co.

Ohta, A. (2005), 'Interlanguage Pragmatics in the Zone of Proximal Development', *System*, 33: 503–17.

Olshtain, E. (1989), 'Apologies across Languages', in S. Blum-Kulka, J. House and G. Kasper (eds), *Cross-Cultural Pragmatics: Requests and Apologies/Instructors Edition*, 155–74, Norwood, NJ: Ablex Pub. Corp.

Olshtain, E. and Cohen, A. (1990), 'The Learning of Complex Speech Act Behaviour', *TESL Canada Journal*, 7 (2): 45–65.

Olshtain, E. and Cohen, A. D. (1981), 'Developing a Measure of Sociocultural Competence: The Case of Apology', *Language Learning*, 31 (1): 113–34.

Olshtain, E. and Cohen, A. D. (1983), 'Apology: A Speech Act Set', in N. Wolfson and E. Judd (eds), *Sociolinguistics and Language Acquisition*, 18–35, Rowley, MA: Newbury House.

Owen, M. (1983), *Apologies and Remedial Interchanges: A Study of Language Use in Social Interaction*, Germany: Mouton De Gruyter.

Pallotti, G. (2009), 'CAF: Defining, Refining and Differentiating Constructs', *Applied Linguistics*, 30 (4): 590–601.

Park, H. S. and Guan, X. (2009), 'Culture, Positive and Negative Face Threats, and Apology Intentions', *Journal of Language and Social Psychology*, 28 (3): 244–62.

Pavlidou, T. (1994), 'Contrasting German-Greek Politeness and the Consequences', *Journal of Pragmatics*, 21 (5): 487–511.

Pavlidou, T. S. (1998), 'Greek and German Telephone Closings: Patterns of Confirmation and Agreement', *Pragmatics Quarterly Publication of the International Pragmatics Association (IPRA)*, 8 (1): 79–94.

Pawley, A. and Syder, F. (1983), 'Two Puzzles for Linguistic Theory: Nativelike Selection and Nativelike Fluency', in J. Richards and R. Schmidt (eds), *Language and Communication*, 191–225, London: Longman.

Plonsky, L. and Zhuang, J. (2019), 'A Meta-Analysis of L2 Pragmatics Instruction', in N. Taguchi (ed.), *The Routledge Handbook of Second Language Acquisition and Pragmatics*, 287–307, New York/London: Routledge.

Qi, Y. and Ding, Y. (2011), 'Use of Formulaic Sequences in Monologues of Chinese EFL Learners', *System*, 39: 164–74.

Ranta, L. and Meckelborg, A. (2013), 'How Much Exposure to English Do International Graduate Students Really Get? Measuring Language Use in a Naturalistic Setting', *Canadian Modern Language Review*, 69 (1): 1–33.

Rau, D. V. and Rau, G. (2016), 'Negotiating Personal Relationship through Email Terms of Address', in Y. Chen, D. V. Rau and G. Rau (eds), *Email Discourse among Chinese Using English as a Lingua Franca*, 11–36, Singapore: Springer.

Reinhardt, J. and Sykes, J. M. (2014), 'Special Issue Commentary: Digital Game Activity in L2 Teaching and Learning', *Language Learning and Technology*, 18 (2): 2–8. Available online: http://llt.msu.edu/issues/june2014/commentary.pdf (accessed 12 August 2019).

Riddiford, N. and Newton, J. (2010), *Workplace Talk in Action: An ESOL Resource*, Wellington: Victoria University of Wellington.

Rintell, E. and Mitchell, C. J. (1989), 'Studying Requests and Apologies: An Inquiry into Method', in S. Blum-Kulka, J. House and G. Kasper (eds), *Cross-Cultural Pragmatics*, 248–72, Norwood, NJ: Ablex.

Roberts, C., Byram, M., Barro, A., Jordan, S. and Street, B. (2001), *Language Learners as Ethnographers*, Clevedon: Multilingual Matters.

Roever, C. (2005), *Language Testing and Evaluation: Testing ESL Pragmatics: Development and Validation of a Web-Based Assessment Battery*, Frankfurt am Main /New York: Peter Lang.

Roever, C. (2011), 'Testing of Second Language Pragmatics: Past and Future', *Language Testing*, 28 (4): 463–81.

Roever, C. (2013), 'Technology and Tests of L2 Pragmatics', in N. Taguchi and J. Sykes (eds), *Technology in Interlanguage Pragmatics Research and Teaching*, 215–35, Amsterdam: John Benjamins.

Rose, K. (2000), 'An Exploratory Cross-Sectional Study of Interlanguage Pragmatic Development', *Studies in Second Language Acquisition*, 22 (1): 27–67.

Rose, K. R. (2005), 'On the Effects of Instruction in Second Language Pragmatics', *System*, 33 (3): 385–99.

Rose, K. R. and Kasper, G. (2001), *Pragmatics in Language Teaching*, Cambridge: Cambridge University Press.

Rose, K. R. and Ng, K. (2001), 'Inductive and Deductive Teaching of Compliments and Compliment Responses', in K. R. Rose and G. Kasper (eds), *Pragmatics in Language Teaching*, 145–70, Cambridge: Cambridge University Press.

Sabaté i Dalmau, M. and Curell i Gotor, H. (2007), 'From "Sorry Very Much" to "I'm Ever So Sorry": Acquisitional Patterns in L2 Apologies by Catalan Learners of English', *Intercultural Pragmatics*, 4 (2): 287–315.

Safont Jordá, M. (2004), 'An Analysis on EAP Learners' Pragmatic Production: A Focus on Request Forms', *Iberica*, 8: 23–39.

Salazar, P. (2003), 'Pragmatic Instruction in the EFL Context', in A. Martinez-Flor, E. Uso-Juan and A. Fernandez-Guerra (eds), *Pragmatic Competence and Foreign Language Teaching*, 233–46, Castello: Publicacions De La Universitat Jaume I.

Sánchez-Hernández, A. and Alcón-Soler, E. (2018), 'Pragmatic Gains in the Study Abroad Context: Learners' Experiences and Recognition of Pragmatic Routines', *Journal of Pragmatics*, 146: 1–18.

Sasaki, M. (1998), 'Investigating EFL Students' Production of Speech Acts: A Comparison of Production Questionnaires and Role Plays', *Journal of Pragmatics*, 30 (4): 457–84.

Savić, M. (2016), 'Do EFL Teachers in Serbia Have What They Need to Teach L2 Pragmatics? Novice Teachers' Views of Politeness', in K. Bardovi-Harlig and J. César Félix-Brasdefer (eds), *Pragmatics Language Learning* (Vol. 14), 207–33, Hawaii: University of Hawaii: National Foreign Language Resource Center.

Savvidou, C. and Kogetsidis, M. (2019), 'Teaching Pragmatics: Nonnative-Speaker Teachers' Knowledge, Beliefs and Reported Practices', *Intercultural Communication Education*, 2 (1): 39–58.

Schauer, G. A. (2004), 'May You Speaker Louder Maybe? Interlanguage Pragmatic Development in Requests', in S. H. Foster-Cohen, M. Sharwood Smith, A. Sorace and M. Ota (eds), *EUROSLA Yearbook No. 4*, 253–73, Amsterdam: John Benjamins.

Schauer, G. A. (2006), 'Pragmatic Awareness in ESL and EFL Contexts: Contrast and Development', *Language Learning*, 56 (2): 269–318.

Schauer, G. A. (2007), 'Finding the Right Words in the Study Abroad Context: The Development of German Learners' Use of External Modifiers in English', *Intercultural Pragmatics*, 4 (2): 193–220.

Schauer, G. A. (2009), *Interlanguage Pragmatic Development: The Study Abroad Context*, London: Continuum International Publishing Group.

Schauer, G. A. (2019), *Teaching and Learning English in the Primary School – Interlanguage Pragmatics in the EFL Context*, Cham: Springer.

Schieffelin, B. B. and Ochs, E. (1986), *Language Socialization across Cultures*, Cambridge: Cambridge University Press.

Schmidt, R. (1993), 'Consciousness, Learning and Interlanguage Pragmatics', in G. Kasper and S. Blum-Kulka (eds), *Interlanguage Pragmatics*, 21–42, New York: Oxford University Press.

Schmidt, R. (2001), 'Attention', in P. Robinson (ed.), *Cognition and Second Language Instruction*, 3–33, New York: Cambridge University Press.

Schmitt, N. (2004), *Formulaic Sequences Acquisition, Processing, and Use*, Amsterdam: John Benjamins Publishing Co.

Schmitt, N. (2010), *Researching Vocabulary: A Vocabulary Research Manual*, New York: Palgrave Macmillan.

Schmitt, N. and Carter, R. (2004), 'Formulaic Sequences in Action', in N. Schmitt (ed.), *Formulaic Sequences*, 1–23, Amsterdam: John Benjamins.

Searle, J. R. (1969), *Speech Acts: An Essay in the Philosophy of Language*, London: Cambridge University Press.

Searle, J. R. (1976), 'A Classification of Illocutionary Acts', *Language in Society*, 5: 1–23.

Shardakova, M. (2005), 'Intercultural Pragmatics in the Speech of American L2 Learners of Russian: Apologies Offered by Americans in Russian', *Intercultural Pragmatics*, 2 (4): 423–51.

Shively, R. L. (2008), 'Politeness and Social Interaction in Study Abroad: Service Encounters in L2 Spanish'. Unpublished doctoral dissertation. University of Minnesota, Minneapolis.

Shively, R. (2010), 'From the Virtual World to the Real World: A Model of Pragmatics Instruction for Study Abroad', *Foreign Language Annals*, 43 (1): 105–37.

Shively, R. and Cohen, A. D. (2008), 'Development of Spanish Requests and Apologies during Study Abroad', *Ikala, Revista De Language Y Cultura*, 13 (20): 57–118.

Shively, R. L. (2011), 'L2 Pragmatic Development in Study Abroad: A Longitudinal Study of Spanish Service Encounters', *Journal of Pragmatics*, 43 (6): 1818–35.

Siegel, J., Broadbridge, J. and Firth, M. (2019), 'Saying It "Just Right": Teaching for Pragmatic Success in ELT', *ELT Journal*, 73 (1): 31–40.

Sifianou, M. (1992), *Politeness Phenomena in England and Greece: A Cross-Cultural Perspective*, Oxford: Clarendon Press.

Sinclair, J. and Sinclair, L. (1991), *Corpus Concordance and Collocation (Describing English Language)*, Oxford: Oxford University Press.

Spencer-Oatey, H. (2000), *Culturally Speaking: Managing Rapport through Talk across Cultures*, London: Continuum International Publishing Group.

Spencer Oatey, H., Dauber, D., Jing, J. and Wang, L. (2017), 'Chinese Students' Social Integration into the University Community: Hearing the Students' Voice', *Higher Education*, 74: 739–56.

Su, I. R. (2010), 'Transfer of Pragmatic Competences: A Bi-Directional Perspective', *The Modern Language Journal*, 94 (1): 87–102.

Suszczyńska, M. (1999), 'Apologizing in English, Polish and Hungarian: Different Languages, Different Strategies', *Journal of Pragmatics*, 31 (8): 1053–65.

Swain, M. (1996), 'Three Functions of Output in Second Language Learning', in G. Cook and B. Seldlhofer (eds), *Principle and Practice in Applied Linguistics: Studies in Honour of H.G. Widdowson* (2nd ed.), 245–56, Oxford: Oxford University Press.

Swan, M. (2017), 'Chunks in the Classroom: Let's Not Go Overboard'. Available online: https://mikeswan.net/wp-content/uploads/2017/08/Chunks-in-the-classroom.pdf (accessed 7 November 2019).

Sydorenko, T. (2015), 'The Use of Computer-Delivered Structured Tasks in Pragmatic Instruction: An Exploratory Study', *Intercultural Pragmatics*, 12 (3): 333–62.

Sykes, J. (2009), 'Learner Request in Spanish: Examining the Potential of Multiuser Virtual Environments for L2 Pragmatics Acquisition', in L. Lomika and G. Lord (eds), *The Second Generation: Online Collaboration and Social Networking in CALL, CALICO Monograph*, 199–234, San Marcos, TX: CALICO.

Sykes, J. (2013), 'Multiuser Virtual Environments: Apologies in Spanish', in N. Taguchi and J. Sykes (eds), *Technology in Interlanguage Pragmatics Research and Teaching*, 71–100, Amsterdam/Philadelphia, PA: John Benjamins.

Sykes, J., Oskoz, A. and Thorne, S. (2008), 'Web 2.0, Synthetic Immersive Environments and Mobile Resources for Language Education', *CALICO*, 25 (3): 528–46.

Taguchi, N. (2002), 'An Application of Relevance Theory to the Analysis of L2 Interpretation Processes: The Comprehension of Indirect Replies', *International Review of Applied Linguistics*, 40: 151–76.

Taguchi, N. (2006), 'Analysis of Appropriateness in a Speech Act of Request in L2 English', *Pragmatics Quarterly Publication of the International Pragmatics Association (IPRA)*, 16 (4): 513–33.

Taguchi, N. (2008a), 'Cognition, Language Contact, and the Development of Pragmatic Comprehension in a Study-Abroad Context', *Language Learning*, 58 (1): 33–71.

Taguchi, N. (2008b), 'The Role of Learning Environment in the Development of Pragmatic Comprehension', *Studies in Second Language Acquisition*, 30 (4): 423–52.

Taguchi, N. (2010), 'Longitudinal Studies in Interlanguage Pragmatics', in A. Trosborg (ed.), *Handbook of Pragmatics Vol.7: Pragmatics across Languages and Cultures*, 333–61, Berlin: Mouton De Gruyter.

Taguchi, N. (2011), 'The Effect of L2 Proficiency and Study-Abroad Experience on Pragmatic Comprehension', *Language Learning*, 61 (3): 904–39.

Taguchi, N. (2012), *Context, Individual Differences and Pragmatic Competence*, New York/Bristol: Multilingual Matters.

Taguchi, N. (2014a), 'Instructed Pragmatics at a Glance: Where ILP Studies Are, Were, and Should Be Going', *Language Teaching*, 48: 1–50.

Taguchi, N. (2014b), 'Development of Interactional Competence in Japanese as a Second Language: Use of Incomplete Sentences as Interactional Resources', *Modern Language Journal*, 98 (2): 518–35.

Taguchi, N. (2015), '"Contextually" Speaking: A Survey of Pragmatic Learning Abroad, in Class, and Online', *System*, 48: 3–20.

Taguchi, N. (2017), 'Interlanguage Pragmatics', in A. Barron, P. Grundy and G. Yuego (eds), *The Routledge Handbook of Pragmatics*, 153–67, Oxford/New York: Routledge.

Taguchi, N., Li, S. and Xiao, F. (2013), 'Production of Formulaic Expressions in L2 Chinese: A Developmental Investigation in a Study Abroad Context', *Chinese as a Second Language Research Journal*, 2: 23–58.

Taguchi, N. and Roever, C. (2017), *Second Language Pragmatics*, Oxford: Oxford University Press.

Taguchi, N. and Sykes, J. M. eds. (2013), *Technology in Interlanguage Pragmatics Research and Teaching*, Philadelphia, PA: John Benjamins.

Taguchi, N., Xiao, F. and Li, S. (2016), 'Effects of Intercultural Competence and Social Contact on Speech Act Production in a Chinese Study Abroad Context', *Modern Language Journal*, 100 (4): 1–22.

Takahashi, S. (2001), 'The Role of Input Enhancement in Developing Pragmatic Competence', in K. Rose and G. Kasper (eds), *Pragmatics in Language Teaching*, 171–99, Cambridge: Cambridge University Press.

Takahashi, S. (2010a), 'The Effect of Pragmatic Instruction on Speech Act Performance', in A. Martinez-Flor and E. Uso-Juan (eds), *Speech Act Performance: Theoretical, Empirical and Methodological Issues*, 127–44, Amsterdam/Philadelphia, PA: John Benjamins.

Takahashi, S. (2010b), 'Assessing Learnability in Second Language Pragmatics', in A. Trosborg (ed.), *Pragmatics across Languages and Cultures*, 391–422, Berlin: Mouton De Gruyter.

Takahashi, S. (2012), 'Individual Differences and Pragmalinguistic Awareness: A Structural Equation Modelling Approach', *Language, Culture, and Communication*, 4: 103–25.

Takimoto, M. (2009), 'The Effects of Input-Based Tasks on the Development of Learners' Pragmatic Proficiency', *Applied Linguistics*, 30: 1–25.Fmw.

Tanaka, N., Spencer-Oatey, H. and Cray, E. (2000), '"It's Not My Fault!": Japanese and English Responses to Unfounded Accusations', in H. Spencer-Oatey (ed.), *Culturally Speaking – Managing Rapport through Talk across Cultures*, 75–97, London: Continuum.

Tateyama, Y. (2001), 'Explicit and Implicit Teaching of Pragmatics Routines: Japanese Sumimasen', in G. Kasper and K. Rose (eds), *Pragmatics in Language Teaching*, 200–22, Cambridge: Cambridge University Press.

Tatsuki, D. H. and Houck, N. R. (2010), *Pragmatics: Teaching Speech Acts*, Virginia: Teachers of English to Speakers of Other Languages, Inc.

Teng, C. and Fei, F. (2013), 'A Conscious-Raising Approach to Pragmatics Teaching: Web-Based Tasks for Training Study Abroad Students', *Journal of Technology and Chinese Language Teaching*, 4: 50–63.

Thomas, J. (1983), 'Cross-Cultural Pragmatic Failure', *Applied Linguistics*, 4 (2): 91–112.

Timpe Laughlin, V., Wain, J. and Schmidgall, J. (2015), 'Defining and Operationalizing the Construct of Pragmatic Competence: Review and Recommendations', *ETS Research Report No. RR-15-06*, Princeton, NJ: Educational Testing Service.

Trice, A. (2003), 'Faculty Perceptions of Graduate International Students: The Benefits and Challenges', *Journal of Studies in International Education*, 7 (4): 379–403.

Trosborg, A. (1987), 'Apology Strategies in Natives/Non-Natives', *Journal of Pragmatics*, 11 (2): 147–67.

Trosborg, A. (1995), *Interlanguage Pragmatics: Requests, Complaints, and Apologies*, Germany: Mouton De Gruyter.

Trosborg, A. (2010), *Handbook of Pragmatics Vol.7: Pragmatics across Languages and Cultures*, Berlin: Mouton De Gruyter.

Tsai, M. H. and Kinginger, C. (2015), 'Giving and Receiving Advice in Computer-Mediated Peer Response Activities', *CALICO*, 32: 82–112.

Universities UK. (2018), 'Patterns and Trends in UK Higher Education 2018', Available online: https://universitiesuk.ac.uk/facts-and-stats/data-and-analysis/Pages/Patterns-and-trends-in-UK-higher-education-2018.aspx (accessed 20 November 2019).

Usó-Juan, E. (2010), 'Requests: A Sociopragmatic Approach', in A. Martinez-Flor and E. Usó-Juan (eds), *Speech Act Performance: Theoretical, Empirical and Methodological Issues*, 237–56, Amsterdam: John Benjamins

Usó-Juan, E. (2013), 'Effects of Metapragmatic Instruction on EFL Learners' Production of Refusals', in O. Marti-Arnandiz and P. Salazar-Campillo (eds), *Refusals in Instructional Contexts and Beyond*, 65–100, Amsterdam: Rodopi.

VanPatten, B. (1996), *Input Processing and Grammar Instruction in Second Language Acquisition*, Norwood, NJ: Ablex.

Vásquez, C. and Sharpless, D. (2009), 'The Role of Pragmatics in the Master's TESOL Curriculum: Findings from a Nationwide Survey', *TESOL Quarterly*, 43 (1): 5–28.

Vellenga, H. (2011), 'Teaching L2 Pragmatics: Opportunities for Continuing Professional Development', *The Electronic Journal for English as a Second Language*, 15 (2): 1–27.

Wang, J. and Halenko, N. (2019), 'Longitudinal Benefits of Pre-Departure Pragmatics Instruction for Study Abroad: Chinese as a Second/Foreign Language', *East Asian Pragmatics*, 4 (1): 87–111.

Wang, V. X. (2011), *Making Requests by Chinese EFL Learners*, Netherlands: John Benjamins Publishing Co.

Warga, M. (2007), 'Interlanguage Pragmatics in L2 French', in D. Ayoun (ed.), *French Applied Linguistics*, 171–207, Netherlands: John Benjamins Publishing Co.

Warga, M. and Schölmberger, U. (2007), 'The Acquisition of French Apologetic Behavior in a Study Abroad Context', *Intercultural Pragmatics*, 4: 221–51.

Watts, R. J. (2003), *Politeness*, Cambridge: Cambridge University Press (Virtual Publishing).

Weinert, R. (1995), 'The Role of Formulaic Language in Second Language Acquisition: A Review', *Applied Linguistics*, 16 (2): 180–205.

Wen, W. P. and Clément, R. (2003), 'A Chinese Conceptualisation of Willingness to Communicate in ESL', *Language, Culture and Curriculum*, 16 (1): 18–38.

West, R. (1994), 'Needs Analysis in Language Teaching', *Language Teaching*, 27 (1): 1–19.

Wierzbicka, A. (1985), 'Different Cultures, Different Languages, Different Speech Acts', *Journal of Pragmatics*, 9 (2–3): 145–78.

Wierzbicka, A. (1991), *Cross-Cultural Pragmatics: The Semantics of Human Interaction*, Berlin: Walter De Gruyter.

Wik, P. and Hjalmarsson, A. (2009), 'Embodied Conversational Agents in Computer Assisted Language Learning', *Speech Communication*, 51: 1024–37.

Winke, P. M. and Teng, C. (2010), 'Using Task-Based Pragmatics Tutorials while Studying Abroad in China', *Intercultural Pragmatics*, 7 (2): 363–99.

Wishnoff, R. J. (2000), 'Hedging Your Bets: L2 Learners' Acquisition of Pragmatic Devices in Academic Writing and Computer-Mediated Discourse', *Second Language Studies*, 19: 119–57.

Woodfield, H. (2008), 'Interlanguage Requests: A Contrastive Study', in M. Puetz and J. Neff Van Aertselaer (eds), *Developing Contrastive Pragmatics: Interlanguage and Cross-Cultural Perspectives*, 231–64, Berlin: Mouton De Gruyter.

Woodfield, H. (2012), '"I Think Maybe I Want to Lend the Notes from You": Development of Request Modification in Graduate Learners', in M. Economidou-Kogetsidis and H. Woodfield (eds), *Interlanguage Request Modification*, 9–50, Netherlands: John Benjamins Publishing Co.

Woodfield, H. and Economidou-Kogetsidis, M. (2010), '"I Just Need More Time": A Study of Native and Non-Native Students' Requests to Faculty for an Extension', *Multilingua – Journal of Cross-Cultural and Interlanguage Communication*, 29 (1): 77–118.

Wray, A. (2000), 'Formulaic Sequences in Second Language Teaching: Principle and Practice', *Applied Linguistics*, 21 (4): 463–89.

Wray, A. (2002), *Formulaic Language and the Lexicon*, Cambridge: Cambridge University Press.

Wray, A. (2008), *Formulaic Language – Pushing the Boundaries*, Oxford: Oxford University Press.

Wray, A. (2012), 'What Do We (Think We) Know about Formulaic Language? An Evaluation of the Current State of Play', *Annual Review of Applied Linguistics*, 32: 231–54.

Xiao, F. (2015), 'Adult Second Language Leaners' Pragmatic Development in the Study Abroad Context: A Review', *Frontiers: The Interdisciplinary Journal of Study Abroad*, 25: 132–49.

Yang, H. C. and Zapata-Rivera, D. (2010), 'Interlanguage Pragmatics with a Pedagogical Agent: The Request Game', *Computer Assisted Language Learning*, 23 (5): 395–412.

Yates, L. and Wigglesworth, G. (2005), 'Researching the Effectiveness of Professional Development in Pragmatics', in N. Bartels (ed.), *Applied Linguistics and Language Teacher Education*, 261–79, Boston, MA: Springer.

Young, R. (2002), 'Discourse Approaches to Oral Language Assessment', *Annual Review of Applied Linguistics*, 22: 243–62.

Young, R. (2011), 'Interactional Competence in Language Learning, Teaching and Testing', in E. Hinkel (ed.), *Handbook of Research in Second Language Teaching and Learning*, 426–43, Abingdon: Routledge.

Yu, M. (1999), 'Universalistic and Culture-Specific Perspectives on Variation in the Acquisition of Pragmatic Competence in a Second Language', *Pragmatics Quarterly Publication of the International Pragmatics Association (IPRA)*, 9 (2): 281–312.

Yu, M. (2003), 'On the Universality of Face: Evidence from Chinese Compliment Response Behavior', *Journal of Pragmatics*, 35 (10–11): 1679–710.

Yu, M. (2011), 'Learning How to Read Situations and Know What Is the Right Thing to Say or Do in an L2: A Study of Socio-Cultural Competence and Language Transfer', *Journal of Pragmatics*, 43 (4): 1127–47.

Yuan, Y. (2001), 'An Inquiry Into Empirical Pragmatics Data-Gathering Methods: Written DCTs, Oral DCTs, Field Notes, and Natural Conversations', *Journal of Pragmatics*, 33 (2): 271–92.

Zhang, Y. (1995), 'Indirectness in Chinese Requesting', in G. Kasper (ed.), *Pragmatics of Chinese as Native and Target Language*, 69–118, Hawai'i: University of Hawai'i Press.

Zhu, W. (2012), 'Polite Requestive Strategies in Emails: An Investigation of Pragmatic Competence of Chinese EFL Learners', *RELC Journal*, 43 (2): 217–38.

Appendix 1. Living in the UK questionnaire

Chinese and English name:

....

Part A: Using English

On average, **how often do you communicate in English** with native or fluent speakers of
English since coming to the UK?
Since coming to the UK, I try to speak English to:

a. my tutor outside of class
0. never   1. a few times a year   2. monthly   3. weekly   4. daily

b. friends who are native or fluent speakers of English
0. never   1. a few times a year   2. monthly   3. weekly   4. daily

c. classmates
0. never   1. a few times a year   2. monthly   3. weekly   4. Daily

d. strangers who I thought were native or fluent speakers of English
0. never   1. a few times a year   2. monthly   3. weekly   4. daily

e. a host family, if living in an English speaking area
0. never   1. a few times a year   2. monthly   3. weekly   4. daily

f. service personnel (e.g. bank clerk, cashier at the supermarket)
0. never   1. a few times a year   2. monthly   3. weekly   4. daily

On average, **how often do you do these activities in English** since coming to the UK?
Since coming to the UK, I …

a. watch English language television
0. never   1. a few times a year   2. monthly   3. weekly   4. daily

b. read English language newspapers
0. never   1. a few times a year   2. monthly   3. weekly   4. daily

c. read novels in English
0. never   1. a few times a year   2. monthly   3. weekly   4. daily

d. read English language magazines
0. never   1. a few times a year   2. monthly   3. weekly   4. daily

e. listen to songs in English
0. never   1. a few times a year   2. monthly   3. weekly   4. daily

f. watch films/movies in English
0. never   1. a few times a year   2. monthly   3. weekly   4. daily

Part B: Your language ability

In the boxes below, rate your language ability in each of the languages that you know. Use the following ratings: **Poor/beginner 1 2 3 4 5 Excellent/native-like**

Language	Listening	Speaking	Reading	Writing	Interacting
English					

This is the end of the questionnaire. Thank you for your participation.

Appendix 2. Scheme of work for the six-week explicit instructional period

Session	PAPER group*	CAPT group*	Approx. time on task in minutes
Week 1 T1 oral and written DCTs administered in the language laboratory. Study abroad language contact questionnaire administered			50
Main activity: Mind maps Discussion	a) Mind map potential situations where may need to make a request/apologize with familiar settings provided (university, shop, in the street).	a) Mind map potential situations where may need to make a request/apologize with familiar settings provided (university, shop, in the street).	15
	b) Class discussions of cultural differences (China vs. UK). When and where to request/apologize, length and content of apology discussed.	b) Class discussions of cultural differences (China vs. UK). When and where to request/apologize, length and content of apology discussed.	20
	c) 6 paper-based scenarios presented on cards. Groups/pairs grade situations according to imposition/brevity of offence via discussion/oral response. Sociocultural follow-up discussions. China vs. UK differences.	**c) 6 CAPT scenarios presented on PPT.** Groups/pairs grade situations according to imposition/brevity of offence via discussion/oral response. Sociocultural follow-up discussions. China vs. UK differences.	40
Week 2 Request focus Main activity: Listening Reading Role-play	a) SS read 6 paper-based **pre-scripted role-plays in small groups.** 3 role-plays contain examples of infelicitous requests. Group discussions to highlight errors.	a) SS watch 6 pre-scripted **role-plays in small groups via CAPT.** 3 role-plays contain examples of infelicitous requests. Group discussions to highlight errors.	25

		b) Members of groups to highlight error. SS suggest language which may be more pragmatically appropriate for each context. Class feedback and language-focused discussion.	b) Members of groups to highlight error. SS suggest language which may be more pragmatically appropriate for each context. Class feedback and language-focused discussion.	35
		c) T introduces 6 formulaic request sequences which may be appropriate for each situation. Language-focused instruction. SS to use sequences to suggest appropriate alternatives to (a).	c) T introduces 6 formulaic request sequences which may be appropriate for each situation. Language-focused instruction. SS to use sequences to suggest appropriate alternatives to (a).	20
		d) Practice via 6 paper-based exercises as used in activity (a). Test-teach-test approach incorporated. Class discussion of how responses are now different from activities (a) and (b).	**d) Practice via 6 computer-animated scenarios used in activity (a). Test-teach-test approach incorporated. Class discussion of how responses are now different from activities (a) and (b).**	40
Week 3 Apology focus Main activity: Reading Discussion		Review of request language **a) SS are given 7 social contexts and examples of apologies – paper-based format. SS to complete appropriate response.**	Review of request language **a) SS are given 7 social contexts and examples of apologies – CAPT format. SS to complete appropriate response.**	20
		b) SS must identify characters and offence. Discussion on appropriacy of language. Language focus. L1 transfer? Introduction of 5-step apology. Controlled practice. Practise responding to apologies.	b) SS must identify characters and offence. Discussion on appropriacy of language. Language focus. L1 transfer? Introduction of 5-step apology. Controlled practice. Practise responding to apologies.	70
		c) Discussions highlighting cultural comparisons and appropriate social behaviour in the UK. **d) SS shown PAPER materials again for further discussion. Have your ideas changed?**	c) Discussions highlighting cultural comparisons and appropriate social behaviour in the UK. **d) SS shown CAPT materials again for further discussion. Have your ideas changed?**	20

Appendix 2 207

Week 4 Request and Apology focus Main activity: Reading Writing	a) SS given 8 of written dialogues and examples of requests/apologies – paper-based.	a) SS watch and are presented with 8 dialogues and examples of requests/apologies via PPT (CAPT).	20
	b) SS match context with request/apology (there are more examples than required; each may be used more than once). Focus on differences between spoken and written.	b) SS match context with request/apology (there are more examples than required; each may be used more than once). Focus on differences between spoken and written.	60
	c) SS must change characters for each situation (e.g. increased social distance and power relationships) and amend requests/apologies as appropriate. **Focus on typical sequencing in speech acts within spoken and written requests and apologies – paper-based.**	c) SS must change characters for each situation (e.g. increased social distance and power relationships) and amend requests/apologies as appropriate. **Focus on typical sequencing in speech acts within spoken and written requests and apologies – CAPT-based.**	25
Week 5 Request and Apology focus Main activity: Reading Writing Speaking	a) SS highlight intensifiers in apologies and downgraders in requests.	a) SS highlight intensifiers in apologies and downgraders in requests.	30
	b) Discussion of situational appropriate language.	b) Discussion of situational appropriate language.	30
	c) SS transform 6 dialogues to include intensifiers and downgraders. Focus on spoken language and use of intonation and stress – paper-based.	c) SS transform 6 dialogues to include intensifiers and downgraders. Focus on spoken language and use of intonation and stress – CAPT.	40
Week 6 Request and Apology focus Main activity: Role-play	a) SS given 6 individual scenarios (texts) and characters as paper-based activities.	a) SS given 6 individual scenarios (texts) and characters via PPT (CAPT).	15

	b) SS must adopt character and role-play scenes with a number of different SS using appropriate language of apologizing/requesting and responding. **SS decide whether to accept or not. Scenarios presented on cards for reading.**	b) SS must adopt character and role-play scenes with a number of different SS using appropriate language of apologizing/requesting and responding. **SS decide whether to accept or not. CAPT scenarios utilized.**	30
	c) Class feedback and discussions about language used. Alternatives elicited to consolidate previous language work.	c) Class feedback and discussions about language used. Alternatives elicited to consolidate previous language work.	20
T2 oral and written DCTs administered in the language laboratory. Study abroad language contact questionnaire administered			50

Note * Activities highlighted in bold denote where the format was differentiated between paper-based and CAPT activities.

Appendix 3. Sample of communicative practice materials

Communication practice

You have broken a window in your flat.

You go to the security guard to apologise

You say?

Communication practice

You can't find the train station

You go into the coffee bar and ask someone for directions

You say?

Communication practice

You ask a stranger to help you carry your heavy bags

You say?

Communication practice

You need a reference from your tutor to apply for a course.

She is very busy but you go to see her to ask for the reference.

You say?

Index

activity 15, 35, 37, 41, 47–8. *See also* computer-animated production task (CAPT); paper-based activities; written discourse completion task (WDCT)
agency 7, 34, 39
apology language 155–63
apology strategies 8–9, 33, 117. *See also* speech act(s)
   analysis of 117–27
   CAPT and WDCT activities 81–2
   Chinese 28, 30, 59–62
   coding scheme 98–100
   computer*vs.* paper-based activities 164–5
   explicit expressions of 58–9, 64
   explicit instruction of 38, 147–8
   instructional phase 87–91
   lost library book, analysis 117–18, 121
   missed appointment, analysis 120, 121–2
   noisy party, analysis 119, 121
   non-L2-like features of 59–62, 64–5, 125–7, 158–60
   raters' assessment of 115–17
   sequencing 157–8
   study abroad environment 26–7, 165–9
   testing phase 91–3
assessing performance 4, 36–7. *See also* rating scale; self-evaluation questionnaire
   computer-based testing 47
   oral discourse completion tasks 69–70
   rating scales 38, 55–7, 74
   written discourse completion task 68–9
awareness-raising approach 34–5, 37, 89, 147, 153, 179 ch.3 n.1

barriers 6, 28
'book a study room' request analysis 82, 109–10, 150, 153, 155

CALL. *See* computer-assisted language learning (CALL)
CAPT. *See* computer-animated production task (CAPT)
cartoon oral production task (COPT) 70–2
CCSARP. *See* cross-cultural speech act realisation project (CCSARP)
Chinese
   apology language 156, 161
   at British Higher Education institution 9, 74, 79, 147–63
   participants in studies 79–80
   politeness and culture 6, 9, 20–5
   request language 26, 28, 51–4, 149–54
   study abroad environment 27–8, 165–8
classroom access, request analysis 82, 103–4, 107–8, 150, 151, 153, 155
closed role plays. *See* oral discourse completion tasks (ODCT)
coding schemes 94–5
   for apology 98–100
   for request 95–7
collectivist societies 22–4
communicative competence 13–15, 89
computer-animated production task (CAPT) 4, 9, 83
   apology assessment 115–25
   benefits 74, 173
   content of 82
   data collecting instrument 57, 68, 71–2
   instructional phase 88
   questionnaire 75, 78–9, 86–7
   request assessment 101–15
   studies 80–2, 176–7
   testing phase 91–3
   training materials 164–5
computer-assisted language learning (CALL) 45
computer-based performance testing 47–8, 71. *See also* multimedia elicitation task (MET)

Index

control group 74, 79–80, 87–8, 91–3, 157–60, 168, 172
   apology assessment of 115–27
   request assessment of 101–15
   self-evaluations 130–2, 140–2
   testing procedure 91–2
conventionally indirect strategies (CID) 50, 57, 95–6, 107, 109, 148–9
cross-cultural discussions 2, 20, 23, 31, 41, 61, 63, 89, 91, 148–50, 165
cross- cultural speech act realisation project (CCSARP) 54, 58, 62, 97, 99
cultural adjustment 27–8

data collection 9, 68
   innovative method 70–3
   naturally occurring data 70
   oral discourse completion tasks (ODCT) 69–70
   phases in 87–93
   written discourse completion task (WDCT) 68–9
data treatment and analysis
   coding schemes 95–100
   procedure 93–7
   rating scale method 93–4
delayed test 38, 74, 80, 91, 175
developmental research 175–7
digital game 46–8
directives. *See* request strategies
directness 20, 24, 53–4, 95, 148, 150. *See also* indirectness

e-communication 6, 27–8, 30, 55–6
educational game 46–7
email apologies/requests 27–8, 28, 30, 55–6
empirical studies
   on apology 62–5
   on requests 52–7
essay extension, request analysis 82, 84, 108–9, 150, 153
ethnographic approach 36, 72, 178 Ch.3 n.1
experimental groups 46, 74, 79–80, 91–3. *See also* computer-animated production task (CAPT); paper-based activities (PAPER group)
   comparisons in activities 138–40
   listening/reading activities 138
   speaking activities 133–7
explanations, apology strategy 28, 98, 99, 109, 159
explicit instruction 3, 8–9, 17, 37–40, 74, 147–8
   of apology language 155–63
   of request language 148–55
expressions 42, 43, 58–9. *See also* apology strategies
external modification devices 24, 26, 52, 57, 96–7, 151, 153–4

face threatening acts (FTAs) 20–1, 49, 57–8, 64
feedback
   data collection 80
   interactional 2, 27, 29
   online 47, 48
   sociopragmatic 168
formulaic language 26, 41–3, 103, 152, 156, 163, 174, 176
frequency response analysis
   of apology 122–5
   of request 103–7, 111–12

game-based research 46–7, 71
grammatical competence 2, 152, 163
grounders (explanations) 28, 52, 54, 151, 154–5

head acts, request 50, 52, 97
high-context cultures 25
horizontal societies 24–5

IFIDs. *See* illocutionary force indicating devices (IFIDs)
illocutionary acts 18–19, 49
illocutionary force indicating devices (IFIDs) 19
implicit instruction 37, 39
imposition of request 21, 28, 36, 49, 81, 82, 90, 149–52, 176
indirectness 20, 21, 24, 50, 53–4, 148. *See also* directness
innovative data collecting instrument 70–1
input processing theory 17, 18
institutional talk 5–6, 27

instructed second language acquisition (ISLA) 16–17, 37, 171–2
instructional period 9, 80, 90, 175
instructional phase 87–91
instructional studies, study abroad 35–7
instruction 2, 15
  in academic study 27–9
  CALL technologies 45
  vs. exposure studies 35, 172–3
  history of 33
  implicit and explicit 37–40
  and L2 pragmatics 25–31, 33–48
  online 46
  strategy 34–5
  in study abroad 26–7, 35–7
  teaching approaches 33–5
  technology-enhanced 38–9, 45–8
instruments for data collection 68–73
interactional competency 14–15
interaction hypothesis 17, 171
interaction questionnaire 140–6
intercultural competence 15
intercultural pragmatics 14, 16
interlanguage pragmatics (ILP) 1. *See also* second language (L2) pragmatics
internal modification devices 24, 26, 51–3, 64, 96, 153–4
international students 5–6, 9, 27–9, 55–6
ISLA. *See* instructed second language acquisition (ISLA)

L2 pragmatics 1. *See also* interlanguage pragmatics (ILP)
  data collection in 68–73
  and language learning 13–16
  research 3–10, 16–18
language contact profile 86–7, 129. *See also* self-evaluation questionnaire
language learning process 2–3, 13–17
language socialization theory 18
Likert scale rating method 38, 55, 74, 78, 86, 87, 93, 101, 129, 140
linguistic choices, factors influencing 21
linguistic knowledge. *See* pragmalinguistics
listening/reading skill analysis 129–46
lost library book, apology analysis 82, 117–18, 121, 156, 157, 159, 161
low-context cultures 25

methodological approach 38, 67, 173
  CAPT (oral mode) 77, 81–5
  data collection procedure 87–93
  data treatment and analysis 93–100
  instruments 80–73
  participants in 79–83
  perception questionnaire 78–9
  pilot study 77–9
  and research gaps 73–4
  self-evaluation questionnaire 86–7
  statistical analyses 100
  WDCT (written mode) 77, 80–3, 85–7
missed appointment, apology analysis 82, 120, 121–2, 157, 160–1
multimedia elicitation task (MET) 71, 72

native/non-native speaker 8
natural data collection method 70
negative face 20, 30, 49, 62
negative politeness 6–7, 9, 22, 23, 178 Ch.1 n.2
noisy party, apology analysis 82, 119, 121, 158, 160, 161
noncongruent requests 29
non-conventionally indirect strategies 50, 96
noticing hypothesis 17, 171

online technologies 45–8
oral discourse completion tasks (ODCT) 69–70. *See also* computer-animated production task (CAPT)
oral requests 28, 36
output hypothesis 17, 171

paper-based activities (PAPER group) 4, 9, 17, 78–80, 164–5. *See also* computer-animated production task (CAPT); written discourse completion task (WDCT)
  apology assessment 115–25
  instructional phase 88
  request assessment 101–15
  testing phase 91–3
participants 7–8, 79–80
perception questionnaire 77–9
performative verbs 18, 19, 58, 64, *See* apology strategies; request strategies

pilot study 77–9
politeness 7, 148
    and culture 20–5
    and directness/indirectness 20–1, 148
    negative/positive 6, 22
    speech acts and 18–23
politic behaviour 21, 178 Ch.2 n.2
positive face-based culture 7, 20, 62, 157, 161
positive politeness 6, 9, 22–4, 49, 148, 157, 178 Ch.1 n.1
PowerPoint presentation 83
pragmalinguistics 1, 2, 20–5, 30, 46, 54, 63, 94, 103, 163, 168
pragmatic competence 2, 9, 46
    explicit instruction in 147–63
    vs. grammatical competence 152, 163
    sociolinguistic competence and 13–14
pragmatics
    barriers 6, 28
    definition of 1
    importance of 2–3
    improvisation and suggestions 171–5
    and language learning 13–16
    materials 2, 3, 9, 14, 15, 17, 34, 46, 71, 87–90, 147, 164–5, 171–3
    routines 41–3
    in teacher education 44–5
pretest and posttest performance 4, 47, 54–5, 91–2
production task. *See* written discourse completion task (WDCT)
productive skills. *See* speaking skill analysis

quasi-experimental approach 67
questionnaire 77–9, 81–2, 86–7, 91–3, 129–46. *See also* self-evaluation questionnaire

rapport management 21, 178 Ch.2 n.1
raters' assessment
    of apology data 115–17
    of request data 101–3
rating scale 4, 8, 56, 57, 74, 93–4, 173
reading skill analysis 129–46
receptive skills. *See* listening/reading skill analysis
recordings 70, 83, 93

remedial work. *See* apology strategies
request language 22, 24, 47, 111, 148–55
request strategies 8–9, 33, 103. *See also* speech act(s)
    analysis of 50, 52, 78, 103–12
    'book a study room' analysis 109–10, 150, 153, 155
    CAPT and WDCT activities 81–5
    Chinese 28, 53–4
    classroom access analysis 107–8, 150, 151, 153, 155
    coding scheme for 95–7
    computer *vs.* paper-based activities 164–5
    essay extension, analysis 108–9, 150, 153
    explicit instruction of 38, 147–8
    frequency response analysis 103–7, 111–12
    on instructional phase 87–91
    Japanese 53, 63–4, 168
    non-L2-like features of 51, 52, 55, 57, 112–15, 152–3
    raters' assessment of 101–3
    self-criticism strategy 97, 103, 107, 108, 150, 151
    study abroad environment 165–9
    on testing phase 91–3
research 1
    aims 8–9
    contributions to 171–5
    limitations 175–7
    methodological gaps in 73–4, 172–3
    scope 5–8
    theoretical frameworks 16–18
research gaps 73–4
research questions 74–5
    apology language 155–63
    computer *vs.* paper-based activities 164–5
    explicit instruction of requests and apologies 147–8
    request language 148–55
role-plays. *See* virtual role-plays
routines 41–3

second language acquisition (SLA) 1, 13–18, 171
second language (L2) pragmatics 1, 7, 14, 26, 171–5

self-criticism strategy 97, 103, 107, 108, 150, 151
self-evaluation questionnaire 86–7, 92, 129, 168–9
    productive/receptive activities 129–40
    skills assessment report 140–6
skills acquisition theory 17–18
skills evaluation 140–6
social distance 21, 53, 60, 81, 91, 109, 150, 176
social interaction 1, 18, 166, 172
sociopragmatic approach 1, 20–5, 27, 54, 55, 90, 94, 101, 115, 162, 163, 168, 176
speaking skill analysis 129–46
speech act(s) 3–5. *See also* apology strategies; request strategies
    of apologies 57–65
    and politeness theories 18–23
    of requests 49–57
    teaching 40–1
status-preserving strategies (SPS) 6
strategy instruction 34–5
study abroad (SA) 4, 13, 18
    benefits 26–7
    CAPT, PAPER and control group self-evaluations 129–40
    environment 165–9
    instructional studies 26–31, 35–7
    language contact questionnaire 86–7, 129–146
    skills evaluation 140–6

teachability studies 35
teacher education 44–5
teaching
    frameworks 34–5
    routines 41–3
    speech acts 40–1
technology-enhanced teaching 3, 4, 38–9, 45–8. *See also* computer-animated production task (CAPT)
testing phases 91–3
training materials 2, 3, 9, 14, 15, 17, 34, 46, 71, 87–90, 147, 164–5, 171–3
transfer-appropriate processing (TAP) 92

verbosity 28, 57, 113, 154–5
vertical societies 24, 25
virtual role-plays 10, 37, 46, 54, 57, 69–70, 72, 73, 83, 90, 171, 173. *See also* computer-animated production task (CAPT)

written discourse completion task (WDCT) 68–9, 164–5
    apology assessment 115–25
    content of 82
    questionnaire 86–7, 140–6
    request assessment 101–15
    studies on 77, 81–3
    testing phase 92

Xtranormal 83

www.ingramcontent.com/pod-product-compliance
Lightning Source LLC
Chambersburg PA
CBHW072233290426
44111CB00012B/2082